MISSING TIME

MISSING TIME

A Documented Study
of UFO Abductions

by Budd Hopkins

With an Afterword by
Aphrodite Clamar, Ph.D.

Richard Marek Publishers
New York

> *To April, my loving, patient wife.*

The author gratefully acknowledges permission from Prentice-Hall, Inc., to reproduce drawings from *The Andreasson Affair* by Raymond E. Fowler, © 1979 by Raymond E. Fowler and Betty Andreasson.

Library of Congress Cataloging in Publication Data

Hopkins, Budd, date.
  Missing time.

  Bibliography:p.
  Includes index.
  1. Unidentified flying objects—Sightings and encounters.   I. Title.
TL789.3.H66   001.9′42   80-39516
ISBN 0-399-90102-7

Printed in the United States of America

Acknowledgments

I want to declare my immense debt to Ted Bloecher, for both his steady, principled example and his invaluable personal support throughout—and preceding—the birth of this book. The encouragement and stylistic advice I received from writers Paul Brodeur and B.H. Friedman were particularly helpful to me, coming as they did at the very beginning of this undertaking. The precise, critical scientific readings this manuscript received from Anthony Wolff and David Webb steered me around a number of technical sandtraps, and for their efforts I am deeply grateful. Sideo Fromboluti, my friend and fellow painter, provided a spirited, yet carefully neutral overview, and his valuable suggestions have made this a stronger book. Coral and Jim Lorenzen—upon whose pioneering work I have depended—have kindly allowed me the use of some illustrations, as have Ted Jacobs, Betty Andreasson, and Wayne Laporte. Nancy Munro, who typed most of the manuscript, also transcribed hours of emotionally difficult tape recordings, and I deeply appreciate her patient work. Above all I want to thank April Kingsley, my wife, for having put up with this digression from the painter she married. It was, as she understood, a labor of intellectual necessity, and her nourishing support has been crucial to its making.

—Budd Hopkins
December 23, 1980

CONTENTS

There are three visual sightings made by the astronauts while in orbit which, in the judgment of the writer, have not been adequately explained. These are:

1. **Gemini 4**, Astronaut McDivitt. Observation of a cylindrical object with a protuberance.
2. **Gemini 4**, Astronaut McDivitt. Observation of a moving bright light at a higher level than the **Gemini** spacecraft.
3. **Gemini 7**, Astronaut Borman saw what he referred to as a "bogey" flying in formation with the spacecraft.

. . . The training and perspicacity of the astronauts put their reports of sightings in the highest category of credibility . . . . Especially puzzling is the first one on the list, the daytime sighting of an object showing details such as arms (antennas?) protruding from an object having a noticeable angular extension.

> —*Final Report of the Scientific Study of Unidentified Flying Objects* conducted for the U.S. Air Force, Dr. Edward Condon, project director.

So far, only one thing is certain: it is not just a rumor: *something is seen.*

> —Dr. Carl G. Jung, 1954. *(Emphasis his.)*

INTRODUCTION

*Since World War II, tens of thousands of reports of uniden-*tified flying objects have been gathered, officially and unofficial-ly, by the United States Air Force and myriad other governmental and civilian investigative organizations around the world.[1] Like Astronaut McDivitt's "cylinder with antennas," these objects are often described as being mechanically structured, metallic, and very frequently as behaving as if they were under intelligent con-trol. The thousands of similar, enigmatic reports from across the world mean that no matter what realities may lie behind it, the UFO phenomenon exists as an undeniable fact of life.

The question, then, is what we should do about the disturbing mass of material which makes up this ubiquitous phenomenon. There are two polar positions. One group, to which I and a large number of investigators, scientists, and even a few committed sceptics belong, believes that the UFO phenomenon poses a tan-talizing and serious problem—perhaps a profoundly revolutionary one. If there is nothing but smoke to this mass of mysterious reports, then enormous numbers of people, from farmers to astro-nauts, must be hallucinating fire—which in itself would be an alarming state of affairs. The other group is made up of those who, out of lack of information or mere indifference, simply ignore the phenomenon. The first group looks into the data, the other de-clines to. Essentially, UFO "belief" is definable by whether or not one believes that the thousands of ongoing reports constitute a problem worth looking into, regardless of one's prejudices, theories, and assumptions. (And of these there are almost as many as there are investigators.)

It has long been obvious to serious UFO researchers that the majority of UFO reports—some say up to ninety percent—are misidentifications of conventional aircraft, stars, and other natural or artificial objects. As an example, I received a phone call a few years ago from an agitated woman who had seen a UFO from her car as she drove on Manhattan's East River Drive. "It was a bright, hovering light," she told me, "much bigger than a star." She lost sight of it when a building blocked her view; then she saw it again, and then finally it was gone. It appeared not to be moving, and it was very close to the horizon. I asked about its location, and she said that it had been in the northeast. "Near La Guardia Airport?" I inquired. "Why, yes," she answered, "it would have been just about over La Guardia." As she spoke she realized why I had asked the question. Her "UFO" was undoubtedly a distant plane coming in with its landing lights on against a twilit sky, just far enough away for her eyes to blend the two bright lights together into one large one. Since the plane was pointed south, towards her car, it seemed to be hovering.

Reports like these are common, and many investigators pay no attention to them at all apart from their obvious explanations. Even without its transparent cause, a report like this offers an unrewarding paucity of information in the best of circumstances. A number of scientists, naïve about the complexity of the *other* UFO reports, assume that this sort of thing—an odd light in the night sky—is all there is to the phenomenon. Their ritual denigrations (Carl Sagan's, for instance) appear to be *pro forma*, akin to the similar scientific assurances we've heard about the safety of atomic energy and the ongoing flight of *Skylab*. Sagan wittily remarked that no one has produced "even a cocktail napkin" from a UFO. Another astronomer countered by asking, for that matter, how many Brazilian aborigines have a piece of a Boeing 747?

But what about the "other ten percent," the UFO reports which remain unexplained after investigation? These are the detailed cases, like the 1964 Socorro, New Mexico, sighting which was investigated by officials from the White Sands proving grounds, the FBI, the Air Force, and the local police.[2] In fact, the principal witness was a highly respected Socorro policeman. Officer Lonnie Zamora, on a sunny afternoon in April, was in his patrol car following a speeder when he heard a roar and saw a flame in the sky a half mile or so away. He turned away from his chase to investigate and saw a "motionless flame . . . slowly descending." Its "noise changed from high frequency to low frequency and then stopped." Zamora drove up a gravel road and saw a shiny oval object in a gully below. "It looked at first like a car turned upside down. Thought some kids might have turned it over. Saw two people in white coveralls very close to object. One of these persons seemed to turn and look straight at my car and seemed startled. . . . Persons appeared normal in shape—but possibly they were small adults or large kids."

Zamora radioed that he was investigating a possible accident when he heard another roar. His report, written a few hours after the incident in a kind of policeman's telegramese, continues:

Stopped car, was still talking on radio, started to get out; mike fell down, reached back to pick up mike. . . . As I got out of car, at scene area, I heard two or three loud thumps, like someone hammering or shutting door hard. These thumps were possibly a second or so apart. . . .

As soon as saw flames and heard (second) roar, turned away, ran from object but did turn head towards object. Bumped leg on car, back fender area. . . . Object was oval in shape. It was smooth—no windows or doors . . . like aluminum—white. Flame was under the object. Object starting to go straight up— slowly . . . rose straight up. . . . Thought, from roar, it might blow up. Kept running towards north with car between me and the object (for protection in case object exploded). I was scared of the roar. I turned around towards the ground, covering my face with my arms. When the roar stopped, heard nothing. It appeared to go at the same height and in a straight line, possibly ten to fifteen feet from the ground. Object was traveling very fast. It seemed to rise up and take off immediately cross country. Got into the car and radioed to Ned Lopez, the radio operator, to 'look out of the window to see if you can see an object.' As I was calling Ned . . . the object seemed to lift up slowly and to get small in the distance very fast. It seemed to just clear Box Canyon or Six-Mile Canyon Mountain. It disappeared as it went over the mountains. It had no flame whatsoever as it was traveling over the ground and made no smoke or noise.

* * *

Sergeant Chavez of the Socorro Police Department came on the scene moments later in response to Zamora's radio call. "When I arrived," the record reads, "Zamora was sweating and white . . . very pale. I went down to where the object had been. I noticed the brush was burning in several places. I could see tracks on the ground. The object had left four perpendicular impressions in the ground. I noticed smoldering bushes, but they felt cold to the touch."[3] Chavez later remarked to Dr. J. Allen Hynek, then the Air Force's scientific consultant on UFOs, that never in his long association with Zamora had he seen him in anything at all approaching the state he was in when Chavez joined him. Zamora is used to accidents, bloodshed, fights, and even murders. "We all seem to agree," said Dr. Hynek, who conducted a thorough investigation for the Air Force, "that Zamora saw something that really and truly frightened him." And it had been less than one hundred feet away.

Subsequent investigation by the Air Force, which even included a fruitless search for propellant residue on the burnt bushes and a return trip by Dr. Hynek four months later, turned up nothing that would in any way discredit Zamora's account. The Air Force's final verdict? Like the UFO sightings by the astronauts mentioned earlier, the Socorro, New Mexico, landing is officially listed as unidentified. Carl Jung was right; things are being seen which defy explanation—close up and in bright daylight!

Reports of figures, like Zamora's "small adults or large kids in white coveralls," seen in or near UFOs are surprisingly common. In fact, just about eleven hours *before* Zamora's encounter, a dairy farmer named Gary Wilcox of Tioga City, New York, saw what he took to be the wing tank from an airplane in one of his fields. He approached it and found that it was an oval, light-colored craft of some sort, resting on four strutlike supports. And nearby he also saw two small men, roughly four feet tall, dressed in one-piece, apparently seamless coveralls. Researchers Ted Bloecher and David Webb have assembled in their data bank over fifteen hundred reports of such figures—"humanoids"—associated with UFOs and as we will see in the course of this book, most of these figures conform closely to a series of physical types, and have been reported by apparently reliable people.[4] So close are the descriptions in these two cases that one wonders if Mr. Wilcox's visitors didn't leave upstate New York for a flight to New Mexico, where they encountered Officer Zamora later that afternoon.

Whatever all this means, one thing is clear—a larger segment of the scientific community should certainly be joining the investigation of what may turn out to be a watershed event—the arrival of extraterrestrial visitors. No one can deny that this is *possibly* the correct explanation of the UFO phenomenon, and in 1948 the Air Force personnel charged with investigating UFO reports concluded in a top secret "Estimate of the Situation" that UFOs *were* of extraterrestrial origin.[5] The Chief of Staff of the Air Force, General Hoyt Vandenberg, received the report and decided that it lacked proof, but nevertheless it represented the considered opinion of the first official government investigation.

It is ironic but true that the very possibility of an extraterrestrial cause works against scientific interest in the UFO phenomenon. All of our thinking, all of our boundaries are anthropomorphically determined. Science is based upon human intelligence dealing with the empirical world. The nature of other possibly "superior" but surely different intelligences studying *us* is literally ungraspable. The whole business, potentially, is nothing less than a second, more devastating Copernican revolution, and none of us, scientist or not, can ever truly be prepared for that. And, of course, anyone who wishes can deliberately ignore all the photographic evidence, the written reports and radar contacts, and so on, and simply take refuge in the fact that, so far as we know, the one piece of evidence we are lacking is the central one—we don't have a captured UFO parked somewhere as the final, invincible clincher, the *corpus delicti*. As a friend of mine once said to me, "I believe they're up there all right, but I won't be content till I kick the tires on one of them."

Though there was a wave of sightings in the United States in 1896-7, UFO reports in large numbers turn up for the first time during the last years of World War II.[6] In fact, the American Air Force and the Luftwaffe each thought UFOs, which the American fliers called "foo-fighters," were the other side's secret weapon. The first modern wave of sightings in the United States occurred in 1947 and has been thoroughly documented by Ted Bloecher. Bloecher[7] points out the interesting fact that many of the early witnesses automatically assumed that they had seen some kind of secret craft of *terrestrial* origin. References to "alien spacecraft" were often embellishments added by reporters who wished to tart up their news stories. Typically, the witnesses would decide that the silvery disk which had followed their car a few hundred feet away must have been a Russian secret weapon or some new kind of American craft, so they would dutifully report it as such to the Air Force. If they called the local paper, their account most likely would appear under the headline, "Couple Sights Martian Spaceship," ridicule being a particularly instinctive weapon in the hands of uneasy people.

Over the decades, it became obvious that, whatever UFOs were, they were clearly not Russian or American or German advanced aircraft. The reports, which had a surprising consistency of detail, described craft which could move silently at incredible speeds, stop almost instantly, and in general perform like nothing aerodynamic engineers on this planet could even imagine. Instead, earthly designers continue to concentrate on building noisy, expensive rocket or jet propulsion systems, one dead end of which seems to be the Concorde SST. Wars have been fought, invasions attempted, but no nation has come forward with the strategic edge that would be provided if anyone possessed aircraft with the performance capabilities of UFOs.

In 1949 the Air Force intelligence group looking into the UFO problem hired Dr. J. Allen Hynek, an astronomer at Ohio State University, as their scientific consultant. Unofficially his task was to debunk the sighting reports which had grown to what the Air Force considered disturbing proportions. Dr. Hynek, who served the Air Force in this capacity for twenty years, was, so far as we know, privy to more official military UFO reports than any other scientist. His credentials are impeccable. He has directed the Dearborn Observatory and was Associate Director of the Smithsonian Astrophysical Observatory. He has been Chairman of the Astronomy Department at Northwestern University and has served as a NASA consultant. He now directs the Center for UFO Studies in Evanston, Illinois, a central repository for UFO case material. As a result of his twenty years of investigations for the Air Force he became persuaded of both the reality and the crucial importance of the UFO phenomenon, and the strong possibility that UFOs were, indeed, extraterrestrial spacecraft.

Beginning at least as far back as 1947, some reports of landed and hovering craft included descriptions of occupants—humanoids of various types. At the time, these accounts seemed almost impossible to believe. One could accept the possibility that we were being observed, studied from some distance by alien intelligences of some sort. But *creatures* . . . *people* . . . *robots?* And then, in 1965, a story was published in a Boston newspaper about the temporary abduction of two people, Mr. and Mrs. Barney Hill, by the occupants of a UFO. Their memories had been somehow blocked, and the kidnapping, which occurred in 1961, had only recently emerged through regressive hypnosis in the course of psychotherapy. At the time, many serious UFO researchers found the account difficult to believe, though now, a decade and a half later, the Hills' account is only one of literally hundreds very much like it.

Since 1976 I have been involved to varying degrees with the investigation of nineteen similar abduction cases involving thirty-seven people. These nineteen cases have yielded clear patterns, though the thirty-seven people involved form a random cross-section of professions, ages, and social backgrounds. They include two registered nurses, a golf pro, several college students, a Wall Street lawyer, a painter, a news-media writer, a retired public school principal, an insurance underwriter, a college instructor, and so on. Seven of these nineteen cases form the heart of this book. I am convinced of the integrity of each individual witness, a trust that in some instances was reinforced by the use of polygraph tests. (This expensive step is usually not considered necessary when a thorough investigation has been undertaken.)

At this time in the unfolding history of the UFO phenomenon, it seems to me as if these quite similar abductions constitute some kind of systematic "research" program, with the human species as subject. Individuals or small groups of people are involuntarily "borrowed" and most often the memory of such an encounter is effectively erased from the individual's consciousness, presumably by some sort of post-hypnotic suggestion. UFO investigators have come to rely upon regressive hypnosis as the most efficient method of unlocking the forgotten period of time—usually an hour or two—and recovering the often harrowing account of what actually happened; psychiatrists and psychologists who practice hypnosis have thus become our most helpful allies.

What the purposes of these temporary abductions are, and what part of the experience may be purely psychic, we can only guess, but that they have physical dimension seems to me beyond doubt. As we will see, several abductees bear scars on their bodies from incisions made years earlier when the subjects had been children. On separate occasions, I have heard these witnesses, under hypnosis, describe in almost exactly the same words the equipment used to make these incisions. Although these abduction accounts include almost nothing that can be construed as being deliberately hurtful or malevolent on the part of the abductors, the pattern that emerges, nevertheless, leaves me thoroughly alarmed.

A typical abduction account follows one of several basic scenarios; in fact, it is the presence of certain familiar details in what seemed at first to have been only a routine UFO *sighting* which alerts the experienced investigator to inquire more deeply into the case. For this investigator, a mental red flag goes up if the witness seems confused about an unexplained loss of time, or complains of certain physical symptoms. As an example, I shall construct a hypothetical abduction case, a composite of commonly reported details from a number of actual accounts.[8] Let us assume that a young man and his wife and year-old baby are on a trip, driving late at night on a relatively deserted highway. They see a bright light moving in the sky, and suddenly it approaches their car. They realize after a moment or so that it is not a plane or helicopter or anything familiar. It is soundless; it moves erratically; it can halt suddenly; it is totally unlike any aircraft they have ever seen before. Now it passes low over their car and seems to disappear behind a stand of trees. Then, unaccountably, their engine stalls as its electrical system fails, and they come to a stop. Next, the UFO flies off from a slightly different position from where they had last seen it, and their motor starts up again, seemingly on its own accord. They are bewildered but relieved that things are normal again. What they are not aware of is that it is now *two hours* later. They have all three spent that time inside a landed UFO undergoing some kind of examination, and the entire experience has been blocked from their conscious memories. The events immediately before and immediately after the abduction have been seamlessly joined, leaving them with little or no sense of missing time.

I have described UFO abductions as constituting an epidemic; in fact, we have no idea how many such kidnappings may already have taken place, but I believe there are vastly more than the mere two hundred or so incidents which have been investigated. Why these cases remain invisible will become evident when we return to our example. Most people having such an experience—and I mean by this only the sighting of the UFO, the part that has been consciously remembered—would not report it to any authority anywhere. There are indications that roughly seventy or eighty percent of these events go unreported, so the greatest possibility is that we would never have heard of this case in the first place.[9] Such is the fear of ridicule and the confusion about where to go to report such an unlikely event! But let us place my example in the small minority and assume they stop along the way somewhere and call the police to report an unidentified flying object. Chances are the report begins and ends at the police station, probably relegated to the circular file by a weary dispatcher. In this case, however, we will assume a conscientious police officer does take down the account and phones it in, via a national toll-free hot-line, to the Center for UFO Studies, or perhaps he notifies some other UFO investigatory organization, and eventually this family will be contacted by a trained investigator.

These three assumptions we have made against the odds have kept our abduction case from sinking into invisibility. How many cases, one wonders, would have made it thus far? The UFO investigator begins his interrogation of the witnesses. He asks a few questions about the time and duration of the sighting. If the family checked the time at some point after their encounter, they would probably have become aware of the lost two hours. Very subtly, so as not to alarm them, the investigator inquires into the specifics of the time problem. He then asks if they experienced any unusual physical sensations, of heat or cold or whatever, that they can recall. (These are not the precise symptoms he expects to find; he uses them merely to introduce the physical domain without leading the witnesses.) "That is interesting," the husband replies, "because there was something unusual." He and his wife each had strange red marks on their necks, he explains, and they had no idea how they got them. There was even one just like it on the baby, too. And something else. The next day he noticed a round, red mark next to his navel. It burned a little, and hurt when he touched it. In fact, he still has a little scar from it even though it's been a month since they saw the UFO. Our hypothetical investigator, knowing the significance of these frequently reported details, but not wishing for the time being to raise any disturbing possibilities, asks if the witness ever consulted a doctor about his condition. (In one case Ted Bloecher and I are currently investigating, a young man actually spent a full week in 1976 in the hospital undergoing tests for a suspected kidney tumor which turned out to be nonexistent. He neglected to tell his doctors that the peculiar marks on his abdomen, which had led them to suspect the tumor, appeared after a frightening experience in the woods with a landed UFO and a group of humanoids. A period of roughly an hour is missing from his recall. He said he knew the doctors would never believe him, but he was also reluctant himself to face the possible connection between the wounds and the UFO encounter. His companion on the camping trip still bears the faint traces of two small parallel cuts at the base of his spine which his wife discovered a day or so after his return.)

The investigator would then ask the witnesses if they would like to undergo hypnosis with a professional psychologist to help them recall the details of their encounter that they cannot consciously remember. Herein lies the final and perhaps biggest "if" of all. Many people, possibly a majority who find themselves in this position, refuse to explore the matter any further, and for a variety of reasons. First, they are frightened of hypnosis itself, despite its increasing therapeutic use across a wide spectrum of medical situations. Many others may feel that there is really nothing more to remember about their encounter, most particularly in the cases where no physical traces exist, and an investigator is naturally hesitant to argue the point. But very often the witness senses that something odd happened to him in the period of missing time and he simply does not want to find out what it was. Several years ago, I was looking into a UFO close encounter involving seven young people who simultaneously—they were seated in three vehicles at the time—suffered a two-hour hiatus which began as they were approached by a double line of helmeted figures. The mother of one of the young women called me several days after we had discussed the issue of hypnosis with the group. "You think they were abducted that night, don't you?" she asked, surprising me because I had not given voice to my suspicions. "Yes, I do," I admitted. "So do I," she answered, interrupting me, "and I don't want my daughter to know what happened to her." I replied that psychologists usually feel that it is better to ventilate a traumatic experience that might otherwise, if it is kept buried, cause difficulties. "I know that, and I agree," she answered. "But now she's doing well in school and in her social life, and I don't want to bring up any problems. If the day comes when I feel it's causing her anguish, then I'll let her undergo hypnosis. In the meantime, you know the phrase, let sleeping dogs lie." I couldn't argue with her feelings, and there the matter rests.[10]

Having considered some of the numerous—and enormous— obstacles to the discovery of abduction cases, and to their subsequent in-depth investigation, one can only marvel that so many have, nevertheless, managed to come to our attention. And it seems obvious that for each single case we've heard about, investigated, and listed as an abduction or a probable abduction,[11] there may be dozens still totally unknown, and that's only in the few Western countries—the U.S., England, France, and Canada where something of a widespread investigatory network exists. Fragmentary reports from everywhere else, from South Africa to Indonesia, suggest that the phenomenon is worldwide. In fact, one of the abductions I'll consider in depth occurred in France.

And so, starting with the roughly five hundred[12] individuals who, from a study of the reports, we feel reasonably sure have been abducted to date in the U.S., we can logically theorize that there may be tens of thousands of Americans whose encounters have never been revealed—bearing in mind that we are talking about abductions which came to light through the investigation of a routine UFO sighting in which a time lapse and other suspicious details were uncovered.

The discovery which impelled me to write this book is one I believe to be of extraordinary importance. The seven cases stressed in these pages involve abductions of five different individuals. Three, who incidentally have never met, were taken as seven-year-old children, and incisions were made in their bodies, for whatever purposes we can only speculate. Two of them—and possibly all three—were apparently abducted a second time, one at age sixteen, one a few years later. All three were born in 1943, and were abducted in the summer of 1950. None of them had, prior to hypnotic regression, *any recall whatsoever* of a UFO or humanoid encounter of any kind. How they happened to undergo hypnosis in the first place involves a complex series of unlikely events, which I shall describe in later chapters. Each case is in some way intertwined with another involving a young man who was abducted in his early twenties, but who, like the others had *absolutely no conscious memory* of a UFO sighting; all that he had to go on was the "feeling" that "something may have happened" to him one night in 1973, on a particular road in Maryland, as he drove home from his girlfriend's house. Hypnosis revealed a classic abduction. An inescapable conclusion to be drawn from all these cases is that *anyone* could have been abducted, with no memory of it, no conscious recall even of a preliminary event like the sighting of a UFO. It could have happened to any one of us years ago, in childhood, or recently. No signs or clues may necessarily have remained. This, to me, is the most dramatic and disturbing possibility that has yet taken shape in all the years of UFO research. And yet what it finally *means* is as mysterious as ever. For all any of us knows the whole UFO phenomenon may be ultimately, blissfully benign—there is firm evidence for this position—and so having been abducted may turn out to have been a peculiar privilege. No one knows. All I can say is that I'm sure it is going on; people are being picked up, "examined"—sometimes marked for life—and released, their memories conveniently blocked. Beyond this, everything is speculation.

1

CAPE COD GENESIS

How I, a rational, peace-loving artist, ever became involved in something so esoteric as the UFO phenomenon is something I'm really not sure of myself, though one thing is clear: events came to me—I didn't seek them out—in the beginning, at least. I was in high school and college during the late-Forties and early-Fifties when the first flying saucer accounts appeared in the newspapers. I was not particularly interested at the time and I remember barely paying attention to them. By the middle-Sixties, the subject of UFOs, so far as I knew, had completely receded from view, having been explained away by the Air Force investigators during the past decade. Big weather balloons or hallucinations or something or other had definitely caused all this mistaken excitement.

I was living in Truro, Massachusetts, in the summer of 1964 in our recently constructed summer studio, and my first wife Joan and I were entertaining a house guest, Ted Rothon, an English social worker we had met on a European trip. Provincetown, Truro, and Wellfleet constitute a vital summer art colony, and there is an endless procession of openings, cocktail parties, and sundry cultural and social events. On a late-August afternoon, Joan, Ted, and I set out from Truro, heading to Provincetown for a cocktail party. It was about five-thirty and the cloud masses from an earlier storm had broken up. Small clumps of clouds blew quickly in from the ocean as we drove along Route 6. One of us, I do not remember who, remarked upon a darkish, elliptical object in the sky off to our left and ahead of the car. It was small—two car-lengths long one might judge—and it did not seem to be moving. A cloud clus-

ter approached it, floated in front of it, and obscured it from view.
In seconds, the cloud passed by and there was our elliptical object
again, still apparently in the same place, picking up a strong
beam of temporary sunlight and appearing to be dull aluminum
in color. Another cloud mass scudded behind it, silhouetting it for
a moment. What could it be? We were intrigued, I slowed the car
as we came closer to it, and now we were looking up at it at a
steeper angle. It appeared to be circular when viewed more or less
from underneath. At one point, it was swallowed up by another
fast-moving cloudlet which apparently was of little substance; one
could see our round object *inside* the cloud with all local color
eliminated, and thereby appearing as black, like a ship in a fog
bank. By this time, perhaps a minute and a half or so after we had
first seen it, we were all three speculating. "Is it a balloon?" someone wondered. "If it is, it's tied to the ground," I said, "since it's not
going anywhere and the wind is whipping the clouds along." It
was definitely not a helicopter; there were no wings, no tail, no
appendages of any kind—just a smooth circle seen from below,
and a somewhat elliptical shape in profile.

By now, we had passed it. I was driving very slowly and we
were craning our necks to keep it in sight. Suddenly it moved off,
crossing the road behind us, heading for the ocean against the
wind. I stopped the car and we all jumped out and watched it
silently disappear into the clouds that were blowing in from the
northeast. It moved at the speed of, say, a small airplane. We were
stunned, confused, and then excited. What *was* it? One of us, I
forget who, said, "Do you suppose that was one of those 'flying
saucers' you used to read about?" We went to the party, at Hudson
and Ione Walker's, and told about our adventure. One of the
guests said that she had, the summer previously, seen a very similar object do very similar things at just about the same place along
Route 6. Several other people had stories of their own. Intrigued, I
began to look into the matter of UFOs, and was soon made aware,
from a book I bought on the subject, that the situation was far from
being resolved; that it was, in fact, a perplexing and ongoing mystery.

An odd but very human reaction one has to such mysteries is
to be able to accept as plausible only what strange thing one has
personally experienced, and nothing further. I read accounts in
these UFO books of sightings like mine; very believable, I thought.
But then *Look* magazine published an account of the Betty and

Barney Hill abduction, from John Fuller's book-length study of
this first widely publicized kidnapping by UFO occupants.[1] Ridiculous, I thought. Who can believe such foolishness? My logic
remained unexamined. I accepted the possibility that what I saw
over Route 6 might be some kind of spacecraft, some kind of
extraterrestrial probe of our environment—after all, most scientists accept the idea of extraterrestrial intelligence as probable, so
such eventual explorations would seem to be at least possible. I
even vaguely admitted the possibility that there might have been
some sort of living beings inside this possible spacecraft. But that
they landed, and stopped a car, and kidnapped two people, and
administered some sort of physical examination, and took skin and
blood samples, and so on? Ridiculous!

    I continued to follow the UFO reports through newspaper
articles and occasional paperback books, my interest stabilized on
what I thought was a somewhat casual level. The painter's life
does not easily allow for multiple obsessions. The actor Maximil-
ian Schell acquired a 1968 painting of mine, Genesis I, which contained, as most of my work did in those years, a huge, ambiguous
black circle. He remarked that there was something unearthly
about the painting and suggested that I should go see Stanley Kub-
rick's film 2001, because he felt some kind of resonance between
the two works. I disagreed with him after I saw the movie, but in
retrospect I may have underestimated at the time the degree of my
absorption in the UFO phenomenon. The subconscious is a busy
place.

    It took three or four years for me slowly to admit to myself the
possibility that the Betty and Barney Hill abduction just might
have happened exactly as the Hills recalled through hypnosis.
They had not, after all, initially claimed anything about an abduction. They had had a nighttime UFO sighting in 1961 on a remote
highway in New Hampshire, and sensed that there were about
two hours they could not account for on their drive home. Barney
Hill began to have nightmares and to suffer from a recurrent ulcer. He went to a psychiatrist for help, and since some kind of
hidden trauma seemed to be part of the problem, he entered into
hypnosis. Out came a traumatic abduction by UFO occupants! Betty Hill also underwent regressive hypnosis without knowing any
of the content of her husband's sessions; Dr. Benjamin Simon, the
Hills' psychiatrist, gave both of his patients post-hynotic suggestions that they would not remember what had transpired during

their respective trance periods. Dr. Simon tape-recorded the sessions, however, and was struck by the similarity of their descriptions: of their humanoid captors, of the inside of the ship, of the circumstances of their kidnapping, and so on.

As I read about the case in detail—I finally bought Fuller's book, The Interrupted Journey—I began to feel that the Hills were recalling precisely what had happened to them, and the fact that it emerged the way it did, under hypnosis, in two separate accounts, gave it unusual validity. If the UFOs were some kind of spacecraft piloted—if that's the word—by extraterrestrials, perhaps they might be exploring very cautiously, giving us a good long look, picking up "samples" under very safe conditions, really studying us at long range before landing and establishing contact. After all, it was rather puerile and anthropomorphic of us to expect aliens to behave as we had, landing on the moon, jumping out and sticking a little American flag, wired stiff for TV, pole first into the lunar dust—and then posing for pictures in front of it.

Surreptitious examinations such as those conducted on Betty and Barney Hill made a great deal of sense, especially when contrasted with the foolish "landing-on-the-White-House-lawn-take-us-to-your-leader" concept of what we should expect. Years later, I heard Dr. Edgar Mitchell, the astronaut who walked on the moon during the second landing, explain his position. "If we had expected to encounter any kind of living beings, which, of course, we didn't, we would naturally have asked NASA to put us down in some very unpopulated region where we could examine the local fauna in safety and at our discretion. We would have wanted to pick up some living specimens, examine them, and put them back with a minimum of fuss, hoping to get back to earth safely with as much information as possible."[2]

By the time the Pascagoula abduction occurred in 1973,[3] I was able to accept the idea of "human sample-taking" as quite plausible, within the context of the thousands of worldwide UFO sightings. The crucial reason for my ability to accept these accounts as true was the central issue: if these events did not occur as reported by the witnesses, then what caused their recollections? Many abductees have voluntarily submitted to polygraph examinations and voice stress analysis, the two most common "lie-detection" methods; so far as I know, no case reaching the level of investigation in which these devices were introduced has turned out to be a hoax. Clearly, the witnesses believe they are telling the truth.

Then what happened? How can so many normal people with no discernable psychological disabilities have hallucinated in such elaborate corroborative detail, particularly when these very similar "hallucinations" usually emerge through regressive hypnosis? Not even Jung would have claimed archetypes to be so finely honed, nor so consonant.

Over the years, friends began to pass on to me various UFO sightings of their own, and I began to take notes when they were of sufficient interest. Occasionally, during the later-Sixties and early-Seventies, I would bring the matter up at a dinner party and would almost never fail to elicit another report. Being an artist gave me a certain freedom to introduce such a peculiar subject; one can hardly imagine a neurosurgeon, an investment broker, or a psychiatrist admitting in public to a serious interest in UFOs in those years. The freedom an artist has is both an essential working condition and his greatest fringe benefit. He—or she—can keep the salacious novel out on the bed-table while the lawyer has it buried in his shirt drawer; the curiosity might be the same, but there is a different attitude toward concealment.

The summer of 1975 was a crucial one for my interest in the UFO phenomenon. A series of sightings in the Truro-Wellfleet-Provincetown area came to my attention, and I began a slightly more intensified investigation into each one. Betty Bodian, a painter friend of mine, reported a strange white globe in the twilit sky over Provincetown harbor. This glowing object, which appeared to be stationary, blinked on and off irregularly for about three minutes before it vanished. I was not particularly interested until Dan and Jan Boynton, then co-owners of the *Provincetown Advocate*, told me they had seen a glowing white light blinking oddly over the bay, and I learned that the time, location, and July 16 date were the same as the former report; the interesting thing was that the Boyntons were at a location ninety degrees away from Ms. Bodian, separated by a distance of about three miles. Also very interesting was a human side-issue. The Boyntons personally wrote some of the copy for their paper; Dan was the editor and Jan took most of the photographs. They saw the UFO while driving in Truro on Route 6 (the same location, incidentally, where I had had my sighting years earlier), and carried on the back seat of the car all their camera gear. So two newspaper owners-editors-writers-photographers spent two minutes or so discussing this odd thing in the sky without ever stopping a moment to photograph it; an example, perhaps, of why there are fewer UFO photographs than one might expect.

Subsequently, four more witnesses to this UFO turned up, located at different places along a five-mile stretch. One of them, using binoculars, was sure she observed a row of what seemed like windows inside the glowing shape. This particular UFO– if indeed there was only one—turned out to be very busy, for a while almost ubiquitous. Within a six-week period from late June into August, an object fitting its description was seen on many occasions by: (1) two Wellfleet police officers, who watched it moving through the sky around three A.M. on July 3; (2) by a woman and her teen-aged daughter, who saw it west of Provincetown hovering and blinking; (3) on July 17, by a man in Eastham, a town near Wellfleet, who called the Coast Guard in the belief it was some kind of distress signal; and (4) most interesting of all, by David Lind and Bess Schuyler, near their property in Truro. They had returned home about eleven-thirty P.M. on a warm, foggy night— August 12—when they saw, as they approached their house, what they took at first to be a fire below the top of a hill about a quarter of a mile away. They realized in seconds that it was not a fire but was, instead, a large circular light either resting on, or slightly above, the ground. David found his binoculars and through the fog the globe seemed to contain windows, or vertical sections of some sort, like a "southern mansion with columns," in his words. (The next day we found that a split-rail fence was located nearby, and if the object had been behind it, the slats could have caused this illusion.) David also noticed that from time to time the big light gave off individual beams of light, shining out from its circumference.

Though the sight was most unusual, David and Bess decided in the darkness that it must be a house that they had never noticed before; perhaps a neighbor had cut down some foliage which had screened his dwelling from view, or perhaps had installed a huge new floodlight of some sort that was being enlarged by the fog. There must be some explanation like that, so they put away the binoculars and retired.

I share a small house in New York with Bess and David, and know them very well. Bess is curious about the UFO phenomenon and David is rather skeptical, or in the very least, uninterested. In the morning, Bess called to tell me about it and to apologize for not alerting me the night before. She had awakened early and had gone outside with her binoculars. Because of the nature of the shoreline and the location of the little hill, the light could only have been in one specific place, and Bess quickly realized that there was no house near that spot—just low ground cover, what is called on the Cape "hog cranberry," and scrub pine. There are two houses in the general vicinity, one of which had been for years the summer residence of Edward Hopper, the great American painter, but on the night before both houses were lit and visible. Somewhere between them there had been a large, unknown light, emitting beams, and apparently very close to the ground, if not resting on it. I drove over to see what I could find, and in minutes uncovered something else.

Bess remained on her deck in the spot where she and David had watched the light, and I moved out towards the hill. Bess waved her arm to the left or right, steering me to the site, and as I walked along I saw a car approach. A woman and a teen-aged girl drove up to the cottage and stopped; they were the summer tenants in the house closest to the critical spot, so I asked them about the incident after explaining what I was doing. Unfortunately, the night before the mother had retired very early and was asleep by eleven-thirty; her daughter, and a son who was soon to join us, had been in Provincetown that night until one A.M., and so they, too, had not seen anything unusual. But I noticed that all three exchanged quick, meaningful glances.

"Did anyone see anything peculiar three nights ago?" the woman asked, and then told me her story. It had been a Saturday night and for some reason she couldn't fall asleep, so she decided to read. Around one-thirty in the morning, a light began to shine in her bedroom window—a very bright, moving light, whose source was apparently high enough not to be visible. The light streamed in, passing rather quickly and moving towards the bay. It was very bright, white, and very odd, she thought; the area is quite isolated and she was alarmed. Instead of going to her window, which faced roughly south, she went to the stairs and called to her daughter, whose room on the floor above faced west. The daughter awakened in time to see the light stream in her windows and pass by, heading north, as if circling the house. Again no light source could be seen. Wide awake now, and curious, the girl came downstairs to her mother's room, just in time to see the light come by again, this time reversing its earlier path to run counter-clockwise. And that was that. None of the family of three had any idea what it could have been. It was soundless. The Cape is a very quiet place—noise of any sort carries great distances, and neighbors claim they hear each other turn on the lights.

My only theory was that automobile headlights from a car driving on the dirt road that leads to the Hopper house might somehow have been the cause, though it looked unlikely because a ridge intervenes between road and house. Nevertheless, I decided to experiment. Late that night, I returned in my car. The family retired to their rooms, set the lights as they were that evening, and I took to the wheel. I drove forward, stopped, backed up, turned around, flicked from high to low beams; in fact, did everything but drive straight into the sand. They never saw a flicker from my car; the ridge, as I suspected, blocked everything.

Within the week, I learned about a third incident close to the Lind-Schuyler house. In late June, a psychotherapist and his wife, whose home is located about three-quarters of a mile away, had been napping in their bedroom after dinner. They awakened and noticed what they took to be the full moon shining low in the sky, until they realized that the moon was not full at the time, and besides, was not visible in that location. They told me weeks later that the incident had been vaguely unnerving, so without saying anything much about it, they had gone into the front of their house to brew some coffee. The moon *was* visible from the living room windows. They had their coffee and dawdled a bit, and then returned to their bedroom, both of them glancing casually toward the sky: the globe of light was still where it had been. Neither remarked to the other about it, but both decided to go back to the living room. After a second uneasy wait, which again was deliberately not discussed, they went back to their bedroom, saw the peculiar light, and once more found an excuse to visit the living room. They passed the time in casual, unrelated conversation, and eventually wandered back to their bedroom for the third time. The light was no longer there and, much relieved, they retired for the night. They admitted to me that neither mentioned the incident to the other the next morning, nor, for that matter, ever, until they had heard about the strange "Truro Light" from some friends of theirs, who also told them of my interest. In retrospect, they found their behavior at the time very interesting. "Out of sight, out of mind," had been buttressed by "Out of conversation, out of existence." To have discussed the matter would have been to admit a presence they knew to be unsettling and genuinely mysterious.

The writer Donald Barthelme said to me once after he had read an account of a UFO landing I had written for the *Village Voice* that his life was complicated enough not to have to add this issue to the things he had to worry about. He was sorry he'd read the piece in the first place. I know what he means. I certainly never wanted to deal with the UFO problem, a phenomenon that until that 1964 August afternoon on the road to Provincetown I didn't even know existed.

I have deliberately skimmed over these 1975 Cape Cod sightings, not because they aren't interesting in themselves, but because they are far down on the list of cases which warrant thorough investigation, and at the time they occurred I was just beginning to pursue the subject actively. A few months after I returned to New York, everything changed when, one November evening, George O'Barski told me about his experience in North Hudson Park. But this, at least, tells how my interest in the UFO phenomenon began.

2

THE LANDING IN NORTH HUDSON PARK

Across the street from my studio in the Chelsea district of Manhattan, there is a small liquor store. It is typical of hundreds just like it—physically undistinguished, but open fourteen or fifteen hours every day, and a regular neighborhood stopping-off place, like the dry cleaners or the supermarket. The owners are Bill Burns and George O'Barski, and they have been selling me my dinner wine and doing emergency check cashing for me for over twenty years.

In November of 1975, George O'Barski was seventy-two years old. He is street-wise, astute, and reflective—an essential set of qualities for New Yorkers—and he is also a strict teetotaler. On a particular late November evening, I came into his store to buy a bottle of Soave to have with supper. George was pacing back and forth behind the counter, obviously troubled. He began complaining about an arthritic pain in his knee, and then muttered something to me about how you didn't know anymore what might happen. "A man can be driving home, minding his own business, and something can come down out of the sky and scare you half to death." Naturally, I stopped him there. "What do you mean, 'Something can come down out of the sky'?" Slowly and reluctantly, he began to tell me the story, and he continued only because I assured him I was seriously interested in what had happened to him. Two or three other customers entered the store and caused lengthy interruptions, so I told George I'd be back after dinner to hear the rest of his adventure. He had no idea, I realized, that I was interested in "things that come down out of sky," so his hesitation to expose himself to ridicule was natural. And his story was all but incredible.

An hour or so later, I was back in the store with my cassette tape recorder, and George cautiously began to unburden himself. The incident had happened ten months previously, in the middle of January. George had closed the store at midnight, walked "Cognac," his German shepherd guard dog, and had then worked on his bookkeeping and shelf-replenishing. Around one or two A.M., he locked up and started for home in his black Chevrolet.

George lives in North Bergen, New Jersey, just across the Hudson River from Manhattan. That night, according to habit, he was driving through deserted North Hudson Park on his way to a twenty-four-hour diner in Fort Lee. His car radio began to pick up static and "sound tinny," and, as he fumbled with the dial, muttering at the prospect of another costly repair, a low, brilliantly lit object passed his car a hundred feet or so on the left, traveling in the same direction. It was a warm night, George remembered, and the window was partway down on the driver's side. He heard a quiet humming or droning sound coming from the craft, which now had stopped in a playing field ahead of his car. Proceeding very slowly and feeling totally bewildered by what he was seeing, George drew closer to the roundish, thirty-foot-long ship, which now was hovering about ten feet above the ground. It was circumscribed by a series of regularly spaced vertical windows, roughly a foot wide by four feet high. George looked on in stunned disbelief as a narrow panel opened between two windows and a ladderlike apparatus emerged. The ship settled to within four feet of the playing field, and immediately a group of small figures appeared and, one after the other, descended to the ground.

George estimates that they were only three-and-a-half-to-four-feet tall, and they were clad in identical helmeted, or hooded, one-piece light-colored garments. "They looked like kids in snowsuits," he recalled. There were at least nine and possibly ten or eleven of them—he was too shocked to count—but he could not make out their faces. When George was telling me these things, his eyes were round, startled again by the memory of his terror:

"I've been held up in the store lots of times by men with pistols and knives, and I've been plenty scared, but nothing like this, ever." He accents, and repeats, the last phrase. He kept his car moving slowly, but the figures paid no attention to him. Each one carried a large spoonlike tool and a little bag with a handle. They moved quickly. In George's words, "They came down this ladder thing like kids coming down a fire escape. Fast. No wasted motion." They dug, spooning the dirt into their bags. In a few moments, they were back inside and the UFO ascended, moving north. George, at his closest, was sixty feet away. The entire incident took place in less than four minutes.

I asked George what he did when he got home. "Hey . . . I was sweating. I immediately made some tea." Usually he turned on the TV and watched a late movie, but he was too frightened to risk leaving any lights on in his apartment. "I went to bed. I went to bed, I was that scared. I pulled the covers over my head. I got up and took two aspirin. You know, I was scared. I figured the whole damn world had come to an end. I didn't know what the hell to think . . . I thought either I'm going crazy or there's something awfully wrong down there."

The next morning, George went back to the park. He walked over to the spot where the UFO had landed. There in a small area were about fifteen little holes, four or five inches deep. He said, "You know, when I went there and saw those holes, I got even more scared. . . . I'll tell you something. I even felt those holes. I didn't believe it looking at them. I put my hand in one."

Like most people who have had experiences like his, George tried every means he could to wish away the memory. He wanted to believe he had dreamed the whole thing, or even that "I had somehow slipped a gear." He told me that when he saw and felt the holes, he had to go home and make some more tea and take two more aspirin. Though eventually we located a number of other people who also saw, in North Hudson Park and on the same night, what was undoubtedly the same UFO, the confirmation of his sighting has, if anything, made it *more* disturbing for him.

A common misconception about people who report encounters with unidentified flying objects is that they "believe in UFOs." The fact is that very few witnesses have *a priori* beliefs. They are firm about the accuracy of their descriptions of color, shape, height, movement, etc., but they offer few explanations of what they believe the object was. In a reflective moment, George has told me he has theorized that the government or the CIA or perhaps a foundation somewhere has developed a secret method of propulsion, powering totally unconventional craft like the one he saw. "But then," he added, "it makes no sense. Why couldn't they just send up for soil samples? And how could they recruit all those little guys? A normal run would have guys all heights. It doesn't make sense."

As I listened to George's story, I noticed certain internal details which reinforced the conviction I held about his veracity. First of all, probably no one making up a story like this (and for what reason?) would, in effect, leave himself out of the events. George's role is strictly passive. Never once does a small figure notice him, turn towards him, threaten him, or hand him a "message." He merely drives by, watching. Almost all serious UFO reports involve benign, or at least neutral behavior, and George's story, in this respect, is typical.

Second, it seems to me that anyone inventing a sensational encounter with "space beings" would begin by creating a weird, memorable face: huge eyes, pointed ears, or whatever, and then work down to trivial details. George's "snowsuited kids" wore helmets, obscuring their faces, yet he is sure that their boots were of one piece with their trouser legs. And far from giving himself a heroic role in the encounter, George underlined how petrified he had been—"You just stop functioning," he said—and went on to admit that he, a man in his seventies, had gone to bed with the covers pulled up over his head. When the UFO took off, it flew north extremely quickly and lightly, he recalled, as if it were metal and somewhere high up there was a giant magnet attracting it. Listening to George's particular choice of imagery, I had the inescapable impression that an intelligent, careful man was trying his best to find words to describe an almost incredible experience.

It was essential, I realized, to locate an investigator from a serious UFO organization who would know exactly what to do next. A few phone calls led me to Ted Bloecher, at that time New York State director of MUFON (the Mutual UFO Network) and an investigator with twenty-five years' experience. On November 20, Ted came to my studio to listen to the tape I had made in George's store. He was entranced—it is difficult not to be—by George's diamond-in-the-rough account. Everyone connected with UFO research has heard reams of scientific and quasi-scientific speculation about these machines' as yet unknown method of propulsion. George put it this way: "When it took off, I looked underneath, you know. I said. 'There must be a big fan in there or something that runs this thing . . . but I can't see nothin'!'" In subsequent months he returned to this theme. "You know, when I was a kid I saw everything. I saw the dirigibles and they made noise. The little biplanes used to come to the towns, and you'd have to pay a quarter to watch them land and take off, and they made more noise. And then they had the airlines with twin engines and they made a terrible racket. After the war, there were the jets and they practically deafened you. Each time they made somethin' go faster, it was harder on the ears. Now they have the Concorde, and it's the fastest of all and nobody wants it around because when it takes off it shakes all the shingles off the houses. But this thing I saw that night in the park! It made only a little hum, just like a refrigerator starting up. And it went away almost before you could blink an eye! I'll tell you! I've never seen or heard anything like it. It was awesome."

Ted Bloecher introduced me to a young UFO investigator named Gerald Stoehrer, and on Saturday, November 23, we three drove to North Hudson Park to meet George and re-enact his three A.M. encounter. The plain where the UFO landed is a large athletic field, rimmed by trees and used for both football and softball. The UFO crew would have had a nice view of the upper Manhattan skyline because the landing site is directly opposite West 88th Street. In fact, the ship came down less than four miles from the headquarters of *The New York Times*.

North Hudson Park is a pleasant, manicured place, about a quarter of the size of Central Park. It has a lake, a wooded area, and the genteel, well-tended lawns common to civilized city parks. At the precise spot where George told us the ship touched down there is a thick mat of coarse grass, within which we found a series of fifteen or so bare places, about six inches in diameter, where the grass was entirely missing. There are no actual holes remaining, but the dirt in each little grassless circle contained no traces of roots, a fact discovered by Ted Bloecher when he took soil samples for possible future examination. Several weeks later we located the park custodian, whose job includes packing any holes he finds on the playing field to prevent accidents. He remembered that, in the early summer, he had refilled a number of small holes in that general vicinity. He had no idea what caused them, but assumed they must have been dug by unleashed dogs.

On this sunny afternoon, Ted stationed himself at the precise landing spot while Stoehrer and I got into George's car. George took the wheel to retrace his route that January night. With the tape recorder going and Stoehrer timing each incident as George recalled it, we rode along through the park, listening to his story. From the moment his radio started to misbehave till the UFO lift-off, slightly under four minutes elapsed. The drive established a plausible time-frame, and we had a new, more detailed account to compare with the earlier one.

At the bottom of the hill by the park is a tall, circular, modern structure named, ironically, the Stonehenge Apartments. By coincidence, I knew the building because a collector of my work once lived there, and I remembered that Stonehenge is served by twenty-four-hour doormen. The building sits atop the Palisades, and tenants who face the Hudson River have a dramatic downstream view of Manhattan. The main entrance, however, is on the side which faces North Hudson Park. An alert doorman would have had an excellent view of anything coming to earth in the spot George had pointed out to us. I walked down the hill, three hundred yards or so from the landing site to the front door, preparing to ask a few questions. The doorman on duty was a large, hearty, helpful man by the name of Eddie Oberterbussing. I told him that I was investigating an incident that had occurred in the park the previous January, very late at night, that might involve a UFO. I deliberately withheld any other details such as precise date, location, description of the object, etc. Eddie told me that the two night men who worked at the Stonehenge that January had both since left for other jobs. However, one of them, Bill Pawlowski by name, had reported an odd incident: sometime in January, during the small hours, one of the huge plate glass windows at the entrance had been shattered under rather unclear circumstances. Eddie had not been in touch with Pawlowski for many months, but he was kind enough to find his new address for me.

Ted Bloecher is a walking encyclopedia of Air Force and civilian UFO reports. He felt, when I told him about the broken window, that there was probably no connection whatsoever between the accident and the UFO sighting, and it was only in subsequent months that he came across a case or two indicating something of a precedent.[1] There was no such difficulty with landing and soil-gathering reports such as George's. There are scores of similar accounts of small figures digging earth samples and even removing plants from farms. These events apparently have occurred over a span of some thirty years in the United States, France, South America, and elsewhere. And it is extremely com-

mon for witnesses to such preposterous events to hesitate, like
George, for months before telling anyone their stories. Ridicule
and disbelief are predictable responses.

George O'Barski, a widower, did not awaken his son to tell
him what happened that night. Not until the next day, after he had
returned to the park and examined the holes, did he finally unburden himself. George told me that, had he seen a policeman five
minutes after the UFO had taken off, he would not have reported
it. "A man my age telling a story like this—why, they'd put you
away. If you'd come in here a year ago and told me the same story,
I wouldn't have believed you, either." The pressure to share his
perplexity and fear must finally have been too strong, and in a
very hesitant, guarded way he had approached me, though he had
no reason to believe I would be a sympathetic listener.

Bill Pawlowski, the former doorman, proved to be difficult to
locate. I called him at his home in southeastern New Jersey many
times over a two-week period. As I learned later, he was working
nights at a security job and the phone was unplugged during the
daytime so he could sleep. On December 5, I reached him. I said
that I was looking into an incident that had occurred in the park
opposite the Stonehenge Apartments the previous January and
asked if he recalled seeing anything odd. His answer was immediate. He said that he did recall an incident, and that it had been
frightening. It had been two or three in the morning and he had
looked up into the park because he had suddenly noticed some
extremely bright lights shining down the hill towards him. These
lights, he said, were in a horizontal row, ten to fifteen of them,
regularly spaced. He had never seen anything like it. For a moment, he wondered if it couldn't possibly be an evenly parked row
of automobiles shining their headlights towards him, but then he
realized the lights appeared to be about ten feet off the ground. He
could make out a continuous dark mass surrounding the row of
illumination; he knew that he was seeing something disturbingly
unusual.

He walked over to the window for a better view, and then
decided to call a tenant in the building. He turned behind him to
the phone, dialed the number, and began to speak when he heard
a high-pitched vibration and a sudden crack. The lobby window
had broken at a low point near his feet. He hung up and crouched
down to look at the break; when he glanced up a moment later, the
lights were gone. He immediately called the police.

They responded promptly, he said, probably because a North Bergen police lieutenant lives in the building. The two patrolmen and Pawlowski examined the break, which turned out to be peculiar. Whatever struck the glass did not come through. On the outside, there was an indentation as if a marble of glass had been gouged out of the surface; from this little crater radiated a series of cracks. No projectile could be found anywhere nearby. Opposite the front entrance to Stonehenge is a wide driveway bordered by a low wall, and behind the wall there is a ten-foot drop. Whatever broke the window had to have come from above, and it was clear to Pawlowski the "shot" was fired from the hill across the road. He did not, however, tell the police about the lights in the park; again, the old reluctance to open oneself to ridicule. "The lights had disappeared," he said, "and I thought they'd never believe me anyway, so I didn't tell them. I just suggested they drive around up there and see what they could find." They resumed their patrol, but skipped the park altogether; it turns out that North Hudson Park does not fall within the jurisdiction of the North Bergen Police Department.

I asked Pawlowski if he had told anyone else that night about the object in the park, and, to my immense relief, he had. The police lieutenant who lived in Stonehenge—Al Del Gaudio—was on night duty and returned at about six-thirty A.M., some three and a half or four hours after the landing in the park. Bill was on friendly terms with the lieutenant and told him his story. On December 9, I phoned Lieutenant Del Gaudio to ask him about it. He is a brusque, no-nonsense kind of professional, judging by his voice. My questions, specifically, were: did he know Bill Pawlowski, and what had the former doorman told him the night the window was broken? "Sure, I knew him," said the lieutenant. "He used to work nights. I came in about six-thirty that morning and he had some wild story about this big thing with lights on it that came down in the park. He thought it was involved with the broken window, but you can't believe a story like that. He must've been drinking or something." (The all-purpose answer, like "Shut up.")

Each detail of Pawlowski's story confirmed O'Barski's. George had seen the object from a moving car, so it was not easy for him to estimate the number of lighted windows visible from a single point of view. He guessed ten or twelve, and possibly as many as fifteen. Pawlowski remembered seeing ten to fifteen lights; he was nervous enough not to count. George had said that the UFO stopped ten feet off the ground and then settled a bit until it was only about four feet from the field. Pawlowski's guess, from approximately three hundred yards away, was that the *lights* were ten feet off the ground. Since the lights did not extend all the way to the bottom of the UFO, their estimates are quite similar. Both agreed that the entire sighting had lasted only three minutes or so, and both set the time as around three A.M. All this information was elicited separately and voluntarily from each, and neither man had ever met or spoken to the other.

I ended my phone conversation to Pawlowski thoroughly shaken. What had begun as an almost incredible story—which I believed—told to me by a man I had known then for seventeen years, had just turned into something more complicated, more certain, and more disturbing. An unknown craft of some sort had landed one mile from Broadway, and sixty feet from poor George O'Barski driving home from work. The uniformed—and uniform—crew had disembarked and taken earth samples. Why, and why from *this* spot?

Scenarios followed as I tried to put the parts together. Aboard the UFO, had someone, or something, seen, in the large round building down below, a uniformed human looking back up the hill? Bill Pawlowski in his Stonehenge livery unfortunately reached for the phone, and crack went the window. End of phone call. End of soil collection. Somehow the "shot" seemed more like a warning than a miss.

The next step Ted, Gerry Stoehrer, and I planned was to interview Pawlowski in greater depth in hopes of bringing up additional information. And then, more crucially, to take him back to the park so that he could show us exactly where he saw the UFO. We gave him no details whatsoever from George's account—we wanted his memory to be as pure as possible. Under further questioning, Bill remembered something else which intrigued us. At the foot of the hill across from Stonehenge is a large tree made up of three trunks growing from one set of roots. One trunk grew somewhat parallel to the ground, but in a direct line with both the Stonehenge entrance and the UFO site atop the hill. Pawlowski insisted that, when the sun came up the morning of the landing, the large trunk was broken and hanging down. He believes the same "weapon" which cracked the window also sliced through the tree. The park service has since cut back the broken trunk almost to the ground, so we will probably never know if the two accidents had the same mysterious cause.

Central, now, to our investigation was the matter of exactly where Pawlowski remembered seeing the UFO. He returned to the park on December 11—his first visit in months—with Gerry Stoehrer, and, from his old post at the Stonehenge entrance, looked back up the hill. He had recalled a pole which apparently bisected the lights, as if it were in front of, but close to, the UFO. Atop the hill there had been a flagpole, since removed, but it had been located about two hundred feet to the left of the place O'Barski put the landing site. Pawlowski looked, pondered, and finally decided that it could not have been the flagpole in front of the lights, because he remembered them being further to the right, where, in fact, a tall lamppost stands. He walked straight up into the park to the exact spot that O'Barski had named. Gerry had been holding his breath; he relaxed—we had our final detail confirmed.

Bill never saw the diminutive crew members, which is not surprising. First of all, they were working on the ground about fifty feet or so back from the crest of the hill, so they probably would not have been visible from the entrance to the Stonehenge. Also, the difficulty in looking out from inside a lighted room, through the reflections on the glass, obscures small details—Bill was only able to see the unusually bright lights and the darkish shape containing them. He was amazed when we finally told him the other details of George's account. He seemed to be feeling a mixture of both envy and relief that O'Barski had been about a thousand feet closer to the UFO and its busy occupants.

One of the areas one routinely checks in such cases is the FAA's air traffic control to see if a radar operator might have tracked an unidentified object that night. The New York-New Jersey area FAA spokesman I talked to had nothing for me on this case, but he was interested in the report for personal reasons. A number of years ago, he told me, when he was himself a traffic controller for an upstate New York airport, he tracked a UFO at supersonic speeds. Most interestingly, and this is quite uncommon UFO behavior, the object was in *level* flight, parallel to the ground. Controllers at the two airfields closest to his reported that they, too, were tracking the UFO on their radar screens. He explained to me that, in this recent North Hudson Park case, the UFO would probably not have been picked up. Now, a computer system intervenes between the actual radarscope and the screens that the controllers use. Most non-aircraftlike radar targets are automatically siphoned off the controllers' screens, thus avoiding "ground clutter," inversions, and other potentially confusing data. When I explained the location and altitude and incredible speed of the UFO as George described it, he assured me that the computer would probably have automatically eliminated it, and no controller would have ever seen it on his screen.

In the course of interviews we conducted with other Stonehenge staff members, we learned that Frank Gonzalez, the doorman who worked on Pawlowski's nights off, had once confided in a fellow employee about a sighting he had made. Gonzalez had left the Stonehenge months before for a job in Riverdale, where he lived with his wife and daughters. Ted called him at his new apartment and set up an appointment for Sunday, the first of February. We were eager to learn whatever we could about his sighting, which evidently *preceded* the O'Barski-Pawlowski encounter.

Francisco "Frank" Gonzalez is a small, neat, careful man whose English is far from fluent. His teen-aged daughter gracefully helped the three of us over the inevitable linguistic rough spots. Frank's sighting occurred between two and three A.M. on Monday morning, January 6, six days to the hour before the landing in the park witnessed by O'Barski and Pawlowski. He had been standing inside the main entrance to the Stonehenge when he noticed a large, bright light hovering motionless above the playing field in North Hudson Park. Curious, he opened the door and stepped outside. "I saw something round, very bright, you know . . . with some windows. I hear some noise . . . it's not like a helicopter, nothing like that. Like a plane, no, no. Something different. I was afraid, I tell you . . . I come back (*inside*). Then, you know, I see that light go straight up and I said, 'Oh, God!' "

Gonzalez guessed that the object was about as high up as the twentieth floor of Stonehenge Apartments. He described the sound it made as a "heavy sound," which almost hurt his ears, and the imitation he attempted came close to George's "refrigerator motor" drone. Another detail from the later encounter was confirmed when he described the color of the light. O'Barski had been firm about the fact that the light from the windows was of a regular incandescent hue; that is, closer to amber than to the blue of fluorescent lamps. We asked Gonzalez about the hue of the lights he saw. "Jello," he answered, and his daughter delicately removed the Cuban "j" and turned the word into its proper "yellow." With marvelous ingenuousness, Frank produced a drawing for us of the craft he had seen; it had a bottom ringed with rectangular windows, but no top. "I couldn't see the top of it," he admitted. "*It* was dark, but the bottom was all bright." When he first sighted the UFO, he had called the security guard, but unfortunately for all of us, he was in the garage and unavailable as a confirming witness.

We gave Frank a rough map showing some of the landmarks in the park: the flagpole, the various roads, the playing field, and he unhesitatingly placed the UFO directly over the field in exactly the spot where Pawlowski and O'Barski had seen it touch down six days later. Furthermore, Frank described a kind of spotlight on the craft's underside illuminating what was to be its eventual landing site. The entire episode suggested a preliminary reconnaissance flight to check out the terrain in an almost old-fashioned military sense. Our speculation along these lines was strengthened when, about two months later, Gerry Stoehrer located witnesses to yet another preliminary flight, by what has to be the same UFO, and this time only a few hours before the final landing.

Early in January, before I had heard Frank Gonzalez's story, I began writing an account of the North Hudson Park landing. It was published in *The Village Voice* on March 1, and caused something of a stir in the vicinity of the Stonehenge Apartments. One of the reasons I wrote the piece in the first place was that I hoped it might flush out a few more witnesses to an event I knew had to have been seen by more people than just George and Bill. To this purpose, I had deliberately refrained from including certain facts in my article. I did not specify the exact date, saying only that it was in "mid-January." I did not describe the color of the body of the object itself—"Very dark," said George, "almost black." And there was a third crucial fact: the weather. January 1975, as one would expect, was mostly cold, with the temperature remaining in the twenties and thirties. Only twice did it rise into the forties. But at three A.M. on the 12th, when the UFO landed, it was in the high fifties, and at nine-thirty P.M. on the 11th, about five hours *before* the landing, it was a balmy sixty-three degrees. It was important for us to keep these pieces of information undisclosed, to provide a test of the veracity of anyone who subsequently might come forward claiming to have seen the UFO.

Towards the end of March, Gerry Stoehrer gave a talk to a
PTA group in North Bergen on the subject of UFOs. After he finished, twelve-year-old Robert Wamsley and his mother, Alice, approached him to tell of their sighting. At nine-thirty on a Saturday
night—they were sure of the time because the family had been
watching "The Bob Newhart Show" on television—Robert
glanced out the window and saw, to his complete amazement, a
round, domed craft, brilliantly lit, just outside the house. The
Wamsleys live twelve blocks south of North Hudson Park, or
about fourteen blocks from the Stonehenge Apartments. Robert
alerted his mother and the rest of the family. Joseph Wamsley, the
father, and the other children—Joseph, Jr., age sixteen, and Deb-
bie, thirteen—ran outside for a better look.

The UFO was encircled by rectangular windows, which gave
off a yellowish light. It was moving very slowly, perhaps forty or
fifty feet off the ground, and it glided at a slight angle, "as if," Mrs.
Wamsley thought, "it was looking in people's windows." Stoehrer
visited the Wamsleys two days later and collected further details.
The UFO had flown along Boulevard East toward North Hudson
Park. Four members of the Wamsley family ran along the street,
following it for perhaps two minutes or more. The object, picking
up speed, was finally lost from view in the vicinity, as Alice
Wamsley puts it, "of the big round house" (The Stonehenge Apartments). She provided a crucial detail. When she first saw the UFO,
she was lounging in her bathrobe. Not wanting to miss anything,
she had run outside to follow it down the street wearing only her
robe. She was in her bare feet, too, but she remembered that it was
a very mild night and she wasn't at all cold, a real surprise for
January!

We had originally checked the weather conditions for several
reasons. One, as a routine matter to gain background information;
two, to see if it would have been possible to dig up soil that con-
ceivably was frozen; and three, to check on George O'Barski's
statement that he heard the UFO's hum because he had his car
window partway down, due to the mildness of the weather. Mrs.
Wamsley running down a New Jersey street in January in her bare
feet provided a special confirmation of the date and circumstances
of the landing. A final matter was the question of the UFO's color.
Gerry asked the Wamsleys their recollections. "The body was
dark gray or even maybe black," said Robert, and we had a final
verification.

So the North Hudson Park UFO scouted a landing spot on Monday, January 6, 1975, at three A.M., and was seen by doorman Gonzalez. At nine-thirty P.M. on Saturday night, it returned, passing low over the area, and was followed down the street by the Wamsley family, dazzled by its lights and its peculiar hum. It sped over the park again and disappeared somewhere near the Stonehenge Apartments. Then, a scant five hours later, it was back for its mission. It landed in front of George O'Barski, the "crew" disembarked, dug their soil samples, fired a warning "shot" at Bill Pawlowski, and departed. The whole mysterious business took place over six days and must have been witnessed by many more than the eight people I have described. (Alice Wamsley's sister, whom I have not mentioned, provides a ninth.)

In the months following these events, Ted Bloecher, George O'Barski, myself, and the others involved in the case have speculated on what it all may have meant. It seems absurd on the face of it to imagine that the entire episode occurred because a UFO crew, whoever they may be, actually needed soil from North Hudson Park. Could the mission instead have been a species of theater, a display of imagery designed to communicate certain basic information? Ted Bloecher and many other experienced investigators seriously entertain this theory. Looking coldly at the implications, this is what one might deduce, thinking metaphorically rather than literally:

1. The need to take samples of earth connotes a non-Earth origin or habitat; i.e., the idea of "extraterrestrials" is conveyed. (George thought of our astronauts taking rock samples on the moon.)

2. And, the unknown, "magical" propulsion system of their craft suggests a technology far in advance of ours. Scientific superiority is strongly conveyed.

3. Yet, the two-armed, two-legged "kids in snowsuits" suggests a race of people like us, and therefore not terrifyingly alien.

4. Their diminutive size and neutral behavior towards George O'Barski a mere sixty feet away implies definite non-hostility.

5. The "shot" which broke the window at Stonehenge Apartments might imply a warning and the possibility, if threatened, of their turning hostile.

It has been suggested that the entire enterprise involves both information-gathering and, at the same time, a "consciousness-raising" effort by subtly imparting the idea of their presence to us "mere Earthlings" without unduly alarming us. If this is their goal, they are achieving it remarkably successfully. The Gallup Poll on the subject of UFOs shows that a constantly rising proportion of the population accepts the possibility that we are, indeed, under extraterrestrial surveillance. No one I know has yet panicked from the widely published accounts of UFO activity, Orson Welles and his *War of the Worlds* notwithstanding.

The North Hudson Park landing received a great deal of press and television coverage following my rather detailed piece in *The Village Voice*. Frank Gonzalez, the Wamsleys, George O'Barski, and other witnesses were interviewed by various TV crews. (The case itself, I must point out, involves additional UFO incidents which I have not gone into here. Ted Bloecher's excellent and thorough two-part series in *FSR*[2] should be consulted by the interested reader.) One high point of the television coverage was a 1976 talk show hosted by Stanley Siegel and shown over New York City's Channel 7. The guests were Dr. Robert Jastrow of NASA's Goddard Lab; Dr. Edgar Mitchell, the astronaut who headed the second moon landing; Dr. J. Allen Hynek of the Center for UFO Studies; and witnesses Betty Hill and George O'Barski. After recounting the events of that night in North Hudson Park, from the moment his radio ceased playing to the almost unbelievable sight of the UFO lifting-off in near silence, George was faced with this problem: Stanley Siegel, apologizing in advance for the question, said that his viewers would demand he ask it. "George, did you really see these things you've described? Do you have a drinking problem? A history of mental illness?" Was this witness telling the truth?

There was a pause and George leaned back in his chair, and spoke slowly and directly. "I always figure like this: if a man, as I have, has lived a reasonably honorable and decent life for seventy-three years, he isn't going to do something that's crazy, and in one wild burst destroy his whole life's history and decency." There was no studio audience that day, but the cameramen and technicians nodded and smiled at one another, responding with genuine warmth to George's unmistakable integrity.

I noticed one additional thing; when Stanley Siegel asked these questions, George never for an instant mentioned the fact that there were other witnesses, that William Pawlowski independently confirmed the landing. He declined, one might say, to borrow from another man, and defended his account on the sole grounds of his own truthfulness.

At the time of the North Hudson Park investigation, neither Ted Bloecher nor I knew very much, first-hand, about abduction cases. It occurred to both of us, however, that there was a nagging time problem in George's account. If the UFO incident spanned only three or four minutes, and George arrived home at roughly three A.M., then he couldn't have left his Manhattan store until two-fifteen to two-thirty A.M. The twenty-block drive from his shop to the Lincoln Tunnel, and then along Boulevard East to the park, can hardly have taken more than, say, twenty minutes at that time of the day.

George closes his store at midnight, but hardly ever works as long as two and a half hours before heading home. He has also mentioned to me that he has, from time to time, a sense of having been "told" something by the silent figures, something he cannot grasp or remember. I suggested one day that he think of undergoing hypnosis to see if there might be a part of his experience that has been deliberately blocked from conscious memory. "No, sir," he answered. "When the doctors put you under, you're out there somewhere and you may never come back." I told him about a witness who was currently undergoing hypnosis to recall a lost period of time in a similar case. "How's he doing?" George asked. "He's finding out some fascinating things, but it's been emotionally draining for him." George beamed at my answer. "You see what I mean? I was right. You'll never see me getting hypnotized!"

The essential deduction to be made from the North Hudson Park landing is not that it, too, could possibly involve an abduction. It is that we have an example—a vivid example—of the freedom of movement enjoyed by a UFO craft, a freedom which suggests just how widespread such abductions could be. We are not limited to dark country lanes and isolated Nebraska farms. One of the witnesses to a related sighting near North Hudson Park on Boulevard East reported a brightly lit, windowed object just over the top of the Palisade. He stopped his car and got out to watch it. The UFO then moved off towards the George Washington Bridge, and instantly all of its lights blinked off. He watched the dark mass speed away, a nearly invisible blot in the night sky. The UFO that George watched land might have blinked off its lights, and there could easily be a more complicated scenario here than any of us imagines, though it will forever remain speculation. I have only raised the issue to demonstrate the complexity of the problem.

Very recently I was in George's store and we were having a rather philosophical chat. "You know, Budd," he said, "I'm not a religious man. My wife was religious. But I'm getting on, and I figure I haven't got a lot of time left, so I think about it. I figure if there is a God, and I face him sometime, I'll just say, 'Lord, you didn't give me all the brains in the world or all the advantages, but I did the best I could with what you gave me.' And I figure he'll have to accept that. And if he does, I'm gonna say, 'O.K., Lord, here's one I want to ask you. Who were those little guys I saw in the park that night? Where are they from? Are you their God, too, or what?' "

3

A Sharp Right Turn on the National Road

Not everyone having a close encounter with a UFO is as uninformed about the phenomenon as was George O'Barski, who had to ask me one day what the initials "UFO" stood for. When Ted Bloecher, in January of 1978, introduced me to Steven Kilburn,[1] he explained that he and Steve originally met at a Fortean conference, a gathering held by enthusiasts of the writings of Charles Fort.[2] Like Fort in his day, they remain dedicated to the study of various strange and unexplained phenomena, including UFOs. At the time, Steve was an undergraduate at the University of Maryland, but when he moved to New York and married, he phoned Ted to re-establish their friendship. Ted invited him to an informal meeting of UFO researchers at my studio, and there we met.

Steven Kilburn is a shy, intense, and haunted man. He is young—not quite thirty—and strikingly attractive; in fact, more than once he has turned down invitations to make modeling his career. Instead, he is dedicated to a career in the arts, the study of which he supports by his nine-to-five job. His shyness and seriousness are captivating, accompanied as they are by an understated, natural honesty and directness. At our meeting, he was content to listen, making very few contributions to a general discussion of recent UFO cases. But through it all, one felt that things were percolating inside him, and shortly I came to realize that he was, for no immediately apparent reason, uneasy.

From his Fortean connections and his friendship with Ted, Steven was acquainted with the basic shape and complexity of the UFO phenomenon, though he had read very little of the literature or the specific case material. By the time he had attended two or three of our rather sprawling, unstructured gatherings, he had heard some talk about the use of hypnotic regression in suspected abduction cases. One night early in 1978, as a meeting was breaking up, Steve stopped me in the downstairs hall. He has a way of shifting about nervously, his eyes fixed shyly in middle distance, and then suddenly raising his eyes to meet yours in a steady, pleading gaze; the effect is riveting. "There's probably nothing to it," he said, "but something may have happened to me when I was in college. I can't remember anything specific, but something has always bothered me about a certain stretch of road I used to pass through whenever I left my girlfriend's house in Maryland. I don't know if there's anything to it, but I think there may be."

I asked if there had been a UFO sighting connected with his experience. "No, that's just it. I can't remember anything specific, but I just feel something happened to me one time when I was driving home." It cost him a great effort, I knew, even to bring the matter up, but especially to make a request. "Sometime, whenever there's an open appointment, I'd like to try hypnosis, just to see if there's anything to my feeling after all."

The next day, when I talked to Ted by phone, I mentioned the conviction in which Steve had described the uneasiness he felt whenever he was on that particular length of highway. At this point in our understanding of abduction cases, we accepted the Hill case and others like it as a general model. Though witnesses might realize that there had been a period of unaccountably missing time they would still consciously remember having seen a UFO and/or occupants. The surrounding circumstances would have high definition; only the abduction itself would have been blocked from conscious memory. What could we think about a man who, practically speaking, remembered nothing whatsoever of the experience, and who had nothing more solid to go on than a deep-seated fear of a certain stretch of highway? It seemed an almost ridiculously flimsy pretext for entering into the costly and time-consuming process of hypnotic regression. And yet Steven was, himself, a special case. If anything, I believed, he was the kind of man who would naturally downplay his feelings rather than artificially exaggerate them. Ted and I weighed the various factors involved and decided that the situation should be explored.

Towards the end of 1976, I had met Dr. Robert Naiman, a psychiatrist who occasionally uses hypnosis as a therapeutic technique. He is very experienced in this method, having employed hypnosis for over fifteen years to help some of his patients overcome smoking addictions, problems of overeating, and so forth. In one interesting case he told me about, the patient of another psychiatrist could never remember his dreams, so for weeks he came to Dr. Naiman early in the morning, was hypnotized and instructed that he would be able to recall his dreams when he visited his analyst later in the day. This strange two-step process, he assured me, was ultimately successful.

Dr. Naiman had very little information about the UFO phenomenon, and no really strong opinions about it one way or the other. However, he is a generous, thoughtful man with an inquiring mind, so the prospect of exploring the memories of UFO witnesses was evidently interesting to him. He agreed to give us some of his time, and we began, early in 1977, to use hypnosis in several time-lapse cases we suspected might be actual abductions. The results were fascinating and varied. In one case that is still under investigation, two young men and a young woman, driving near Kent, Connecticut, in September of 1973, watched a large, hovering UFO disgorge a series of individually moving lights at treetop level. The three then drove to the place where they had seen the lights glide down a hillside to a lower road. As they sat in their car, about twenty helmeted figures approached them, and the next thing they knew the figures were no longer there—and, somehow, *two hours* had passed! Under hypnosis, one man remembered nothing whatsoever of the missing time period; the second man, a Vietnam combat veteran, had a dramatic breakthrough, however, and recalled at least some of the startling subsequent events.[3]

In another case, Dr. Naiman was working with a man who, he believed, had a serious memory block. In his second hypnotic session, the subject underwent a frightening physical paralysis of both arms, a symptom that has since been observed during the hypnosis of other suspected abductees. In fact, even when these subjects are brought out of their trance states the paralysis of hands and arms has lingered, sometimes for minutes, in a situation only slightly more disturbing for the subject than for the surprised hypnotist.

In the spring of 1978, Bob Naiman introduced Ted Bloecher and me to psychologist Dr. Girard Franklin, a colleague he was training in the use of hypnosis. Since the demands we were making on Dr. Naiman were always at the edge of the unmanageable, he suggested that we ask Dr. Franklin to help with our investigations. And so it happened that in May a two-hour time period conveniently became available and we arranged an appointment for Steven Kilburn.

Dr. Franklin was not curious about the UFO phenomenon. On the contrary, he was very skeptical, and so was hardly prepared for what unfolded. For that matter, none of the four of us—Ted, Steven, Dr. Franklin, or I—expected anything dramatic to occur. On the way to his appointment, Steve apologized to Ted for having inconvenienced all of us, since he felt there may very well be nothing specific behind his fear of that stretch of Maryland highway. Ted assured him, as I did later when I arrived, that whatever did or did not come out of it, the session would function as a kind of control, an experiment aimed at discovering if deep-seated feelings of dread such as Steven experienced might indicate a buried traumatic event, or perhaps have come about for other, internal psychological reasons. Either way, an answer would be helpful.

Dr. Franklin's office is on the ground floor of his Upper West Side Manhattan brownstone. After introductions all around, Steve sat down on the leather couch and began to detail the background of his feelings, while Ted set up his cassette tape recorder. There was a marvelously uncomplicated honesty in Steven's voice and posture as he spoke; his eyes were steady and met Dr. Franklin's scrutiny head-on.

SK: Before I came to New York, I used to have a girl-friend . . . we're still friendly . . . and I used to drive from Baltimore—it was Pikesville—to Frederick, Maryland, to see her. I would take Route 40 west, and for, I'd say, at least ten or fifteen miles of that road, it was very, very deserted. And very often I'd be at her house very late at night and come back, and it was very dark. The streets weren't lighted at all. And, ah—about—I'd say probably at least a year after I was seeing her, I was driving along the road from Frederick to Baltimore; I don't remember wheth-er I actually saw something in the sky—I believe I did—and it was there that I first felt that—something. I felt very strange, for some reason. I didn't know why. It was that feeling someone is watching you as you wake up, that sort of thing. I don't know whether someone was watching me or I was watching something strange. Whatever it was that particular time, I remember I felt that something maybe had just happened to me, or was going to happen, and it was this very weird feeling. Every time I passed that approximate area, I felt for some reason something right there had happened. And I really just put it out of my mind as a sort of a—an event I had experienced, or from reading some novel, or whatnot. But I always wondered if something really had happened to me at that time.

Now, I can't say for sure, but I believe I was a little bit confused about the time, a loss of time on that one main experience I had. It's possible, of course, that I'm mistaken, but there's something about it that I've never quite understood, and I don't even know what—what questions to ask to find what answer I'm looking for, if that makes any sense. I never felt that way in any other place at any other time. I either have a very vivid imagination, or it was just a . . . It was a very dark road, that was for sure, and it did occur to me as I was driving that this is the kind of place that something like that (*a UFO encounter*) should happen. This was part of my hesitation for—wasting your time. I hope I'm not doing that.

GF: It isn't a waste of time, because if nothing happened, that's as informative as if something did happen, so don't worry about that. It's not a waste of your time—either way we would be okay.

SK: Okay, that satisfies my . . . Well, I remember various other details, if that's important. I believe I was driving my sister's car, which is a Toyota, during this particular incident, and I did not always drive her car. For some reason, I have a very strange memory of looking at the dashboard. I don't know if I was looking at the clock or not, but I do remember seeing it, and I don't remember why.

HM: Do you remember any thoughts that you can elaborate on?

SK: Well, I just remembered as you asked. I see my car pulled over to the side—I think it was the center; there was a big median, grass median—and I see me walking. I see the car at an angle, and I see me walking from the *front* of the car to the right, and I see a light—from the car—I *think* it's from the car, I'm not sure, and—I don't see me meeting anybody or doing anything, going any place, but I distinctly have the feeling of me being out of the car, and my car stopping, and again, this is something that flashed through my mind, like a memory, or—or a scenario that *could* have happened.

And also, driving alone, it *(the source of his "being watched")* would have been to the right, overhead, whatever I felt was there over me, or possibly I was looking at it. It's just so very black, very dark, and it was a clear night, I think.

GF: Do you remember what you were thinking about it?

SK: I was scared.

GF: You were?

SK: Oh, I was scared. Yes. I mean, shivers down my spine, that kind of thing. Not—not petrified. But very scared.

GF: Real scared.

SK: Yes. In fact, I had the feeling of being trapped in my car and wishing I could go faster.

GF: And get out of there?

SK: Yes. And someone in back of me, with a faster car, that kind of feeling. Also, I have the memory of looking in the mirror to see if someone was looking for me.

GF: It almost felt like there could have been?

SK: Yes, like I was being watched, or followed, or something like that. The feeling, I think, to sum it up, was that I wasn't there alone.

GF: Right. You had a sense of some presence, or something . . . of being watched, followed . . . ?

SK: Yes. And also some kind of feeling of power that somebody else had. These were feelings that probably went through my mind very quickly, but I had that feeling, and I'd be feeling it every time I passed this area. I distinctly remember, *distinctly* remember it once. I think it was the first time it happened. Also, I remember that driving on this particular patch of road, like on many highways, there was a kind of a large hill-like embankment, covered with grass, and I think there was a fence and trees; there were trees behind the fence. *(Pause)* I think that it was in front of me while I was driving. Must've been a long way off, because I could see my headlights getting lost in the darkness—I couldn't see the road ahead of me. Again, I don't know if this is my imagination, after this many years. And if I were to hazard a guess, it would probably be two or three in the morning. It's just a guess. It's like it had gotten a little bit chilly. I think I had a light jacket—I can't say for sure. I think the rest of it I'd just be guessing.

GF: Would you feel ready now to try the hypnosis part and try to see if we can make anything out of it?

SK: Okay.

GF: All right. How would you feel about lying down?

Steven made himself comfortable and Dr. Franklin began the process of inducing a trance state, but at this point a slight technical error occurred. The tape recorder had been placed on the floor near the couch, but we discovered later that for some reason it did not pick up Steve's very quiet voice with enough volume for us to distinguish his words. Luckily, however, when it came time during the session to turn the tape over, Ted repositioned the machine and the later, more important part of the hour was successfully recorded.

Initially, Steve talked about being in the car, driving home, and feeling drowsy. He described opening the window to freshen the air, and at one point bending down towards the dashboard for some reason. He told of his car stopping and of his confusion about what was happening.

He lay absolutely motionless in a deep trance state. His voice was soft and his words slightly slurred as he described standing alongside the car and looking uneasily towards the metal fence. There was a long pause and he seemed afraid to go on with his account. He was obviously confused and frightened. Suddenly, he cried out as if in pain. "It's on my shoulder . . . a clamp . . . it hurts. I can't move!" Dr. Franklin tried to soothe his fear, but then a curious accident served to deepen his fright. A few feet away from the couch was the doctor's automatic phone-answering machine, which at that moment intercepted a call; it made a sudden loud click and Steven literally almost leaped a few inches off the couch. He cried out again. His fear was palpable; his voice conveyed panic, and tears flowed down his cheeks. Dr. Franklin took immediate measures to calm him, assuring him that he was safe and that he would be able to tell us exactly what was occurring.

Earlier in his instructions, he had explained that Ted or I might also occasionally question him, so now, after the tape was turned over and the recorder moved closer, Ted took up the dialogue.

TB: Are you still standing next to your car, Steven?
SK: Yes.
TB: Can you see what's on your shoulder?
SK: *(Agitated)* Yes.
TB: What does it look like?
SK: Big wrench.
TB: Where is it coming from?
SK: I can't tell. Uh . . .
TB: Behind you?
SK: *(Agitated)* Yes. It's long . . . It's a big . . . not a wrench . . . uh . . .
TB: Grappling hook?
SK: No . . . uh . . . no. A wrench . . . it fits . . .
TB: A wrench?
SK: I, uh . . . *(Steven's body moved as if in pain.)*
TB: You say it fits up against your shoulder?
SK: Yes . . . it's . . . uh . . . yes . . .
TB: How far down does it go?
SK: All the way. A foot, on either side of my body.
TB: How far? Down to your chest?
SK: Yes.
TB: Does it fit closely to your body? Or is it uncomfortable?
SK: Yes. *(Agitated)* Yes. Uh, I think that it . . . *(Inaudible)*. It did hurt. . . .
TB: Are you trying to get loose from it?
SK: No. I'm afraid! *(Inaudible)* There's light . . . in that direction.
TB: Is the light coming from your car lights?
SK: No. *(Frightened)* No! There's something else. Something behind the fence! *(Very agitated.)* Oh! Oh! Black . . . all dressed in black! *(Inaudible)* Can't see their faces. . . .
TB: Can you see how many?
SK: Uh . . . more than two . . . three or more.
TB: But they're on the other side of the fence?
SK: Yes. I think they're waiting for something. I'm afraid! I don't know what's going to happen. . . . Oh . . . I don't know what's going to happen. . . . I don't know what's going to happen! *(Very agitated)* Oh . . . somebody's coming over!
TB: They're coming over the fence?
SK: Uh, I don't know. I think they might.
TB: How tall is the fence?

SK: Uh, higher than me. Six feet or something. They're right up against it. I think I hear their breathing or something . . . or sliding, or some kind of sound.

TB: Hear that sound. Listen for it. Tell us what you hear.

SK: *(Inaudible.)* My side hurts, my back. They twisted me back. I feel like . . . my back . . . I keep feeling it turning me, but I don't see anything. . . .

TB: Which way is it turning you?

SK: To the right.

TB: Is that toward the fence?

SK: No. To the street.

TB: Where are you standing in relation to the car?

SK: Um, within six feet.

TB: On the side or in the front?

SK: *(Inaudible)* left front. I keep seeing, uh, my sister's Toyota. That's the car. I keep seeing it. It's day. It's light. *(Agitated.)*

TB: Is it day or is it just bright lights?

SK: *(Agitated)* I'm confused. *(Inaudible)* it just . . . It's close.

TB: Go on.

SK: *(Frightened, inaudible.)*

TB: Is it on your shoulder?

SK: It's long and brass. It's day . . . but it's night.

TB: Did you see anybody?

SK: *(Vehemently)* I'm scared! It scared me. *(Inaudible)* I mean, I think he has something else.

TB: Where was he, behind the fence?

SK: I'm afraid!

TB: He's behind the fence? Was he behind the fence?

SK: He was. He climbed over and now he's on my side. He's very white. *(Extreme agitation)* Oh. Oh. Oh.

GF: *(An inaudible question about the figure.)*

SK: I don't know. I'm afraid. I don't want to look.

TB: Is he close to you?

SK: Not now.

TB: Where did he go?

SK: Oh! I keep seeing him coming over the fence. When I first saw him, it really scared me.

BH: Was he your size?

SK: Yes. No. No, he was smaller . . . almost our size. It's his . . . his hands *(inaudible)*. Very white neck. Neck, head, face . . . no hair. None on his face or his head. *(Ag-*

itated.) Oh, I don't want to see him! Not like us. I don't want to see him. Everytime I see him, it scares me.

GF: Because he was so different?

SK: Yes. Uh . . . I don't think I really see him, but I do.

TB: Does he touch you, Steven?

SK: *(Very agitated)* Oh! I think he . . . yes . . . but not right away.

GF: But he doesn't hurt you . . . he just scares you.

SK: Yes.

TB: Did he say something to you? Does he speak to you?

SK: No. *(After a long pause)* There's something. I . . . I know there's something. They're coming for something. I don't know what they're doing. Preparing for something. Leather. That's what the noise is.

TB: What is the noise?

SK: Uh, gloves, or, or coats or something. It sounds like leather, like new leather gloves . . . rubbing their hands together. That, kind of . . . that's what the noise is.

TB: Do you know where it's coming from?

SK: The . . . uh . . . yes . . . uh . . . I'm scared . . . they're moving . . . against the fence. It's something behind . . .

TB: How could the one with the white skin get over the fence?

SK: I don't know. I don't see him coming over. They want something. I think maybe they want something from me. I don't know what they want from me.

TB: *(Inaudible question about the skin of the figures.)*

SK: Yes. *(Inaudible.)* It's still . . . I'm afraid! He's, he's ugly. He doesn't have regular skin. It's, uh, funny skin. It's not like skin.

TB: What *(kind of skin)* does he have?

SK: Uh, it looks like putty or something. It looks like you could move it with your hand.

BH: What color is it?

SK: Whitish, like chalkish, whitish . . . a little tint of gray in it. I don't know . . . it's really weird.

TB: Is it just his head that you see?

SK: Yes.

TB: This whitish color?

SK: Yes.

TB: What is he wearing from the neck down?

SK: Black. A turtleneck or something. You can see his neck. It's the same thing. It's scaring me. . . .

TB: Is he standing in front of you?

SK: Yes.

TB: How close?

SK: Very close. *(Agitated)* I'm afraid!

TB: Does he raise his hands?

SK: Uh, yes. *(Inaudible.)*

TB: Can you see his hand?

SK: *(Long pause)* I think so. It's the same as, uh, his face. Like putty or something. All the, all the fingers are perfect.

GF: *(Inaudible question.)*

SK: Yes. Scared me with his fingers.

*(At this point, **GF** begins his instructions to bring Steven out of the trance. It was clear to us all that his ordeal should be broken off.)*

Over an hour and a half had passed since our appointment began. As Steve rubbed his eyes and came back to full consciousness, a profound sense of shared relief flooded the room. After some final reassuring words from Dr. Franklin, we left his office and wandered down Columbus Avenue towards a café, moving as if the three of us were still a little stunned. When we were seated at the table inside, we ordered three richly desired drinks and began trying to understand what we had learned.

One of the most persistent misconceptions about hypnosis is that once the subject is no longer in a trance state he or she immediately forgets the content of the hypnotic recall. On the contrary, the subject remembers exactly what has transpired, and usually with great vividness. Stage hypnotists—the kind, unfortunately, many of us are most familiar with—as part of their act often give their subjects some kind of silly post-hypnotic suggestion: "When someone says the word 'cat,' you will stand up and sing 'The Star-Spangled Banner,' " or some such. Then the hypnotist gives the additional instruction that the subject *will not remember* anything that occurred during the hypnotic trance. This artificially induced amnesia is essential to their act. The volunteer is brought out of the trance, returns to his seat, and hears the hypnotist say the word "cat." To his amazement and humiliation he finds himself on his feet singing the national anthem. This kind of performance has led many people to assume incorrectly that hypnotic subjects normally do not remember what transpired during the trance state.

Steven Kilburn remembered more, perhaps, than he would have wished. Though he was thoroughly shaken by what he had re-experienced, he was also actually relieved to know that there had been a cause, after all, for his peculiar dread of that specific stretch of Maryland highway. He was precise when we questioned him about the clamp. Its edges were rounded. It was metallic, and it fitted over his shoulder from behind, holding him immobile and turning him around painfully. We attempted a few sketches, but he did not want to deal with the faces of the white-skinned creatures. We knew—all three of us—that we were only at the very beginning of a search to uncover all the details of that night. This first hypnotic session had ended only when Dr. Franklin saw that Steven was undergoing so much obvious fear and physical discomfort that to extend it would have been unthinkable.

I went home full of an odd kind of sadness and sympathy for Steve. What was going on? Nothing that he remembered about the UFO encounter implied deliberate malevolence, but the fear and pain it engendered were devastating. Certain details stayed firmly fixed in my mind, the description of the creature's skin, for example. "He's very white. . . . Neck, head, face . . . no hair. . . . He doesn't have regular skin. . . . It's not like skin. . . . It looks like putty . . . like you could move it with your hand."

In the months to come, I was to see that image reinforced. Travis Walton[4] published an account of his Arizona abduction and described his captors in strikingly similar images:

"They were a little under five feet tall. . . . Their thin bones were covered with white, marshmallowy-looking flesh. When they extended their hands towards me, I noticed they had no nails on their fingers. Their hands were small, delicate, and without hair on the backs of them. Their thin round fingers looked smooth and unwrinkled." Steve Kilburn's rather cryptic observation took on meaning: "All the fingers are perfect," he had said at the end of his hypnotic session.

Steve's Maryland encounter happened in 1973. Travis Walton was abducted two years later, in November of 1975. In October of that year, two young men from Norway, Maine, had a similar encounter and under hypnosis one of them described their captors this way:

"It looked like skin, but you know how somebody was indoors, say, a year, a year and a half, how it would look? It looked really white." His image of their overall effect is precise: They looked "like a mushroom."[5]

On March 18, 1978, Bill Herrmann experienced a two-hour time lapse while standing outside his home in Charleston, South Carolina, observing a UFO. Hypnosis revealed another classic abduction. The figures were very white-skinned, "the color of a marshmallow," he recalled.[6] "Their eyes were dark with a brown iris. They have large heads . . . without any hair." In 1953 Gerry Armstrong, twelve years old at the time, experienced a similar trauma.[7] Under hypnosis for the first time very recently, he said that "the two that took me to the ship are a little taller than I am. They have, is it, whitish-gray skins?" The list of examples can be extended many times over, but centrally important is the sense one has of honest, frightened people trying to be as precise as possible about what they saw. They were taken by humanoid creatures whose skins were whitish-gray in color and disturbingly soft looking, like a mushroom, or a marshmallow, or like putty. These three images denote consistent textural, coloristic, and kinetic qualities, all apart from the repeated description of the figures being between four and five feet tall.

Air Force Sergeant Charles L. Moody described his August 13, 1975, abductors vividly, adding a detail that we shall encounter many times again. They were between four-feet-eight-inches and five feet tall, had heads larger than ours, and "there was no hair, no eyelashes, no eyebrows . . . the skin was whitish-gray in color." But this skin, Moody said, was "almost like a mask . . . you know . . . if you just had a face-lifting job or something like that."[8]

When I talked to Steven a few days after the session at Dr. Franklin's, he told me that he was calm about his experience, and that he was trying to put it out of his mind. He was definitely not eager to resume the hypnotic process for the time being. It was the end of May, and following our usual practice, my family moved—wife, daughter, houseplants, cat, art materials and myself—to our summer house on Cape Cod, where we lived and worked until the beginning of September. Ted continued to see Steve from time to time but it was not until December 1978 that Steven decided he was ready once more to try hypnosis.

This seven-month gap between hypnotic sessions presented us with an unforeseen advantage. Steven had never heard the tape recording we made of his first session, nor had he seen the transcript. Apart from two or three days immediately after his May hypnosis, neither Ted nor I had talked to him in any detail about the events he had recalled. We were therefore in an ideal position to see if any new material that might surface would dovetail with what we already knew, or instead might in some way contradict it and thereby cast doubt on the accuracy of Steven's recall.

In the months since the session with Dr. Franklin, Ted and I had met still another psychologist, a charming and incisive woman of Greek-American background whose exotic name never fails to elicit surprise. In a world full of Marys and Bettys, when people ask Dr. Aphrodite Clamar how she came by her first name, she looks them straight in the eye and says, "My parents gave it to me," thereby invariably laying the matter to rest. Dr. Robert Naiman originally met Dr. Clamar at a party and happened to mention that a group of UFO researchers he was acquainted with were looking for a female psychologist versed in hypnotic techniques. Our problem had arisen because a woman who had been abducted in April of 1977 near Tucson, Arizona, had agreed to undergo hypnosis only if the psychologist were female.[9] Her experience, parts of which she recalled consciously, evidently contained events that were unnerving in a particularly intimate way, so this shy, fifty-three-year-old woman requested a psychologist of her own sex. For a complex series of reasons, the hoped-for regressive hypnosis never occurred, but the situation nevertheless led to our meeting Aphrodite Clamar, whose subsequent help and cooperation have proved to be invaluable.

The appointment we made for Steven was for December 1, 1978. Ted had described to Aphrodite the obvious fear Steve experienced in his session seven months earlier and she adapted her technique accordingly. After conducting a short interview, she led him into a deep trance state and gave him as a protective image a "warm, solid house to stay within, safe from everything threatening, but from which you will be able to watch any events which might unfold outside."

She carefully established this imaginary refuge. "There is a wooded area, a wooded area of your choice. There's lots and lots of land. . . . Sit yourself in such a way that you can look out. . . ." and then she led him back to his experience of 1974.

AC: Do you see a car?

SK: Yes.

AC: Let the car drive up . . . see where it's going.

SK: Yes . . . I'm going fast. I'm very tired. That's all I want to say. Yeah, I'm really tired. Sleepy. Yeah, that's all.

AC: Had a long day?

SK: Long day. Really sleepy. It's late.

AC: Is there a clock on the dashboard?

SK: Yeah, but it's not working. I turn the light on in the car to see something. And then I turn it off. I think I have a watch on. Yeah, I think I do.

AC: Do you see what time it says?

SK: No. I'm not looking at it. But the light was on in the car just for a minute. (*Long pause, and then with a less drowsy voice:*) I think I'd gone off the road just onto the shoulder . . . and that wakes me up. . . . Going down a big hill. Yeah. Big hill. Really going fast. I'm reaching down for something. I dropped something, or I'm adjusting the seat or doing something. . . . That's when I see the light go on. I'm leaning forward to do something. Down on the floor—something. I'm reaching with my right hand. . . . Yeah . . . I don't know what it is. It's dark. There's almost no other cars on the road. . . . I'm all alone in that whole—well, in my direction. (*Long pause*) I just want to get home. (*Another long pause*) Oh, no! What's happening? No! I don't want this to happen!

AC: (*Asks an inaudible question about what he sees.*)

SK: Oh! I don't see anything on the road. I don't see anything at all and the right part of the car turns violently, and I'm going pretty fast but it jerks to the right. Really hard, and the car doesn't skid. It's like a huge magnet just sucked it over to the right! I have to stay away from the car (*in his recall*) and I feel better. 'Cause then I'm not in it. When I'm in it, it really scares me. (*Steven pauses and then resumes.*) We're coming . . . coming over to the right side of the road, the car's pulling over and I feel like somebody's looking over my right shoulder. . . . I don't see anything there in the back seat . . . but it's scary in the car 'cause I don't know what's going on. I'm confused. Why did I pull over? I don't see anything. I just pulled over. And there's the fence . . . trees. One really big tree, and I hear the rustling of the leaves because of the wind. There's kind of a ditch.

Yeah, kind of a steep ditch. There's a fence that's going
down. There's a hill and it goes down because I look at it to
the left. And then it goes up further over there . . . it keeps
going along the highway. There's an oil drum, I think,
and . . . some rocks and dry kind of mud, only not too dry,
'cause it rained recently . . . maybe even that day or the
day before.

I'm out of the car . . . and I'm looking at the fence.
And a car is passing on the road. My car is off the
road . . . but it's on concrete. It's on something solid, like
they were going to build a road there but they
didn't. . . . I'm not really scared. I just don't know what
I'm doing there. I have some kind of sweater on. Some kind
of coat, also, I think. I know I'm warm enough. I keep thinking of warmth. In the car, I thought of it, and here, walking
outside of the car, I thought of it. *(Steve paused, and then
spoke to Dr. Clamar as if he had chosen to break off his
recall:)* I'm afraid to go any farther. I don't mean then, I
mean right now. I'm afraid to look any farther.

AC: Are you safe inside your house?
SK: No . . .
AC: You can go back to your house. There's a very clear view, a
      fantastic view.
SK: Yes. Oh . . . oh . . . yeah . . . yeah. I am protected. But
      I wasn't then. I was really exposed. I was really out. Yeah.
      I'm protected now, yeah, and I'm looking at the fence 'cause
      I hear a noise against it, the fence rattling. I don't know why
      I'm not scared, but I'm just looking at the fence . . . a little
      bit bent over . . . I'm still afraid to see. *(Very softly)*
      Yeah . . . yeah.
AC: You're comfortable in your house. When you want to, you
      can see everything.
SK: *(After a long pause)* I'm out there all alone. In front of the
      car . . . looking across the ditch over to the fence. I don't
      even know what I'm looking at there . . . but I am. I'm not
      supposed to look there. *(He begins to tremble slightly, and
      fear wells up with sudden force.)* I know! Oh, God! I know
      why I pulled over! Oh, no! *(Agitated breathing.)* I see two
      lights in the sky when I'm driving. I'm hunched over, look-
      ing up. It's a reflection in the windshield and then I turn the
      light on to see if it's still there. And it is. And I turn it off.

And it's going to the right, way up high, over the highway, over the trees, and it's going kind of slow . . . and I didn't know what it was. It was moving fast, but not that fast. I don't hear anything. . . . Two lights, kind of diagonal to each other. One to the right and the lower to the left . . . they're whitish, with kind of a haze around them. I see a shadow of something . . . they go to the trees to the right and they disappear in front of me. Right in front of me. As I'm coming down the hill. And I finally get to about the spot where I think it would be, and I pull over. No! Ah . . . I don't really want to go over there but I . . . I don't know. It was really violent the way the car went to the right. Yeah, hard. On the wheel. Hard. A really hard right. I thought it was dangerous. . . .

When I first saw those lights, they were more than a mile away, and the sky was dark, but not that dark. I could see clouds. Dark clouds, and the sky was lighter. Yeah, the sky is lit and that must be the moon behind the dark clouds . . . almost directly in front of me, slightly to the left. And the moon isn't that high.

I'm back over looking at the fence. I still am . . . I don't know what. No. I just . . . I don't want to look down there. I'm going to be really scared if I go over there. I am curious to see what's going on. I don't really expect to see anything. And then I remember driving home. Yeah, just driving home. And I'm OK. Back in the car and driving home. And I don't want to remember. I'm not supposed to remember.

AC: Who said you're not supposed to remember?
SK: Just . . . not. I just know I'm not. *(His voice is tense, anguished.)* It's really serious! I might die. I mean, I know I won't, if I remember. But I feel really, really afraid to see. I believed it then, but I don't believe it now. I'm just scared. . . .

At this point, there is a slight break in the recorded continuity as the tape ends and it is turned over. As this was being done, Steven's fear abated, and he began to speak in a slightly different, firmer tone of voice, repeating the sentence, "There's nothing to be afraid of," several times. It was eerily as if the calming words had been delivered by an outside source.

SK: There's nothing to be afraid of. There are these things
     standing around me . . . and, uh . . . there's nothing
     to be afraid of. . . . I keep looking over the
     fence . . . there's something back there. I think there's a
     field or something they came from. It's really quiet. There's
     that light back of me . . . again. And it's light now. It's not
     like it's dark; I mean, it's light all over that area. And my car
     is still there . . . partly lit in front. . . .

     And there's one . . . at least three . . . in front of
     me. And they're . . . uh . . . really strange . . . and I
     am scared. *(Deep, agitated breathing and slight moaning.)*
     I'm not supposed to remember. There's one . . . he's boss.
     He's the boss. And one of them is doing something in back
     of me, over at the right . . . bending down and doing
     something. They're interested in me. I'm not scared now.
     There's something over on the fence to the left. And I see
     that leathery stuff again. I remember it. Like a black leath-
     ery . . . like a breastplate or something . . . or a chest. I
     hear it, too. It's like leather rubbing . . . sliding against
     leather, but not real thick leather . . . kind of sticky and
     thin. It looks like that, but it's not real shiny. And I don't
     know what it is. I think I also see dark arms and gloves, but
     they aren't all black. . . .

     These things in front of me aren't black. They're
     not supposed to. . . I see the faces and they're
     white . . . chalky . . . ah . . . they look like they're
     made out of rubber, or . . . ah . . . not rubber, ah
     . . . what do you call it? Putty or something. Like an artist's
     eraser. That's what it is. It's like a big . . . and they're not
     shiny at all . . . really a dull finish, kind of chalky and
     white, only not pure white. They touch me. And it hurt. I
     don't know what they want. And this one is motioning to the
     others with one of his arms. It's got some kind of suit on. I
     don't know whether it's part of him or it's a suit or what it is.
     It doesn't look like skin. Everytime it hurts, I see these fin-
     gers. Those fingers I remember. They're . . . ah . . . like
     tubes. That's exactly . . . they're tubes. White plastic
     tubes, only . . . yeah . . . they touched me. They didn't
     feel hard, though, but they looked hard . . . they were
     kind of shiny.

     They're small. Below my shoulder . . . that height.

We're standing there. I don't know what we are doing.
They're doing something. Digging. The one is digging.
The . . . boss there is motioning to this one in back of me
to dig or do something with his left hand, and he is pointing.
I think he means to hurry up or something, and the one is
bending down. . . . He's got something . . . I can't really
see it . . . and he's digging a hole. Not a deep
hole . . . he's just kind of poking, sort of. He's bent down
on his right knee. The dirt's kind of grayish . . . right off
the side of the highway . . . next to the car; in
fact . . . just a few feet from the right front wheel of the
car.

I don't get the feeling that he's real strong. . . . I don't
know what he's digging for. . . . One of the others is
watching. I think they're four. Four or five. We're all just
having a good old time standing there. I don't know what
we're waiting for.

He's kind of crinkly . . . whatever he has on
. . . legs and top and everything. He's skinny . . . really
skinny. I don't think he'd weight very much. In fact, he'd
probably weigh . . . not even fifty pounds.

The intense fear Steven had experienced earlier seemed now
to have melted away. He appeared tranquil, as if he were enjoying
these outrageous circumstances in a thoroughly detached manner.
Some of his comments were punctuated by small, ironic chuckles.
It was hard for me not to conclude that Steven had been artificially calmed somehow at this point in his encounter.

SK: I'm wondering when another car is going to go by. I can see
us just standing out there. I'm not really afraid, though. The
boss there . . . his eyes are really shiny. They look black. I
don't see any pupils or anything . . . and they're big. His
head is not round, it's like, uh, an inverted teardrop. With
a big round bar on top. He looks like he's not
alive . . . maybe just because I can't really understand
what he is doing or what he is thinking or anything . . . it's
like everything's very stilted. . . . He's not very comfortable there . . . he doesn't want to stick around. He's not
telling me, but it's obvious. He wants to leave, I think, more
than I do. I think he wants me to tell him something or help
him or something. Why me? He'd have to pick on me. It

figures. I don't feel that tired anymore, though. I don't understand. He wants something from me. I don't understand
what it is. . . .

I want it to be over. I want the whole thing to be over. I
mean, I'm not sure. I'm not believing what I am seeing at
all. I don't . . . ah . . . there's no way to explain it away.
I've been aware that I can't do what I want to. They've really got something on me . . . and I don't know what it is.
They can just make me do whatever they want.
They're . . . understanding each other, but they're not
talking. I don't hear anything.

AC: Do you think it's mental telepathy?

SK: I guess it is. 'Cause they're somehow understanding each
other. There's some conflict, I think. I don't think they're
getting along so great. *(Chuckles.)* I think there's an argu-
ment about something 'cause this boss wants one thing and
one of the other guys wants something else. I think they're
arguing about a place . . . about where to dig. And the
boss, there, is pointing—this is it. And the other guy is pointing over toward the fence there, over to the right where it's
dark.

It's very bright. The light is coming from something in
back of me. Brighter than daylight. It's really harsh light, but
it's not in my eyes. It must be in theirs. That's why I see the
reflection. Yeah, there's something really shiny coming off
this character's eyes. It's almost like they're black and endless. Like they're liquid or something. But they're perfectly
shaped. They're really kind of walnut-shaped. Not perfect
circles, but almost. I keep looking at these eyes looking at
me. God. I feel like I'm under a microscope. But he doesn't
really . . . I don't think he really cares about me. I don't
think he's really concerned about what I'm thinking.
They've got it all figured out.

He moves like a . . . like . . . he's standing still, but
when he walked, it was almost like he had two really bad
knees. He was hobbling almost . . . shifting his weight to
the left and right. Almost rocking back and forth. And he
drags his feet a little bit. I mean, I don't know whether
they're feet or they're boots. They're almost white. They're
not like his head, his face. They're shaped like cat's eyes,
very almond-shaped. I don't see any toes or anything, but
the almond shapes are pointed in the front and the back so

that, ah, they're kind of club feet. Yeah. Skinny ankles, legs. Really skinny. Not bony, nothing like that, but he's so little.

And I think he's just as interested in me. No, I mean, I don't feel threatened at the moment. I'm kind of looking at his feet and he kind of looks back. Just to sort of check on where I am. Make sure I don't go anywhere.

Arms, too, really skinny, like he has no biceps. He's got almost no shape. He's kind of straight down, kind of almost flat. I'm really afraid to look at him. I don't want him to think I'm being aggressive. . . .

And, ah, his shoulders . . . they're really square, but they're really small. Skinny. And he has a neck, but it's small, like the rest of him. Skinny. His chin is really pointy, too. I don't see any ears, although there's something there. There's a slit where his mouth should be, but it's not open . . . just kind of across. He absolutely does not change expression. I'm kind of . . . I feel like . . . if only my friends could see me now! I don't think . . . but it's O.K., I can handle this. I'm doing O.K., just watching him. I look back at the car and now another part of the car is lit up . . . the part of the right side of the car that I'm looking at. Yeah, the light's all over. Then he looks over, the boss there, he looks over my head, 'cause it's something moving down. There's a light moving or something moving that's really bright . . . and the shadows change. . . .

That guy is still digging. God, what is he digging for? He's digging with something he's got in his hands. It's not easy for him. I'd offer to help him, but I have the feeling it would cause problems. And then there's another guy in front of him, watching him. They all look kind of alike. I mean, they're all small and whitish and not real coordinated. They're kind of fumbling at things. I think he's having trouble digging. God. I mean, talk about an unlikely place to dig. It's right near the road. Not even a field or grass or anything. Just ugly, blackish, grayish dirt. It's getting deeper. He's digging a hole. He sure is. Yeah, it's like a foot deep. I can see that. He's still digging.

At this point, it was obvious to the three of us that, despite his deep trance state, Steven was resisting moving ahead in his narrative. He seemed to be deliberately avoiding any recall of what happened next, and was, in effect, marking time by dwelling on details of the moment. Ted signaled Dr. Clamar and she began to bring him out of the hypnotic state, assuring him that he would easily be able to integrate these newly conscious memories into the texture of his life. It had been a long, illuminating session, though the tension had been emotionally draining.

Today's most important revelation was the sense we had of a consistent, though still-unfolding, sequence of events. Seven months before, we knew that Steve's car was stopped alongside the road, and that he had stepped outside of it, a piece of the story to which I will attach the letter "B." Letter "A," how the car came to stop in the first place, we had not known until today, accompanied as it was by his description of the involuntary swerve at high speed, as if "a huge magnet just sucked it over to the right." As he stood by his car, "C" occurred—he saw and heard the still-mysterious black leather objects. And then "D"—the approach of the white creatures. Interestingly, in today's retelling he did not include their actual arrival on the scene, an obviously extremely frightening moment which he had recalled vividly in the earlier session. This time, he began with their presence as a *fait accompli* and coupled it with a new detail—the repeated, calming message: "There are other things standing around me . . . there's nothing to be afraid of." This situation, "E," immediately follows "D" (their arrival).

Steven moved on to "F," the episode of the figure digging while he was somehow held motionless. "G" we will designate as the placing of the clamp on his shoulders, another part of the story omitted here, and obviously another particularly terrifying memory. So, one could say, his first hypnotic session dealt with "B," "C," "D," and "G". Seven months later, we learned of "A," some new details of "C," and "E" and "F," a perfect narrative dovetailing.

On a smaller scale, other revelations served to illuminate a few unexplained and dangling memories from before. In May, Steven recalled bending down—perhaps to turn on the car's interior light—for a reason he could not supply: "I have a strange memory of looking at the dashboard. I don't know if I was looking at the clock or not but I remember seeing it, and I don't remember why." In his later session, this apparently inconsequential act was again described: "I'm reaching down for something. I dropped something, or I'm adjusting the seat or doing something . . . that's when I see the *(car)* light go on. I'm reaching with my right hand." Minutes later, the significance of his move came back with a shock: "I know! Oh, God! . . . I see two lights in the sky when I'm driving. I'm hunched over, looking up. It's a reflection in the windshield and then I turn the light on to see if it's still there. And it is. . . ." Steven's recall was so vivid because it was the moment he first saw the UFO flying overhead. His instinct was to try to convince himself it was only some kind of reflection, but his flicking on the interior light told him otherwise.

A few days after his appointment, I phoned Steve to ask how he was, and what he was thinking in retrospect. I told him that it had seemed during his hypnosis that he was reluctant to move ahead in his recall. "That's true," he said, in his characteristic shy, understated tone of voice. "I didn't want to go any further. I'm afraid the worst is still to come." The hypnotic process apparently contains its own built-in safety valve; subjects usually recall only what they can handle comfortably at that moment. There seems to be a careful, unconscious doling out of disturbing material, and despite moments of near panic, such as Steven experienced during both sessions, the mind is able, self-protectively, to shut off the flow.

At this point in our investigation, Steven Kilburn's account paralleled many other abduction reports, such as the Betty and Barney Hill case, in precise ways, but there was one basic and striking deviation from the model. In every case I had ever heard about, the witness or witnesses consciously remembered at least seeing a UFO. The odd circumstances—such as a period of lost, unaccounted-for time—that accompany such a UFO *sighting* are what alert investigators to the possibility of an abduction. Steven had nothing more to go on than a vague feeling that something he could not remember happened to him one night on a particular stretch of highway. Since beneath these feelings there turned out to be, indeed, a UFO abduction, how could one guess how many other abduction experiences lay buried and ticking within how many other unconscious minds? The prospect was staggering; if it happened once, it could happen ten thousand times and no one would necessarily ever know!

Months after Steven's second hypnotic session, Ted Bloecher told me about a California case that had recently surfaced. It had not been made public, and he had only learned of it through private communication with one of the investigators. On Nov. 26, 1972, a young legal secretary named Judy Kendall[10] and her sisters, Danon and Becky, visited their grandmother in the town of Bodega Bay. They left at six P.M. for the two-hour return trip, and

arrived home at midnight—four hours late. Their parents had already called the state police, fearing their daughters had been
involved in an accident. The girls had no explanation for their
delay, though they reported a peculiar detail: Danon and Judy
both remembered driving over the same bridge twice, but in the
same direction! They passed the flashing yellow light at Cash
Creek bridge, continued on their way, but felt confused as to
where they were or what was happening. Then they passed the
same flashing light and re-crossed the bridge, and shortly thereafter arrived at home. There seemed to be no explanation. They
definitely weren't lost, since they knew the territory well. The car,
for that matter, did not have enough gas for a six-hour drive. The
strange episode was put aside by all three women until a sequence
in a movie three years later re-established the incident. Judy was
watching "Escape to Witch Mountain," and at one point in the
film an "RV"—a van—supernaturally lifts off to the sky. Judy felt
oddly uncomfortable, recalling the sensation of being in her own
car and somehow floating. Her sister Danon, sitting beside her in
the theater, felt the same unease. It was clear to both of them that
this disturbing half-memory was connected with their peculiar
experience in 1972 when they lost four hours driving back from
Bodega Bay.

Again, Judy put the mystery out of her mind until 1977 when,
after visiting a friend near Yolo, California, she sighted a UFO on
her way home. It was a typical distant "nocturnal light." When she
told her friend about it, she was urged to report it to the Center for
UFO Studies. Her friend asked if she had ever figured out what
had really happened in the "lost hours" incident five years earlier,
and when Judy said she still did not know, the friend suggested
she also report this episode. Dr. Hynek at the Center was curious.
In 1977, Judy was hypnotized, and the story that emerged was similar in many details to Steven's. The first odd thing that she
recalled was her car somehow not responding to her control, but
moving of its own accord, as if it were not actually on the ground.
Later, this dialogue ensues:

Dr. McCall: What can you see?
JK: I think I see a . . . transparent head-shape thing
              with funny-looking eyes. I don't want to see it!
Dr. McCall: Why don't you?
JK: It scares . . .
Dr. McCall: What's happening now?

JK: *(Sobbing)* Coming towards . . . me. It scares me!
Dr. McCall: Where are you, Judy?
JK: I don't know! I don't know! I'm scared. I don't want
                   to see it anymore!

Dr. McCall asked her to describe her captors' heads. "They look like ordinary people's heads, but they don't have any hair. No hair anywhere. Their cheekbones are funny-looking. *(Their skin is)* kind of white and milky. . . . I don't remember seeing a mouth. . . . I don't see any ears . . . all I see is holes. . . ." Inside the UFO, Judy recalled seeing three distinct types of creatures, one of which, a woman, seemed entirely human. The description immediately above, taken from the transcript of her hypnosis, describes what seems to be the same white-skinned, hairless type that Steven remembered.

At the time I first heard about the Kendall case, its most striking similarity to Steven's was the fact that neither Judy nor Danon (Becky apparently was asleep throughout the encounter) had any conscious recollection of a UFO sighting. The Kendall and Kilburn cases, one could guess, came to light only because of an unlikely series of accidents: Steven's chance meeting of Ted Bloecher, his relocation to New York, etc., and Judy's having seen "Witch Mountain" and later having a UFO sighting, which she reported to the Center. The unmistakable deduction to be drawn is that we had happened to notice the tip of the proverbial iceberg.

Other similarities between the Kendall and Kilburn cases eventually came to light, but there is one detail that should be mentioned here, and that is the question of the two automobiles appearing to be under external control. In hundreds of UFO encounters, drivers have reported that their electrical systems have failed and their engines have died, only to come back on as if by magic when the UFOs depart. More startling still are the reports, which probably by now also range in the hundreds, of automobiles literally lifted off the ground and moved, with driver and passengers inside. Steven could not understand how his car, traveling downhill at about seventy miles per hour, could make a violent right turn without rolling over, moving as if "sucked by a giant magnet."

Betty Hill, under hypnosis in 1964, described her experience this way: "We're driving along on a tarred road and all of a sudden . . . without any warning or rhyme or reason or any-

thing . . . Barney made a . . . he always . . . the brakes
squealed, he stopped so suddenly and made this sharp left-
handed turn off the highway. . . ." In a case I investigated in late
1978, two nurses in central Tennessee were stopped late at night at
a village traffic light. A large domed craft landed on the road
ahead of them and D.S., in the driver's seat, was startled when her
vehicle began to move without her "pushing gas or anything . . . or accelerating the car." They traveled about five
hundred feet before the car halted "all of a sudden, and the motor
just kind of stopped."[11] In another episode, Sandra Larson[12] and a
friend were abducted in 1975. Under hypnosis, she said that,
when the UFOs (there were several) landed, the car stopped automatically, and that she had the sensation of floating. "I saw the car
being brought right up to it. Like the car was pulled."

A witness in an Alaskan case noticed that her car was driving
itself. She could neither guide it, nor accelerate, and they pro-
ceeded for many miles at twenty-five miles per hour, a period
during which the car apparently used no gasoline.[13]

Less lucky were the terrified women in the Casey County,
Kentucky, abduction of January 6, 1976.[14] The three friends noticed a blue light behind their automobile just as it began to escape
their control. The speedometer was registering eighty-five miles
per hour, though the driver had her foot off the accelerator and
was crying for help in steering the car. The women experienced a
burning sensation in their eyes, followed by more excruciating
pain, and then the inexplicable sense of their car being pulled
backwards. When they finally reached home, they discovered an
hour and a half of missing time, and through hypnosis their abduction and "examination" aboard a landed UFO was uncovered.

If an abduction case contains, let us say, one hundred separate bits of information, probably eighty of them can be found in
previously investigated cases—but twenty "information bits" will
be new. The phenomenon repeats itself, but never exactly. The
shapes cohere, but without forming an *identical* pattern, and in a
strange way these new details add credibility to each case.

Getting through to buried traumatic material by means of
hypnosis is usually a time-consuming, laborious undertaking. Dr.
Clamar has described the process of slowly uncovering the core
memories as being a little like peeling an onion—layer upon layer
must be patiently stripped away. By the fall of 1979, Steven had
consciously recalled a few later events from his experience, including the sense that he had been examined by his captors inside

the UFO. From the moment he first realized that his encounter had included an involuntary physical examination, he had avoided pursuing the matter through hypnosis. So reluctant was he that he was not ready to explore it specifically until January of 1980 in his fourth hypnotic session. (The third session, in February of 1979, was recorded by an NBC film crew and will be discussed in chapter 5; it did not reveal many incidents not already known from the two earlier hypnotic regressions.)

In the fourth session, Dr. Clamar instructed Steven to imagine himself in a spacious movie theater, feeling relaxed and very comfortable, and about to view film concerning his experience on the Pikesville road in Maryland . . . an experience which affected his shoulder.

His memories began as he stood beside his car, facing his white-skinned captors. His nervousness was palpable, and the first image clearly frightened him.

SK: When I first see it, it scares me. All by myself. That's why I'm hesitating.

AC: (Reassuringly) You can watch as much as you care to watch. . . . Turn it off whenever you want to.

SK: (Chuckles.) I may not be watching it today. (A long pause follows.) I see the . . . uh . . . I don't know what it is . . . a long clamp kind of thing. And there's a joint in the middle like an elbow, almost like an arm, and it's . . . around my shoulder. And I see it just, just holding me, over my right shoulder. It's connected to this . . . I don't know what this is. . . . It looks like a saucer . . . that's what it looks like. It's whitish. And it's sitting on something . . . looks like it's white also, a kind of platform. It looks like an erector set or something . . . some kind of girders, criss-cross . . . latticework . . . it sits on. Like an egg sitting on it, and, uh, I see the car.

(Deep sigh) It's holding me . . . if it grabs me, I feel . . . it hurts my back, my lower back on the right side.

AC: (After a long pause.) What happens next? Films have a continuity, Steven. (She prods his memory very delicately.)

SK: They're watching me now. They're standing there watching me, and the one guy starts motioning . . . now starts walking past me, on my right, and he goes in back of me and . . . uh . . . (sighs) and he's looking inside the thing, and he turns me around slowly. I don't think I could move if I wanted to . . . that thing is really on my body. And he's, uh, just standing there, and I'm turned now, looking at the thing. And he's looking inside and it's dark. I can't see what's in there. My back hurts.

AC: Breathe into your back. You can make that pain disappear. . . . (Dr. Clamar instructs Steven in ways to overcome the pain.)

SK: (After a long pause) They want me to come in. It's a ramp . . . a little ramp. He wants me to walk up before him. And . . . I think there's some kind of noise. I'm not sure I even hear it. It's like . . . it's coming from the thing, whatever it is, the saucer. I think the whole thing is vibrating, but it doesn't look like it's moving. It's like a very, very quiet hum. Uh, the thing pushes me in. (Chuckles.) You'd think they'd realize I was going. . . .

And, uh, now he's alongside me at my left, and there's a passageway. . . . It's round, almost like a tube we're walking through. The thing's not on my back anymore and I'm very relaxed.

They're not going to hurt me. I want to look back, but I feel like I'm almost paralyzed. It doesn't hurt, though. I'm just very relaxed, very calm. We make a right turn. It's funny, this thing didn't look that big from the outside. Didn't look like there was that much room in it.

And now we're coming back. (Chuckles.) I think we went the wrong way. Now, he . . . I don't think he knows which way to go . . . what to do now . . . and he looks at me. I wasn't looking at him. (Sighs.) I'm not really afraid of him, but I'd like to know what he's thinking. Now we go back, yeah, to that right turn where he turned me around. We turn around again . . . we're in the passageway at the right and we go into a room . . .

And the door closes behind us. This room, it's all white. It's almost the color of the outside of the ship . . . whatever the thing is . . . the saucer. It's . . . Oh! My back!

AC: Just breathe deep into your back and the pain will diminish (etc.).

SK: (Shouts) Oh! They put . . . they put a thing on my back. I'm sitting on a table in the middle of this room. Oh! (Arches back, as if in pain.) Oh . . . Oh! (Arches back.) When I think about what they did, it really hurts.

AC: (*Calming him again with instructions to overcome the pain.*)

SK: (*Rapid breathing, obvious signs of distress.*) This room is, uh, whitish. It's really big. It's curved on the inside . . . the walls aren't . . . I don't think there are any angles in the room. That's what it is. Everything looks kind of whitish. Even when I look at my own hands . . . they look kind of whitish. It doesn't glow. . . . These little guys . . . there are two of them in the room . . . the one other . . . oh, no, there are a few others over there against the walls, circled around. There are two guys who seem to be running the show. One is . . . the guy who came in with me, and they're, uh, they almost blend in with the white. I almost want to say that the air in the room is white also. Something strange about the color of everything. I don't know how to describe it . . . everything is kind of milky or misty or something. It doesn't shine, but everything has almost that metallic kind of glow to it . . . including me . . . as I look at my legs and . . . I don't know where my clothes went.

(*There is an obvious gap in his recall at this point, between his entering the room and finding himself nearly naked, seated on the table.*)

AC: What are you wearing?

SK: It looks like a wrapped diaper of some sort . . . very soft. It's wrapped in a criss-cross. There's a thing over my head . . . it's coming out of the ceiling. It looks like it should be made of metal or something, but I can't tell if it is. It looks kind of like something I saw in a planetarium. A big thing. It has a kind of bulbous head on one end. It looks like a big insect. It's about twice the size of me. It's nine feet long or so, and maybe three or four feet across. It's really intricate. There are all kinds of little . . . it's a gadget, whatever it is. (*Chuckles.*) At one end, there's like . . . I don't know if it's a needle . . . it looks like a fancy ray gun of some sort. I don't know what it is.

   And it's, like, on a pivotal point in the center of it, so it's suspended in the center. And it turns down by itself; they don't touch it. It turns so the needle part is pointing down towards me, and that's what runs along the bottom of my back. And I'm just sitting there, and when they put it against my back—I don't know whether they're sticking something into my back, but it hurts. That's what hurt before.

And the guy who brought me in is just sort of watching everything. He seems to know what's going on. The walls around the room are curved, so the inside of the room would be the shape of a saucer. Even the ceiling is curved. It's like a big oval. Yeah, the room is a big, circular, flattened-out oval. It has a really calming effect, being in this room. (Chuckles.) It's almost like being hypnotized. This is really . . . you almost feel as if you could float. It's very peaceful.

And there is not a sound. Nothing. I think it's the quietest place I was ever in. This table is so . . . I don't know, it's like it grows out of the floor. It's perfectly smooth. The same color. There are no drawers or anything. No cabinets, no handles. Nothing. It's just like a pillar. And . . . it's a perfect temperature, so I'm perfectly comfortable.

It's a flat kind of thing on the end, yeah, that's digging into my back. Whatever they're doing there . . . it's feeling the bone. On my back. (Sighs.) Just touching my back. I don't know what it's doing there. It doesn't hurt now . . . it's not a needle. Feels like it would be almost as wide as my hand if my hand were flattened out.

And, uh . . . they take it off and it hurts when it comes off. And the thing goes back up into the ceiling. It's still up there, it doesn't go out of sight or anything. I can look straight up . . . directly over my head. In fact, I feel a little bit dizzy. My back hurts a little bit. All this time I've been sitting with my legs over the edge of this . . . I guess it's the doctor's table. (Chuckles.) It's one doctor's office I didn't have to wait to get into, I guess.

Now I'm lying down on my right side. It's kind of a . . . Oh! My back hurts. It's . . . soft, where I put my head down and it moved up. The table itself moved up to support my head. It's very comfortable. Almost like a cushion or something. (Inaudible.) They're taking the thing I'm wearing off.

AC: (Inaudible question.)

SK: The other guy who was in the room when I walked in. And he's (lifting?) it up with his hand. I didn't know they did anything with their hands. And it slides against my leg . . . (inaudible). These two are talking to each other . . . I mean, or they're communicating with each other, 'cause there's something going on between the two of them. They're looking at each other . . . Oh! Why are they waiting until it starts hurting to (inaudible). They're awfully interested in my back. I'm just lying there now, just . . . waiting for what's next.

I think the joy has gone out of this relationship. It's not that interesting anymore. Uh . . . (sounds of pain). That thing has come down and it's pushing against my back again. It's pushing . . . at an edge . . . pushing against the lower . . . oh . . , whatever they hit   uh   . . it's a version of the old hit your knee and see if it jumps up in the air . . . 'cause that's what my right leg did. (Chuckles.) They're testing my reflexes. (Sighs.) It hurts when they do it, too. Kind of a sharp edge. Oh! (Sudden cry.) That only makes my right leg twitch . . . wherever they're hitting, on my back. Oh . . . (sighs) . . . No, I'm really not that thrilled with being there now. I don't think they really care whether it hurts or not. And I . . . my back itches. I can feel it now. It itches now, too.

AC: Continue to breathe deeply. . . . (Instructions to calm the pain and end the itching.)

SK: (Inaudible) I'm lying there. My back is just kind of in dull pain . . . and . . . uh . . . I think the guy who brought me in, the leader, I think he's getting impatient. He's kind of . . . he turns to look at where we came in. That's why I think a door must have closed or something, 'cause I don't see a door there or anything. It's just all smooth.

There are a few other characters in this room also, there are like one, two, three, four, five . . . there are about five or six of them, 'cause they're kind of scattered around against the walls with their hands behind their backs. (Chuckles.) They look like guards or something. I don't know what they need guards for. I'm sure not going anywhere. Especially the way I feel.

It's kind of a light now, out of the ceiling, out of the center. It's coming actually out of the center where this big device is hooked up. And it shines on me. Kinda warm. Feels good. It was getting a little bit cold in there. It feels good now. My back feels better, too.

Now it hurts . . . hurts again. (Winces.) They want me to turn over . . . on my stomach. And, uh, I don't think

they're going to miss anything . . . they're going to get me
from all angles. *(Sighs.)* I'm really getting bored being in
there. I want this thing to be over. Whatever they plan to do,
do it. Get it over with.

   I feel something touching that spot where it itched. I
don't know . . . what . . . I think it's the mark on my
back that they want to look at. To see what it is, I think. I
think I have something on my back, some kind of a mole or
something. Yeah, they're touching it.

AC: How does it feel when they touch it?

SK: Uh, it's hard. I mean, his finger, or whatever he's touching it
with, is hard. Yeah, I think . . . *(chuckles)*. He sure is looking closely. He's leaning over, and his head is
like . . . strange the way his head turns down. I didn't notice any of them do that before. It's like on a joint or something . . . his head is very . . . and I do see his neck. I
didn't know he had a neck *(chuckles)*, but he does. It's a
little skinny thing. But he turns and it's just like . . . I think
his neck can bend . . . it's strange. Anyway, he's looking . . . he's really getting close to my back.

AC: Where on your back is it?

SK: It's on the right side, a little bit lower than the middle, and,
uh, he kind of pushes on it and it hurts a little.

AC: What does his finger feel like as it touches you?

SK: Very solid. It's heavy.

AC: Does it feel warm?

SK: No, I don't feel any temperature. I mean, it must be the
exact same temperature as my body, or something, 'cause I
don't feel any difference. It's very hard. Like, uh, just the
way it looks. It looks like hard plastic and it feels hard. I
don't know how he could possibly feel anything with a hard
finger like that.

   Oh! He had some kind of . . . *(chuckles)* . . . pushed
at it with his finger . . . on the edge. That's funny, when
he touched it, the little thing on my back, it hurt farther
down.

AC: Where does it hurt?

SK: Farther down, where, my back hurt, where that thing was
hitting my back and hurting . . . lower. *(Sighs.)* Now he's
just pushing on it, pushing down on it. I think he just wants
to feel it. I don't know what the great fascination is.

   It's strange, but what I can't figure out is he's so short

and this table sits up really high. And yet when he leans over to touch it he can look down on it. I really don't understand how he can do that. It doesn't make any sense to me. I'm trying to look down at his feet but I can't see them. He must be standing on something, is the only thing I can think. (Chuckles.) Unless he's floating. (Chuckles.) Maybe he is.

Oh! He pushed that spot on my back with his hand. He should leave it alone. It hurts.

The other guy, the boss there who walked me in, now has his back partially turned. Maybe he can't stand the sight of blood. I keep getting the feeling that my back is open, but there's no blood. Or that it's not cut or anything. I get the feeling that they're looking inside of it.

My leg, my right leg especially, going down my right leg, it feels a little bit numb. Also like it's falling asleep. And the pain goes up my back, the right side.

Now, it's my stomach. This thing, uh, they turn me on my left side now and I'm lying on my left side. My stomach hurts. Right side of my stomach, almost right on the opposite side of where my back hurts. A dull pain. Sort of a stomach ache.

I'm getting sleepy there. I don't know whether they're doing it or if I'm just getting sleepy. Yeah, I'm really comfortable. (Sighs.) Awkward position to be lying in. I'm lying on my left arm. My arm is straight down along my side.

Something is poking my stomach. I mean, not poking into . . . on the outside it's poking. (Chuckles.) I keep thinking an X-ray would be quicker. Ah. Clamp. Kind of like the thing that was on my shoulder, only it's rounder, it's on my hip, my right hip. That's what . . . (Very short break as tape is turned over.)

Oh! A rod now, it's just poking into my . . . (chuckles). I can see the color of this. This is dark, this is like a dark gray. Just poking it up against, like almost tapping, really . . . it comes from that thing. That thing has come down again, and I see it's like a rod, it's like a wand, tapping against my stomach, slowly. I see it sliding back and forth . . . tap, slowly it moves back, tap, and it pushes against my stomach.

It . . . almost looks as if it's made of lead. It's almost that color. I don't see any lines or anything. It's perfectly shaped. Cylindrical . . . kind of very skinny, though. And

it's flat on the end. Not hollow. Sure is poking into my stomach, though. Right on the . . . *(sighs)* . . . on the side.

I'm looking back at that other guy standing there, the
one who brought me in, and I see the back of his head,
now. . . . It's almost perfectly round. Ugly little thing. And
I think there's a line. I don't even know if that's skin on his
head. A very, very faint line like a ripple . . . like a seam.
(Chuckles.) Right down the middle. I can't tell if it's skin or
something he has over his head. It fits well, though. *(Chuckles.)*

He has the tiniest little chest. I can't see any ribs.
Just . . . there's no muscular definition or anything. He
turns around, and he sees I'm looking at him, and I don't
think he's too crazy about the idea. *(Chuckles.)* So I look
away.

The supervisor in this room is the other guy, though. It's
like he's the boss and he just took over once we got into this
room.

That thing is gone, now. The thing moved up into the
ceiling and the light isn't on me anymore. And I'm lying on
my back now. I do that myself, though. I knew they wanted
me on my back and maybe they just let me do it . . . instead of forcing me. Now the . . . our doctor . . . I don't
know what else to call him . . . he's coming over and he's
looking at . . . that spot on my stomach. It tickles a little
bit. *(Chuckles.)* He feels it. A little sensitive. Still don't understand how he can be looking down . . . he's so short.

I almost feel, lying there, I'm almost high, just a little bit
dizzy. But I'm very relaxed. I feel like a frog. *(Chuckles.)*
Now there's a metal thing comes up around both my legs.
It's very skinny. Moves my legs apart a little bit. It's almost . . . a . . . comes right up under my legs as high as it
can go. And they want to feel what's on my skin. My right
leg . . . moves my right leg all the way up—that's why I
feel like a frog. The doctor now touches my skin under
that . . . my leg . . . inside my leg . . . it feels . . . I
got goosebumps a little bit. It feels kinda rough. Anyway . . . he's certainly interested in it. He goes back and
feels my stomach again, the spot on it . . . on the right
side.

My right hand is now paralyzed. I want to move but I
can't. My left one is just relaxed, but my right one

isn't . . . it's falling asleep, there's no feeling in it. Now my left one's getting numb. It's happening fast. It starts from the—God, it happened fast—it starts from the fingertips and it goes right to the elbows, right up to the shoulders. They're both totally paralyzed. There's no pain, though, I just feel that I have no feeling.

God, I'm even more relaxed than I was before. (Sighs.) I'm almost asleep, but not quite. Now my legs. My leg is down again. The two metal things—I saw the color, they're dark also—they come off and they're gone. I don't know where they went. My legs are now paralyzed. My back still hurts a little bit, though. I think they're trying to knock me out. They sure did it. . . .

This seemed to be a logical place to end the session, so I signaled Dr. Clamar and she began the process of bringing Steven out of the trance state. He was told that he would be able to integrate this experience into his life, that it would not cause him any difficulty, that he would be relaxed. Immediately upon awakening from the trance, Steve complained that his ears bothered him. He felt a peculiar pressure not unlike that experienced in an airplane during a sudden shift of altitude. It was an unusual reaction—one I had never observed before—but the problem was gradually eased by repeated yawning and swallowing.

The hypnotic period had lasted for about an hour and had been filled with precise and fascinating new details, but it had been unnerving for all three of us. Steven and I said good-bye to Aphrodite and went out to a coffee shop on Lexington Avenue to talk further about what we had learned. These "debriefing sessions"—to use the wooden NASA phrase—have always yielded important information, and the basic reason is this: as the subject in the hypnotic state re-experiences the encounter, he (or she) tells only what seems to be most "tellable" at the moment, what he judges to be most immediately significant. But other peripheral things are also being re-experienced, and it is only later, in a more leisurely setting, that these other, less obviously important details can be recounted. For instance, Steven now mentioned what we had perceived as a gap in his narrative. When he first entered the big, whitish room, he walked towards the table, which he said grew straight out of the floor "like a mesa," and which was about chest-high. The next moment, he was seated on the table nearly naked, and his clothes were nowhere to be seen. One can specu-

late either that he has repressed the disturbing experience of being stripped and lifted onto the table, or that he may have been, in
fact, unconscious during that operation. My observations of the
hypnotic recall of various abductees suggests that in almost every
case there seems to be a period of missing time when the subject is
probably unconscious, and thus unable, even through hypnosis, to
remember anything.

During a phone conversation two days later, Steve recalled
some other details—particularly about the final moments of his
"examination." The thin, round metal loops which raised and
slightly spread his legs must have come up from the surface of the
table. They completely encircled his thighs very high up—almost
at the level of his hip sockets—and, the ultimate effect was to force
him into a posture not unlike that which results from obstetrical
stirrups. As he phrased it at the time, "I feel like a frog."

He also mentioned a peculiar emotional reaction he had after
he had relived this examination through hypnosis. "I felt embarrassed, somehow ashamed . . . the way you would feel if you
had flunked a test or something and tried to conceal it from your
parents." He recalled that, when he came home that fateful morning in 1973, he felt physically dirty, and wanted very much to
shower, though he was so tired that he gave up on the idea and just
went to bed. He definitely had the sense that he had withheld
some details of his ordeal from Dr. Clamar and myself, though he
wasn't sure what they might be. "I really don't like to think about
it," he said. "I'm trying to put the whole thing out of my mind."

One final detail, however, was particularly interesting. At
some point towards the end of the examination, Steven said that
the "doctor" held a whitish, cylindrical object "like a wand" in his
hand. I asked how thick it was in relation to Steve's thumb. "Over
twice as thick," he answered, and about seven or eight inches
long. It appeared to be very heavy, and seemed to be regarded by
the others as highly significant, "As if it were the most important
part of the entire operation." For a short time, he recalls, this tubular implement with a rounded end was placed against his chest.

As we shall see when we consider other abduction cases, this
short, plain cylindrical device is indeed a ubiquitous tool. Sergeant Charles Moody, taken from his car near Alamogordo, New
Mexico, in 1975,[15] described being touched on his back by a
"small, rodlike device" while sitting on a "slablike plastic or metal
table which was like a solid block sitting on the floor." In the

Casey County, Kentucky, abduction,[16] Ms. Mona Stafford described while under hypnosis, lying on a white table while experiencing the impression that her right arm was somehow pinned or fastened and her leg was forced back under her rather painfully; similarly her friend, Ms. Elaine Thomas, recalled a "bullet-shaped" object, about an inch-and-one-half in diameter, being placed on her left chest. Like so many other aspects of the UFO phenomenon, the patterns closely repeat themselves and the descriptions from case to case contain remarkable similarities. We have the data but lack the explanations, and it is partly my purpose in writing this book to stimulate others—psychologists, neurologists, physicists, statisticians—in fact, intellectuals and scientists of whatever disciplines, to examine the data and to begin the task of deciphering meaning.

A few months before this final hypnotic session, I met a young neurosurgeon who was also an art collector interested in my work. A conversation in my studio one day led around to the subject of UFOs. He was immediately curious about my investigations, though he remained neutral in his judgement of the phenomenon. One evening we listened together to a tape recording of a hypnotic regression and he was struck with the obvious sense one has of hearing a believable person recalling a frightening and very real experience. I told him about cases I had uncovered involving scars on the bodies of UFO abductees. Screwing up my courage, I asked him if he would ever do me the favor of examining one or two people, just to see what could be deduced from the character and location of these wound traces. He agreed, out of a mixture of friendship and curiosity.

Steven Kilburn's final hypnotic session had been so connected with the recall of what seemed to be a neurological examination that he became the logical candidate for the first appointment. Dr. Paul Cooper received Steven at his Brooklyn Hospital office about ten days after this last hypnosis. I was not present, but a few hours after the time of the appointment, Dr. Cooper called me.

"I've just had the spookiest two-and-a-half hours of my life," he told me. "Steven is a remarkable young man. He's extremely bright, an excellent observer, and totally believable. And really very, very decent . . . a nice human being. I was spellbound. Everything he told me about what they did to him and how his body reacted accorded exactly with what should have happened if they stimulated the different nerves he said they touched. I tried to

mislead him," Dr. Cooper added. "He said when they pressed
here, and he indicated his femoral nerve, his thigh moved. I said,
'Are you sure? Are you sure it wasn't elsewhere? He said, 'No, it
was right here, I'm sure of it.' I'd insist it couldn't have been where
he said, just to try to mislead him, but he would always stick by his
memory of it. He exactly described the motor reaction that happens when the femoral nerve is stimulated. And he has no particular knowledge of the nervous system. He'd have to have known a
great deal to make it all up, and I'm certain he's not the type to lie.
He's a very decent guy, and I'm really impressed with him. It's
remarkable, the whole thing.

"He asked me what I thought they were doing when they
went up and down his back with their machine, stimulating various nerves. I told him that it seemed to me they just wanted to find
out how he worked."

Dr. Cooper was unable, during the two-and-a-half hour interview and examination, to find any unusual scars or puncture
marks on Steven's body. (The tiny scar near his navel could have
had any number of causes.) But, then, Steve said it had only *felt* as
if he had been opened up—he had never seen any blood or
noticeable scar, and the encounter had happened seven years before. "I don't know what it all means," Paul Cooper told me, "but
it's remarkable. Fascinating! Really fascinating." I had to agree
that no one else knows what it means, either—not I, not Dr. Clamar, not Ted Bloecher, and not even Steven Kilburn, and he was
there!

4

The Blue Light in the Pine Barrens

Judy Kendall and her sisters, Barney and Betty Hill, Elaine Thomas, Mona Stafford, and numerous other people were, like Steven Kilburn, abducted from automobiles by UFO occupants, who somehow took control of their vehicles. But there is a second basic abduction scenario, one that is, if anything, even more disturbing to contemplate. Many people have simply been taken from their homes while they were either asleep or involved in some quotidian activity, like watching television or reading. On October 7, 1979, I received a phone call from a good friend of mine, a man I shall refer to as Howard Rich. He was very distressed about what had happened to him the night before, yet he was unclear as to why it had affected him so deeply.

Last night, I was just relaxing and watching television. I was visiting my mother in Toms River, New Jersey, and I was alone in a groundfloor bedroom. About eleven-thirty or so, as I was watching this program, the room started to fill with light, very bright light, with a bluish tinge to it. It didn't seem to be shining in the window—it seemed to be there in the room with me. It got brighter and brighter, and then it began to diminish. The whole thing only lasted, say, about three seconds, but when it was over, it left me very frightened. I felt a deep sense of dread. It was really strange. I've never had anything like it happen before.

I was really shaken. I got up and . . . I keep a gun in the house. I found it and loaded it and went outside to look around. I was that nervous. I didn't see anything unusual, so I came back in, *but I still couldn't settle down and go to sleep. I took a Valium, but I couldn't relax. I finally got to sleep, but this morning I just thought I should call you and tell you about it.*

Howard is a gentle and pacific man; I was shocked to hear that he owned a pistol, and even more so that he loaded it and went outdoors. I asked him how much time he spent outside.

"Not very long . . . four or five minutes, probably. I walked around behind the house and didn't see anything unusual."

Just to double-check, I inquired if the same television program he had been watching was still on when he came back inside.

"Yes, it was, I think. I'm pretty sure. There wasn't any time problem or anything like that. I don't think anything really happened. It was just that it was so strange, and it left me so . . . feeling so nervous and apprehensive."

Toms River is near Fort Dix, so I suggested he first call the police and report the incident, just to see if anyone else reported something similar, and then, I felt, he should call Fort Dix to inquire about any possible flare drops or nighttime military exercises. Finally, I said that he should ask his closest neighbors if they noticed anything unusual.

Ironically, Howard's call came as Ted Bloecher and Patrick Huyghe, another UFO investigator, were in my studio going over with me the tape recording I had made of a recent hypnotic regression session involving still another abduction. I finished my conversation with Howard and relayed it to Ted and Patrick. I told them that I had been struck by his deep and continuing uneasiness, though there seemed to be no time lapse nor any other clues that might imply a more complex experience than he could consciously recall.

Howard knew a little about the UFO phenomenon, but had no real sense of the abduction cases we were investigating. He had served in the Air Force for three years and had heard of a number of Air Force UFO incidents. The loaded gun, I found out later, he acquired when a job he held for a year or so involved his driving alone back and forth across the country, sometimes carrying a respectable amount of cash.

I called Howard the following day to see what he had learned from the various lines of inquiry I had suggested. The local police had received no other reports of unusual lights or flares. When he spoke to the information officer at Fort Dix, he was told that there had been no nighttime military exercises of any kind. An interesting side-light here, however, was the way the information officer began to question Howard about what he had seen—almost, he felt, as if the officer had a prepared list of questions to ask anyone reporting "unusual lights." The neighbors also had seen nothing out of the ordinary, though they mentioned the fact that they had had an unusually restless night.

A few weeks after his initial call to me, Howard and I were together at a dinner party. He mentioned again how unnerved he had been by the incident of the blue light. I said that, if he was curious, perhaps I could arrange an appointment with Dr. Clamar so that he could undergo hypnosis, and, at the least, he would recall all the details of his experience and would most probably be able to put the matter to rest. I honestly did not think that there was much to discover. I felt that the vivid light might have been some kind of half-dream in the mind and eye of a drowsy, late-night television viewer. The only thing that I did wonder about was his intense reaction. On the stimulus side of the ledger, there wasn't much—just a bright, momentarily light-filled bedroom. But on the other side of the ledger, the response side, there was a very deep, very sustained, fearful reaction that did not seem to have an adequate cause. I should have known from Steven Kilburn's case that an intense reaction with this kind of vague stimulus is itself a definite clue, an indication that perhaps there is more stimulus, and that it has just been effectively blocked.

On March 8, 1980, almost exactly five months after the incident, an appointment I had set up for someone else with Dr. Clamar was canceled, and, almost on a whim, I called Howard and asked if he wouldn't be interested in taking it himself. He agreed. We went to her office by cab, talking all the while about everything except UFO's and the mysterious, light-filled bedroom. On the first appointment, Dr. Clamar usually conducts an informal interview with the subject to gather background information and to better understand his or her general character and psychological make-up. After this, she induces a trance state so that the subject can experience hypnosis in a relaxed and neutral way. Regression to a specific earlier event is something that is usually not attempted until the second appointment.

Howard entered Dr. Clamar's office feeling somewhat apprehensive and nervous, but her direct and cheerful style immediately won him over. I waited outside during the obviously confidential interview. When she had completed the conversation and preliminary "trial run" hypnosis, she asked me to join them. Howard looked relaxed, though there was a slight cloud over his usually happy and open countenance. He is a youthful thirty-eight years old, tall, the kind of man women find very attractive in an easy, brotherly way. Prior to his interview he had told Dr. Clamar and me his story once again, and I tape-recorded it before leaving the room.

It was in a place called ~~Toms River, New Jersey,~~ *near the pine barrens, which is near Fort Dix, and it's kind of a strange place. I don't know how really to describe it,* ~~but it has a funny ambience about it~~ *. . .* ~~at least, I feel it.~~ *I was staying at my* ~~moth-~~ ~~er's house. She has a condominium in a retirement community.~~ *It was a Saturday night, probably around* ~~midnight~~*, and I was* ~~watching television and doing some reading. And I think I had~~ ~~maybe a glass of sherry, and I was tired. . . . . I was halfheartedly~~ ~~watching TV—the TV was on the desk—there was a small light~~ ~~on the desk, probably a sixty watt bulb, in a pretty big room, so it~~ ~~wasn't very bright. There was one window in the bedroom that~~ ~~faces east.~~ *Suddenly, the* ~~room~~ *seemed to have an incredible, intense light in it, with a blue tinge to it, that built in intensity the way a strobe light would, but it was of longer* ~~duration~~*. I'd guess it was almost three seconds.* (**HR** *is an accomplished photographer, so these descriptions and estimates are probably quite accurate.)* It ~~built~~*, peaked, and then became dim again, and then the* ~~room~~ *seemed to be darker than it was originally, as if the bulb had gone down a bit, and I had an incredible feeling of fear and apprehension . . . and almost . . . see if I can find another word to fit it . . . but I guess fear and apprehension fit it best. And maybe it's my mind, but everything seemed to become very quiet at the same time. Do you know how, after an automobile accident, in the city when you hear cars crash, for a split-second after that everything stops? Well, that kind of sound happened, or lack of sound. . . . There are always background sounds, woods sounds, animal sounds. . . .*

But I guess there was a pause there, and I still had that feeling of fear and apprehension. ~~I used to travel a lot and I kept a loaded~~ ~~pistol in the house, and for some reason I got the pistol and went~~

out of the house, outside, looking around, because I felt there was danger out there. I felt it outside, all around . . . all around the house there was this feeling that there was something there, or . . . something happened. And I guess nothing happened. I didn't encounter anything. There was nothing out there, and eventually I came back in. I guess I was outside maybe four or five minutes, walking around the grass and woods. Then I went back in and I was still shaken. It took me a long time to calm down. I had another glass of sherry, and finally went to sleep about thirty minutes to an hour after that. And that was it. There was residue after that, the next few days. I still felt tense and apprehensive.

After the session, Howard and I left the office and went out to the street in search of a cab. "Let's not walk so fast," he said to me. "The whole experience was very strange." I glanced at him and sensed his unease. "As soon as she had me in a trance, I suddenly had a flash of being back there at my mother's house, outside, and I just said, 'They're coming for me.' It frightened me. I don't know what it means. I didn't want to explore it, and she brought me out of the trance right after that." I did my best to assure him that it had probably been just a momentary flash of imagination; though it disturbed me, I thought it best, for the moment, to play it down. I was surprised that this had occurred without any specific instructions by Dr. Clamar for Howard to return to the past, to that night in October at his mother's house.

On the way home, we talked of other things, but I did ask one specific question. The program he had been watching was "The Night Stalker," a one-hour mystery show. "When you went outside, after the program had been on a half-hour or so, you would have interrupted a suspenseful plot. Can you remember, when you came in, how close it was to the end? All those kinds of programs work up to the dramatic denouement, so it should be easy to remember how close you were to the end of the hour."

"It's a funny thing, Budd," he answered. "The more I've been thinking about it, the more I think there was a different program on when I came back inside. I might have been out there longer than I thought."

My feelings at this moment were unusually complex. Howard was not just a recent acquaintance, as were most of the other people I had dealt with in similar UFO cases; he was a good friend, whom my wife and I regard with real affection, and he was clearly troubled. The incident had happened not years earlier but only five months before, within the period of our friendship and his awareness of my interest in the UFO phenomenon. I was the first person he called the morning after, and it was I who suggested he pursue the matter through hypnosis. In some oblique way, I felt responsible for his dilemma. I found myself assuring him that there was probably nothing unusual behind the incident, that he shouldn't worry, and that time would undoubtedly reveal a logical explanation for the strange light and for his feelings of unease. But in my heart, I was afraid for him. The signs were beginning to accumulate.

Sixteen days elapsed before Howard's next session with Dr. Clamar. During that time, neither he nor I mentioned the Toms River incident in any way and we referred to this forthcoming appointment as if it were a dental check-up or something equally routine. I didn't want to alarm him in any way nor to suggest that I regarded it as potentially significant. When I went to his apartment to meet him that Monday morning, we talked avidly about art and photography and women, as if to bury any apprehension either of us might have about the impending hypnotic experience. The taxi ride uptown was a continuation of our conversation, except that art and photography pretty much yielded the floor to an exclusive discussion of women. Sex is always a great attention-fastener, and it was clear that neither of us wanted to think about the next hour.

Dr. Clamar received us warmly and I began to set up my tape recorder. Just before Howard went into the office, he laughingly said that he thought the whole effort would probably turn out to be a waste of time. "We'll probably find out there was nothing out there but a couple of raccoons."

When he stretched out on the couch, Dr. Clamar asked him, as she does routinely, how he felt after the last preliminary hypnosis. He told her that he became quite tense before going to bed that night, so he used the deep breathing mechanism she had taught him to help him relax. "I just put myself on that little indestructible cloud which got rid of the tension, and then I seemed to almost have a vision of being back in New Jersey again, and a very strange feeling again of being outside, and that was it."

Dr. Clamar began the hypnotic induction using the image of a movie theater. Howard was told he will be comfortable, relaxed, and safe as he rests in a soft theater seat preparing to watch a film concerning that night in Toms River at his mother's house. She set the scene: he is in his bedroom, it's late in the evening, and he's watching television.

HR: (Deep, irregular breathing.) It's . . . on Channel 2, and it's a series with Darren McGavin . . . a series called "The Night Stalker" at eleven-thirty . . . it's a fantasy-horror . . . kitsch-horror show . . . but it doesn't seem to be on at eleven-thirty . . . it seems to have started later. . . .

AC: Is it delayed?

HR: Yes. I turned it on . . . I was tired . . . and I was watching it.

AC: What are you feeling as you're watching it?

HR: (Irregular deep breathing.) Tense. Tensely tired. And apprehensive.

AC: What's making you feel apprehensive?

HR: (Long pause) It doesn't feel safe. It's getting later. I feel . . . tension and pain in my back and up to my neck and head. (Irregular shallow breathing followed by a long pause.)

It's really bright. (Shields eyes with right hand and appears to be very agitated.) Incredibly bright. It's done something to me . . . such a bright light.

Getting up. And I take a loaded pistol from a drawer; and look out the window and walk out to the front, and I look outside and it's bright and quiet out there . . . it's just the moon. Put a sweater on and walk outside. (Agitated.) Walk . . . walk to the back of the house and look around. Look at the sky and look at the house and the ground. There's another bright light.

AC: Where is it coming from?

HR: It's . . . it's trees . . . behind the house . . . (Agitated. Inaudible words.) . . . with a bright light coming out. (Covers eyes with right hand.)

AC: Your eyes will become accustomed to the bright light and they won't feel so sensitive.

HR: I drop the pistol. I remember dropping it. And I feel like I can't move. I feel like there's some people there . . . and . . .

They're looking at me . . . there are people

there . . . *(agitated)* and they're trying to move me.
They're trying to move me, and I can't see it . . . I can't see
it, though.

That bright light again. It's all around me. I feel like I'm
floating. They're like dark black shadows in the light.
There's light all around and the shapes are just
black . . . just black . . . the shapes . . . the figures. It's
cold, too, It's very cold. *(Shivers and crosses arms over
chest. Agitated breathing, and then he arches his back and
bends his neck as if in sudden pain.)*

Oh . . . there's a pain in the back of my
neck. . . . Oh, God! It hurts . . . it hurts . . . Oh!

*(At this point **HR**'s memory leaves this scene and shifts ahead to
his return to the house.)*

HR: I think I'm back inside now. There's a different program
on? A different program.

AC: What's on now?

HR: It's the late show . . . it's a movie . . . it's the second, the
late, late movie on 2. It's two o'clock? It looks like two
o'clock. And I don't remember . . . coming in. . . . I put
the pistol down and clean it . . . it must have been dirty . . . and I clean the pistol and put it away.

AC: What kind of dirty was it?

HR: I don't know . . . fingerprints on the barrel or something,
and it was wet . . . it was wet. . . .

AC: Had it been fired?

HR: No. No. I took the ammunition out. It hadn't been fired and
I put the ammunition away separately. I always do that. It
hadn't been fired. It hadn't been fired. I lay down to go to
sleep . . . turn the lights off. I'm frightened somehow. I'm
frightened. Have a . . . took a drink of cognac so I could
sleep. I took a Valium. I couldn't go to sleep. There's blood
on the pillow though, a little bit, a spot of red, a couple of
spots of blood on the pillow. Some tiny spots of blood on the
sheets when I woke up. I feel stiff and achey when I wake
up. Ache in my joints. . . . *(Agitated breathing.)* My
shoulders hurt, my neck hurts. . . . It still hurts sometimes. . . . *(Sighs.)*

AC: Is there any blood on your body? Where did the bloodstains
come from?

HR: I don't know. I looked . . . I thought maybe it was just a
pimple or something. They were very small . . . they were

just tiny spots . . . just a few on the pillow and sheets. I
couldn't see anything on my body . . . I didn't. . . .
Maybe it was a mosquito. There are mosqui-
toes . . . *(Sighs.)* It's cold. *(Shivers, folds arms over
chest.)*

AC: Your body temperature is going to go up to normal and you
won't feel cold any more.

(HR *shivers and sighs.)*

AC: Your body temperature will rise to normal.

HR: *(After a long pause)* It's morning and I'm dressed. Walking
around outside the house in the light, and it's late. I slept
late. I don't do that too much. By eleven o'clock, I'm tired,
really feel tired. And I'm walking around outside the house
and the back and the grass. *(Sighs.)* I feel really apprehensive and strange . . . and I go outside . . . I feel silly and
foolish. And I think I called Budd. For some reason, I feel I
should call Budd up, and talk to him . . . or talk to somebody . . . so I did that. Talked to Budd. And then he suggests I call the police and see if there are any lights or flares,
Dix . . . it's an army base nearby, and I call them and they
say no, there were no lights or flares . . . that night, and I
talk to this officer who asked me lots of questions . . . lots
of questions. *(A long pause ensues.)*

AC: What is your neck feeling like?

HR: It hurts . . . it's stiff . . . there's a dull pain there. *(Sighs.)*
I feel strange for a few days. I get in my car and I drive over
to the base. There are a lot of back roads and pine forests,
and for some reason in the late afternoon I'm driving
around over there and just get out of the car at this spot and
walk around, and I really don't know why I do that . . . I
just look around . . . drive to another spot . . . and look
around. It's late afternoon, and sunset, and then drive back
home.

    (Long pause. Sighs.) Looking for something. Looking for
something. Something happening down there I'm looking
for, there's something happening down there . . . I can
feel something happening down there.

    Oh! *(Loudly, and then in a whisper)* Something's hap-
pening down there. *(Long pause.)*

    Something in the face. And there's pain in my stomach,

too. *(Agitation. Long pause, and his recall moves to the ear-lier events of the night before.)*

They're coming for me again.

It's . . . my . . . it's my . . . my stomach really hurts . . . it really hurts. *(Inaudible words, then* **HR** arches his back, stretching, as if in pain.) People are touching me. Why are they touching me? *(Sighs deeply.)* Oh . . . I want to wake up . . . I want to wake up.

AC: All right. Can you just tell me what's happening that makes you want to wake up?

HR: It's . . . I'm on the grass and they're taking me into this black cloud. It's a black cloud, and a bright light comes out of it. It's really just a dream . . . it's not happen-ing . . . it's . . .

AC: A bad dream.

HR: It's a bad dream. It's just a dream. It's so bright, though. It's so bright . . . into this black cloud . . . it's light and these figures are black . . . and . . . there's no shape to them . . . and they're small . . . just . . . my body just moves. I didn't want it to move, it just moves. I didn't want it to move, it just moves into this black cloud. . . . It's . . . it's cold. I'm so cold. So cold, It's real-ly . . . cold.

AC: Let me get you a blanket. *(Leaves room.)*

HR: It's cold. *(Shivers.)* It's cold. *(Sighs.)* What are they doing? What is he doing this for? It's bright again . . .

AC: *(Returning, she spreads a cover on him.)* Here's a light-weight blanket. You'll be much warmer now.

HR: Oh . . . it's cold. There are different lights now and they're all around the room and they're touching me with the lights. I'm floating . . . it feels like I'm float-ing . . . and . . . and . . . they don't say any-thing. . . . I want to talk to them, but they won't say any-thing . . . they won't say anything.

It feels very pleasant . . . it's soft and warm . . . I feel very good. I feel very good. It feels all right now. Noth-ing happened. Friendly.

I'm coming out of the cloud . . . I'm walking out of the black cloud . . . I'm on the grass . . . again. Back into the house. I feel very tired . . . feel very tired. *(Sighs.)* Oh! *(Loudly)* Oh! Oh. *(Breathing eases.)* It's all right now. Noth-ing happened. It's all right now.

AC: Would you like to sleep a little bit? Take a little nap?

HR: *(After a long pause)* All my energy . . . they took all my energy.

AC: Just take a short, five-minute nap, and that will energize you. It will bring your energy back, and refresh you.

(**HR** breathes deeply, rests.)

AC: *(After a long pause)* You will feel relaxed and detached from the experience. You will be able to see it well. Your perception will be good. You will feel detached. After all, you are in a theater watching this performance . . . this movie. Let yourself have a flashback, a movie flashback, to the people. Can you tell me who they were, what they looked like?

HR: *(Suddenly, firmly.)* No! No. No, I can't tell you that. No. No. *(Whispering)* No. Small. Black. Small. Bright eyes. *(Agitated breathing.)* I'm stronger than they are, though. *(Whispering)* I'm stronger than they are. They have no real will. They're frightened.

They're frightened. I frightened them. I can feel it. They feel hollow and empty. They're like shadows.

They look like shadows with eyes . . . long arms. . . . *(Long pause. Agitated breathing.)* They don't like sunlight. I feel that. They don't like sunlight. So small. They're small . . . small. Cold. Cold, too. They're cold. Feel cold.

(**HR**, still under a blanket, begins once more to shiver and clasp his arms to his chest.)

AC: I'm going to touch your right hand with mine and you will feel warm again. (**AC** notes that his hand is actually warm.) It's much, much warmer now. Your body temperature is returning to normal.

The lights are now coming up in the theater. The film is over. You are feeling very relaxed and very much in control of things. (**AC** continues her calming reassurances and brings **HR** out of the trance state.)

Howard sat up, rubbing his eyes. He had been in the hypnotic trance for about an hour and he appeared haggard and worn. The tape recorder was still operating. There was a long silence and then I spoke.

BH: You don't have to get up just yet.
HR: I want to sit up. *(Hand on neck, soothing it.)* Oh! Whew! It really feels like it was wrenched or something.
BH: Was there anybody near you when it happened ~~to your neck~~? Where were they standing in relation to you when it happened?
HR: I don't know . . . I think I was floating somehow, and they were floating around, but I don't remember that. I just remember being touched. ~~But that seemed to happen when I went out of the house.~~ *(Early in the encounter —**BH**.)*
BH: The neck?
HR: Yeah.
BH: Did you drop the gun at that time?
HR: I must have. I don't remember doing that. I felt like I had it with me all the time. And when I went back inside, into the house, I remember looking at it and it was damp and I cleaned it and unloaded the chambers, and it had six rounds in it. I always keep the ammunition separate from it, so I separated those six rounds, and it hadn't been fired. Whew! *(Hand on neck again.)*
BH: When you went out driving around the next day, you don't remember anything happening then?
HR: No.
BH: It wasn't clear whether . . .
HR: I don't think so, no, I don't think that anything happened.
BH: . . . because you said they're coming for you again . . . or whether that was something connected with that other time.
HR: I don't remember that. I think that it was just a bad dream *(nervous chuckle)*. Or . . . something happened.
BH: What about the blood? Did your mother see the blood on the pillow?
HR: No. It was miniscule. It was just like a couple of spots on the pillow and a couple of spots on the sheets about waist level.
BH: You didn't notice any marks on you?
HR: No. They were just almost microscopic spots, but they were bright red.

BH: Do you sleep on your stomach or your side or back or what?

HR: Usually, I start on my side and do about three revolutions, and then end up on my back.

BH: Yeah. What about the pain in the stomach that you had?

HR: That just seems to be muscles that are tight. I don't know, that seemed to be up here *(indicates area a little above the navel)* and I've had that, I thought, since I moved to New York, but it seems to have started back then. I've never had stomach problems. I used to have, when I was being divorced, incredible tension in the back of my neck and shoulders, but this seems different. That felt like it was muscular and that would relax. A chiropractor could relax that. And Valium would relax that. But this doesn't seem to relax that well.

BH: So you still seem to have the pain?

HR: Not as much, no. But it comes with a feeling of apprehension. I just got it in my stomach again.

BH: The stomach thing—does that feel digestive, internal, muscular, or what?

HR: It feels muscular.

BH: When you remember being touched . . .

HR: Oh! I just got tired.

Howard looked so devastated at that moment that Dr. Clamar suggested he lie down and rest for awhile. She asked if he wanted a cup of tea, and he gratefully accepted. When he lay down, I shifted to Aphrodite's chair close to the couch. Howard turned and looked at me, his expression an unforgettable mixture of shattered disbelief and helplessness. He could not for the moment find any more words. Instead, he reached out and took hold of my hand and held it tightly in his, all the while looking at me with wide, pleading eyes. I will never forget his expression. It was as if he simultaneously needed to touch another human, to feel the solid ground, and to receive some kind of explanation for whatever it was that had happened to him. I have never felt so inadequate.

Moments passed in silence. Finally, I told him that it was not important now to treat his experience as anything specific—a dream, a recollection, or a real event. "It doesn't matter now what it was." I knew this was not an explanation but an attempt to make something frightening disappear, at least temporarily.

Shortly thereafter, Dr. Clamar returned with the tea and Howard began to pour spoonful after spoonful of sugar into his cup. When she pointed out that he was using an extraordinary amount of sugar, he was surprised; he had not been aware of what he had done. The conversation resumed and inevitably more questions were asked. I sought details about the figures.

BH: Did they have arms, legs?
HR: Yeah. Long fingers and skinny arms.
BH: Do you remember being close to them?
HR: Yeah. They were touching me. Or something was touching me. It was so physical. I could feel so many physical things happening.
BH: When they were touching you, where were they touching you? Were you standing up, sitting down?
HR: It felt like I was floating. It felt like they were touching me when I was standing up outside . . . in the grass, and moving or floating me. I don't remember my legs walking. I don't remember my limbs moving. I don't remember articulation. Like I was floating into this black cloud. Occasionally, there was a blinding light . . . a bright light, and I could feel them touching me . . . all over.

I asked about the figures and Howard made an interesting psychological observation.

HR: It really felt like they had no will. . . . I somehow felt . . . stronger than they were. Somehow. Like . . . there was fear there from them. Somehow, they were fearful. There was something there . . .
BH: And yet you weren't really able to move.
HR: No . . . essentially. But I didn't seem to want to. I don't remember wanting to get away.
BH: And there was a point when you said you felt very good.
HR: Yeah. Yeah. Very calm and relaxed.
BH: Do you remember when that was?
HR: That seemed to be towards the end. That seemed to be before I went back into the house. But there was no physical shape. I can't really remember any physical enclosure that I was going into because the foliage is really tight. There is not a large expanse there. The biggest expanse of open

space for any kind of space to go into would be no more
than thirty feet in diameter.

BH: We'll have to go out there and take a look.
HR: No. There's nothing there.
BH: Well, I'd just like to take a look.
HR: No, I don't think there's anything there.
BH: There wouldn't be anything there still, but I'd like to go out
      and take a look at the space and get a sense of it.
HR: I don't think there's anything . . . (nervous laugh).
BH: It fleshes it out for me a little bit just to see the area.
HR: Well, maybe in the spring when it gets a little warmer, or
      something. There really is nothing.

A half-hour later, during lunch, Howard suddenly said that
he had no idea why he was so opposed to my visiting the site of his
encounter. He said that he, himself, thought it was odd to so
strongly oppose it, and he could provide no reason for his behavior.

The impact of Howard's revelations were almost as unnerving for me as they were shattering for him. I sensed not only what
he had gone through, but what he was about to experience. I
phoned him the day after to ask how he was.
      "I'm feeling O.K. right now, but I had a terrible night. I really
didn't sleep very much."
      I suggested he call Dr. Clamar if things got to be really bad,
because she could ease his anxiety through hypnotic therapy. He
said he would call her but only if it seemed absolutely necessary.
At any rate, we did not talk about the content of his experience—
his immediate peace of mind was the uppermost priority. I called
him each day for the next several days, but it took a week or so
before things began to return to normal. He told me later that he
had suffered from a powerful sense of having done something for-
bidden, of having betrayed an important injunction not to remember and not to tell what happened to him. I thought immediately of
Steven Kilburn's "I'm not supposed to remember." When Dr. Clamar had asked him why he said he was not to remember, Steven
had answered, "I just know I'm not. It's really serious. I might die.
I mean—I know I won't, if I remember, but I'm really, really
afraid to see." Howard's repeated refusals to allow me to visit the

site of his encounter seemed a product of this same kind of deeply implanted threat.

One aspect of these abduction accounts must be constantly kept in mind, and that is the dramatic similarity of the basic sequence of events. By comparing these two typical cases, one can construct a step-by-step scenario that suggests on the part of the UFO occupants a thoroughly preconceived *modus operandi*. The very first element is the establishment of some sort of contact or control. Under hypnosis, Steven described the drive in Maryland and mentioned that he was tired. Dr. Clamar suggested he stop and rest. "No, I don't want to do that. Don't stop me. Something will happen if I stop." The suggestion is unmistakable that Steven's mind is somehow being prepared for what is about to happen. Howard, at the beginning of his hypnotic recall, explains how he feels: "Tense. Tensely tired and apprehensive." Aphrodite asks what's making him feel apprehensive and he answers, "It doesn't feel safe." It is possible, of course, that both of these men were simply afraid to proceed with a full recollection of their encounters, but the evidence of other cases, as we shall see, suggests the more literal interpretation.

The next step is an *overt* seizure of control over the victim. A lighted object flies over Steven's car, and then, seconds, later, his car is somehow pulled off the road. Howard, sitting quietly indoors, sees a strange light fill the room and says, "It's done something to me." Near total control having been established, each man next does exactly what he is supposed to do: Steven climbs out of his car and stands near the front fender; Howard gets up, puts on his sweater, and goes out to the back of the house. Each man still has a rational, self-protective impulse that he is unable to act upon: Steven thinks he should go to a nearby house and try to get help; and Howard takes a loaded gun with him when he goes outside. Neither action is realized. Apparently under external control, Steven does not move away from his car, and Howard drops his weapon.

If these events in the scenario can be seen as the initial "setting up" of the subject, the next step is his literal immobilization and capture. In almost every abduction case I know about, this is the most frightening part of the entire experience. "I feel like I can't move. . . . There are some people there and they're looking at me. . . . They're trying to move me." Howard's description of paralysis is vivid. "It felt like I was floating . . . I don't remember my legs walking. I don't remember my limbs moving. I don't remember articulation." Steven said, "They're standing there just looking at me. . . . I can't do anything. . . . My hands are still, I can't move! I can't take one little step! They know it, too." This terrifying and absolute loss of body control usually occurs seconds before the captors come into view, thus combining two kinds of trauma into one devastating experience. The next, and obvious event, is the transporting of the captive into the UFO, and this seems to be accomplished by a variety of means. Steven's "shoulder clamp," so far as I know, is unique in the literature, though Howard's being floated bodily inside is common. One interesting similarity, however, is the way they describe their small captors. "I'm stronger than they are," said Howard. "They're frightened. I frightened them. I can feel it." "I don't get the feeling he's real strong," recalled Steven. "He's not very comfortable here . . . he doesn't want to stick around. He's not telling me, but it's obvious. He wants to leave, I think, more than I do."

The technological implications of these accounts are as disturbing to me as they must be to the reader. Telepathic communication? Mind control? Paralyzing people without affecting their heartbeats or breathing mechanisms? All of it sounds unimaginable, yet we are presented with these particular details over and over again. Logic prohibits us from discounting specific elements simply because we find "C" harder to accept than "L." Unfortunately, we must deal with these accounts whole, and suspend for the moment the luxury of particularized disbelief.

If this phenomenon represents some kind of high-level examination of humankind by very advanced extraterrestrials—a theory not easily discounted—one may have to accept the reality of technological feats far in advance of ours. Since our space program has become a reality, one can imagine a scientist saying of the UFO phenomenon something like this: "They may have the technology to get here from there, wherever 'there' is, but I will never believe they could physically float people or communicate telepathically. Those ideas are just too wild to consider." One can also imagine a scientist as brilliant in his day as Leonardo da Vinci saying something like this: "I can almost accept the idea that they can make my exact likeness turn up on a piece of paper after treating it with chemicals in a darkened room. But I will never believe that that little box over there can receive sounds and likenesses sent through the air invisibly from thousands of miles away." All-

en Hynek likes to point out the smugness with which a twentieth-
century scientist looks upon a thirteenth-century practitioner of
science and medicine. "And yet," he adds, "there will be, if we're
lucky, twenty-fifth-century scientists who may regard us as equally quaint." We must not forget that man has traveled literally from
the horse and buggy to the surface of the moon in fewer than sev-
enty-five years. Any extraterrestrial civilization, say, twenty thousand years ahead of us scientifically, just may have come up with
technological feats more staggering to us than color television
would have been to Leonardo da Vinci.

Steven Kilburn and Howard Rich both described a curious
plateau in a sequence of events which make up the abduction
experience. We have seen the establishment of external control as
a three-step acceleration: a gradual sense of dread, of something
"about to happen," followed by a definite response to some kind
of (telepathic?) order: get out of the car, go outside behind the
house, etc., and finally an absolute muscular paralysis which renders them helpless. In the fourth step, they are moved aboard the
UFO. This is followed by the "examination"—if that is what it
is—which takes place almost invariably on a high, flat table inside
a curved room. What can be described as an odd "emotional plateau" occurs at this point. The captive is somehow tranquilized,
made to feel at ease, sometimes even quite happy and contented.
The analogy here to anesthesia is inescapable. Even though the
subject very often experiences intermittent pain, it is rapidly
eased by some method which evidently does not involve loss of
consciousness. Howard's words as he relived this "examination"
are typical. "What are they doing? What is he doing this
for? . . . There are different lights now and they're all around
the room and they're touching me with the lights. I'm floating . . . it feels like I'm floating and . . . they don't say anything. . . . I want to talk to them, but they won't say anything . . . they won't say anything. It feels very pleasant . . . it's
soft and warm . . . I feel very good. I feel very good." Steven
Kilburn, describing the sensation of sitting on the table in the center of a big curving room, says, "It has a real calming effect being
in this room. . . . You almost feel as if you could float. It's very
peaceful." Later, he describes a light near the center of the ceiling
and above the table. ". . . It shines on me. Kind of warm. Feels
good. It feels good now. My back feels better, too." And still later,
near the end of the encounter: "I almost feel, lying there, I'm

almost high, just a little bit dizzy. But I'm very relaxed." Many of us have described similar feelings after experiencing various kinds of anesthesia.

Two days before Howard's original ordeal in Toms River, Dr. Clamar met with another UFO witness, an accountant named David Oldham, and I was present for what turned out to be a very harrowing hypnotic session.[1] It is important to examine his encounter for the ways in which it bears out the patterns we have been considering. On a September evening in 1966, when David was sixteen, he and two other boys drove out to a small nightclub near Greensboro, North Carolina. It was seven-thirty when they arrived, but they were told that the place didn't open until eight. They decided to buy a six-pack of beer and drive around killing time until things got underway at the club. David was in the back seat and the other two boys were in the front when, for some reason, the driver turned down a side road and stopped. This unexpected and unexplained turn off the highway strongly suggests an imposition of control not unlike Howard's being "lured" outside and Steven's swerve off the highway to a dead stop.

A large orange light hovered motionless over the trees. As they watched it, it began to swing back and forth like a pendulum. There was absolutely no conversation among the three boys. Later, David said, "All I can remember is thinking to myself I really want to talk to these guys, but I can't talk to them. It's like something's got control of my mind or something, but I just can't talk for some reason."

David's next conscious recollection is driving back to the club and going inside with his friends. Things were in full swing and a clock on the wall indicated ten-thirty. They could not understand what had happened to the time—it was at least two hours later than it should have been. They stayed only a short while, but nevertheless told some friends about having seen a UFO. When David went home, he described to his mother the strange orange light, and she told him of UFO sightings near the Greensboro Airport that she had heard about that evening.

The problem of the lost two hours continued to bother him, however, and led to his decision years later to try hypnosis. David had had several appointments before his October 5th session with Aphrodite, but this latter one turned out to be the most revealing. As he relived that night in North Carolina, and as one relistens to the tape, the parallels of his experience with Steven's and Howard's are unmistakable. At the very beginning of the trance, he exhibited great fear and very irregular breathing; in fact, throughout the session, Dr. Clamar had to calm him again and again. One must remember that these three events happened, respectively, to a sixteen-year-old boy in 1966, to a twenty-year-old in 1973, and to a thirty-eight-year-old in 1979. Variations in their individual reactions—particularly in their ability to control fear—may well have to do with their ages at the time of their abductions. Regressive hypnosis involves a reliving, with all the attendant emotions, of experiences which happened at earlier times in one's life.

David began by remembering the orange light above the trees.

Oh! What is that light? (Long pause) *Getting . . . getting out . . . feeling   helpless. . . . Walking . . . walking   out. There's a light. . . . Can't . . . can't talk!*

One recalls Howard's feelings that the light in his room has "done something to him," and then his apparently involuntary action: "Getting up . . . walk to the back of the house. . . . There's another light." David, with almost unbearably palpable fear, next describes something coming towards him:

WHAT IS IT? WHAT . . . WHAT IS IT? (Very agitated breathing) *What is it? Why . . . why . . . getting numb . . . all over . . . getting numb . . . . Oh! Oh! Oh! Can't move . . . can't move. Oh! Oh! What's going on? Can't move. Oh! What . . . what do you . . . want? Let me relax . . . I can't . . . I can't . . . Help! Help! Help! Help!*

Dr. Clamar intervened at this moment to calm him and to remind him that he was only watching these events from a safe distance and not participating in them. But this moment, as I have said, is the one that is most traumatic of all—the coming together of total physical paralysis with the approach of the captors. David's terror was deeper and more harrowing than I had ever before witnessed. It was all one could do to keep calm in its presence.

He is taken inside the ship and the examination begins. He cries out in obvious physical pain and complains that he is unable to breathe. He describes something above his head which makes him vibrate. Next, he is shifted to another part of the ship and he describes the process this way:

I am not walking. I am moving . . . without . . . thinking. I'm feeling relaxed . . . very relaxed.

Howard had described the same phenomenon this way: "I don't remember my legs walking. I don't remember my limbs moving. I don't remember articulation."

When David is returned to his car, his friends are still inside, apparently in a state of suspended animation. (This phenomenon, as we shall see, has also been reported a number of times.) It would seem that David had somehow been "selected" for abduction and examination. The car in which the boys were riding was a two-door sports car; David had to push the seat forward and clamber awkwardly past his rigid companions. The least "convenient" of the three was apparently the only one taken.[2]

The end of his account is worth quoting at length.

My hands are tingling . . . hands are getting . . . cramps. . . . Something is . . . holding my hand . . . and it's all right. I guess . . . I'll go back . . . to the car . . . got to get in. . . .

They look . . . petrified. (Soft laugh. At this moment, evidently, the others regain consciousness and the memory of the experience is wiped away. They talk, resuming the conversation that had been interrupted two hours before.) *'There . . . there . . . that's not the full moon. Let's go back to the club and tell the others . . . we saw a UFO. We really did.*

'Backing up . . . now he's doing a U-turn and we're heading back. We're talking about . . . about the UFO. We're getting there . . . near the club . . . and we go . . . to the front door.

'What . . . what time is it?' 'It's . . . ten-twenty-seven.' Ten . . . twenty- . . . seven. 'Why are we late? Never mind. Let's . . . let's go inside.'

'We . . . saw a UFO. No kidding. We really did.' (Whispering) *'I know they don't believe us.' 'Let's go. Come on, it's getting late.' 'I'll . . . see you later . . . see you guys later.'*

'Mom . . . I saw . . . I saw a UFO tonight . . . I really did.'

'That's very unusual, David. Are you tired?'

'Yes.'

'Oh.'

'Good night. I'm going to bed.' I really . . . feel . . . very weird. For some . . . some reason . . . I want . . . to cry.

Dr. Clamar, at this point, brought David out of the trance. Many other specific details had emerged during the hour, but the central issue to focus upon now is the way David's account echoes those we have been examining in depth. Immediately after the session ended, I asked him if he remembered why he had gotten out of the car in the first place. "Something was . . . drawing me. I don't know why. Like it was luring me. It's all I can remember. It was very frightening. I was scared and I was lured and then I felt really calm." A nice distillation of three steps in the standard abduction scenario.

There is, of course, a crucial difference between David's case and the others. David consciously remembered the UFO sighting and the fact that there was a two-hour time lapse. Neither Steven Kilburn nor Howard Rich consciously remembered either. In their cases, there were almost no clues to indicate any sort of UFO encounter. David is one of perhaps five hundred people who can be reasonably sure they suffered this kind of abduction experience, based on investigations which have been carried out to date. When one tries to estimate how many abductees there may be with *no* conscious recollection of a UFO sighting or a time lapse, one realizes that Steven and Howard are a visible two out of what could be an invisible multitude.

5

NBC—THE CATALYST

In January of 1979, I received a phone call from Harry Lynn, a producer for New York City's "Channel 4 News," seeking information for a projected series of features on the subject of UFOs. Originally, he had contacted Ted Bloecher but, at this point in his life, Ted was reluctant to deal with news people, so he referred Harry to me. During the twenty-five years he has doggedly pursued the UFO enigma, Ted has had some unfortunate experiences with the press. Distortions, mistakes of fact, and outright ridicule of frightened witnesses have been all too common in the press's handling of this difficult subject. Ultimately, however, Harry Lynn's seriousness and integrity won him over, and Ted cooperated with what turned out to be probably the best TV documentary on the UFO phenomenon ever made.

When Harry first called, I suggested that he accompany me on a current Rockland County UFO investigation. It would be helpful, I thought, for him to see first-hand how a case unfolded. In December, I had appeared on a WRKL radio interview and call-in program, and a young man named Denis "Mac" McMahon[1] had phoned to tell of two UFO sightings he had in 1969. Though these incidents had happened a decade earlier, they were both extremely interesting. One, witnessed by more than a dozen people including a few policemen, involved a UFO traveling slowly about fifty feet above the railroad tracks in downtown Pearl River, New York. The second, I suspected, was an abduction. Before I met Harry Lynn, I had already traveled to Pearl River, interviewed McMahon, visited the sites of both encounters, and satisfied myself about the character and truthfulness of the witness.

The sighting which I suspected might have been an abduction was described to me this way: shortly after dinner on a Friday night, McMahon, according to a long-established habit, drove to West Nyack and picked up his friend, Paul Federico. They drove to a narrow road overlooking DeForest Lake where they parked and began to talk over the events of the past week and plan what to do the rest of the evening—where there was a dance that night, where they might find some girls, and so on. Federico noticed, on the flat top of the black enamel dashboard, a reflected light which seemed to be slowly increasing in size and brightness. He pointed it out to McMahon. They both jumped out of the car and looked up at the underside of an oval UFO hovering about thirty-five feet above a nearby telephone pole. The object had a large beam of light radiating downwards from its center, and a line of multi-colored lights around its outer edge.

McMahon ended his account by saying that his car wouldn't start, even though he had recently installed a new battery. He waited a few minutes, and when he tried again, the engine instantly fired. They drove off towards Clarkstown—the location of the nearest police station—to report the incident. As they moved along, the UFO seemed still to be above them, but then it pulled ahead, changed direction, and shot off to the northeast, disappearing in seconds.

When I located Paul Federico, he told me essentially the same story, though he had not seen McMahon or discussed the sighting with him for almost three years. He said that, when he first saw the reflection on the dashboard, he assumed for an instant that there must be a streetlight above the car. When he jumped out, he realized there were no streetlights anywhere in the vicinity. The object causing the reflection was close, large, silent, and unlike anything he had ever seen before. Next, he too recalled the fact that the car would not start.

I had heard McMahon's account several times, and Federico's once, before I noticed an odd gap in their narrative: they saw the reflected light, got out of the car to see what it was—and the very next event they mention is that the car wouldn't start. Nothing about how long they stood there watching the UFO, or when they decided to get back into the car. Not even a single, "Then I said to Federico, 'Let's get the hell out of here.' " Their story had a beginning and an end, but no middle. I asked McMahon directly how long he stood outside the car. He was not certain. His memory was hazy about everything except the very beginning—getting out of the car—and the end—the trouble with the starter and the drive to the Clarkstown police station. Federico was equally uncertain about what happened in between. The time sequence was as follows: both men were sure they arrived at DeForest Lake immediately after supper, which would have been no later than seven-thirty P.M. This was their established custom—to park by the lake to make plans for the rest of an evening which had to end by eleven P.M., when they were expected home. Their stay at the lake would not have lasted in any case more than a half-hour or so, but neither man could recall doing anything else that night except driving straight from the lake to the police station and then going home. It was crucial to find out what time they arrived at the police station, because if they got there at, say, eight P.M. or thereabouts, there could be no strong evidence for a period of lost time and little reason to suspect an abduction.

I filled Harry Lynn in on all these details. We drove together to Pearl River so that he could visit the sites and meet Mac McMahon. Harry was impressed by his obvious integrity and the puzzling incompleteness of his recall. After we left McMahon in Pearl River—he was off to his job as chief of security for a school district—Harry and I drove to the Clarkstown police station to begin a search for the official police record of the incident. None of us were sure of the exact date, but "complaints" are filed by the names of the complainants, and in short order a ten-year-old UFO police report was read to us. The time of the sighting of course was the crucial point, and the first item on the sheet confirmed my suspicions:

10:23 P.M. on 4-5-69. Denis McMahon, seventeen. Approximately ten-fifteen this date they observed a UFO while they were on Snake Hill Road in West Nyack. They got a reflection of light on the hood of their car so they stopped and got out. There were two boys with McMahon at the time—Paul Federico, age seventeen, and Douglas Sharkey, seventeen. The three observed the following when they got out of the car: a round, flat object about fifty feet in diameter. The object had red and white revolving lights going around the edge, and a white light in the center. The object hovered about one hundred and fifty feet over their heads and made

no sound. After a few minutes the object took off, heading in a
westerly direction. The boys stated that they saw a similar object
in Pearl River last Friday around eleven-forty-five P.M.

Putting together what we knew earlier with the report, this is
what seems to have happened: at roughly seven to seven-thirty,
three boys—not two as we had thought[2]—drive to Snake Hill Road
above DeForest Lake, park their car, and begin to plan their evening. Soon they see a strange light, jump out of the car, and a time
lapse ensues. They come to themselves seated back inside the car,
drive immediately to the police station, arrive at ten-twenty-three,
and explain that the sighting has occurred a mere fifteen minutes
earlier, the time it took them to drive from Snake Hill Road to
Clarkstown. Then they leave and go home, excited and undoubtedly confused about why it was suddenly so late. They never did
find a dance or locate any girls.

Sitting in the car, seeing the UFO, and then making the fif-
teen-minute drive to the police station, should have taken them, at
the most, up to eight or eight-thirty; a full two hours is unac-
counted for, the period of missing time most commonly noticed in
UFO abduction reports. The next step, obviously, was to suggest
that McMahon and Federico undergo hypnosis, but, as is often the
case, I ran into problems. Paul Federico lived and worked quite
far from New York City and, though he said he would like to
explore his experience through hypnosis, his time was severely
limited. Mac McMahon was willing to meet Dr. Clamar and discuss his situation with her, but he was ambivalent about undergoing hypnosis.

The factors which influenced their decisions—and those of
everyone else in such a dilemma—were threefold. First, and most
complex, were the personal, psychological factors. Commonly
held false fears about hypnosis abound, and abet the hesitancy
many people feel about the process itself. Will I reveal something
embarrassing, something completely different than the UFO business, if I really "go under"? Do I really want to submit my will to
the will of the hypnotist? Can something happen while I'm in a
trance that will unsettle my hard-won present stability? And, beneath everything, the big one—do I really *want* to find out what
happened to me that night during the missing two hours?

The second set of factors are practical. In this particular case,
the round trip to and from Rockland County plus the session itself

would take at least four hours. Mac McMahon had a time-consuming job, was attending a local college, and had responsibilities to his family and to his girlfriend. Federico's problems were similar. The third set of factors are hidden, but, I believe, very real. There is convincing evidence, as I pointed out earlier, that the abductors implant strong post-hypnotic suggestions, as it were, that their captives not reveal what transpired. Almost every abductee I've seen under hypnosis at some point nervously alludes to warnings not to remember, and not to tell anyone. I often wonder in the face of these obstacles that so many people have been willing to undergo hypnosis.

In addition to this, people have changed their minds in midstream. Howard Rich willingly walked into Dr. Clamar's office and joked about there having been probably "nothing but raccoons out there" in the Jersey pine barrens. An hour later, and thoroughly undone by what had been out there, we knew better. When we left the office, I made the mistake of referring to his next hypnotic session. He looked at me in disbelief, as if I had asked him to go back to the dark alley where he had just eluded a pack of muggers. "Maybe someday I'll try hypnosis again," he said, "but I can't imagine when I'll ever be ready for that." Further details of his experience, therefore, are hostage to the basic and profound human battle between curiosity and self-protection—the desire to know and the need to forget. Ultimately, Mac McMahon accepted a first appointment with Dr. Clamar. She explained the hypnotic process to him but he finally decided against even the preliminary "dry run" trance experience. For the time being at least the investigation seemed to be hanging fire.

Harry Lynn, busily assembling material for his UFO television feature, had been following the McMahon-Federico case with great interest. Abduction accounts particularly fascinated him and he had hoped for a chance to put a hypnotic regression session on film. McMahon's change of mind, therefore, was a distinct disappointment.

My involvement with Rockland County had begun in September, 1978, when I accepted a teaching position at the Rockland Art Center in West Nyack. The painter Stephen Greene had recommended me for a job which he had once held, a one-semester painting class. Greene and his wife, Sigrid, are good friends of my wife's and mine, and we had frequently visited them at their home near—of all places—DeForest Lake. As I was to learn later, they lived only a half mile from the site of the McMahon-Federico encounter. (For better or for worse, coincidences abound within the UFO phenomenon.)

One of my students at the Rockland Art Center told me about a friend of hers who had had, with her daughter, a strange UFO experience. The incident probably happened in August of 1965. The mother, whom I shall call Mrs. Bennett, was an astronomy buff, and liked to sleep outside occasionally with one of her children to observe the summer sky. She and her daughter, whom I shall call Renata, were lying on cots side by side, locating various stars and constellations, when a light appeared traveling from the northeast. It was larger than a star, and it approached swiftly. When it was directly overhead, but apparently quite high, it stopped. A very bright beam of light shone down and illuminated the woman and roughly one-quarter acre of the surrounding terrain. Mrs. Bennett, reconstructing the experience later for Harry Lynn's camera crew, said, "When this light came down and shone on us, I can only tell you the feeling that you get is that you really are . . . dead."

When I first interviewed the Bennetts, it was thirteen years after the event. Renata is married and lives in New Jersey, so I spoke with each woman away from the presence of the other. Each made the same interesting point quite strongly. Immediately after their encounter they rushed into the house to tell the rest of the family what they had seen. Separately, they made drawings of the UFO. But at that moment they realized a peculiar fact: there were differences in what each had experienced only seconds before. Renata surprised her mother by claiming she never saw the huge beam of light, and her mother did not recall her daughter's sighting of two small objects which seemed to come out of the larger object and then fly off in a different direction. When the women first entered the house, they found Mr. Bennett and another child still awake, so we can assume the encounter did not end late at night. Neither woman, however, can recall what time they went outside at the beginning of the evening, so we cannot determine if their experience may not have lasted longer than they consciously remember.

The circumstances of this case, as I reviewed them for Harry Lynn, are quite interesting. The fact that mother and daughter recalled two dramatically different aspects of their encounter only moments after its end suggests two possibilities: first, that one or both is an unusually poor observer, or second, that each was recalling different aspects of a longer sequence of events. Equally important to bear in mind is the *focused* quality of the sighting. The UFO approached from a long distance away and stopped when it was directly over them. They were for a moment apparently the center of interest, and the beam of light seemed clearly aimed at them. It isn't as if Mrs. Bennett and her daughter accidently happened to see something passing by: rather, it is almost as if they were the reason for the UFO's trip in the first place. When my student first told me about this sighting, I jotted down its location. Now, in looking over various Rockland County cases that might interest Harry Lynn, I was amazed to find in my notes that Mrs. Bennett lived on DeForest Lake, and that her experience took place only about a mile from the site of the McMahon-Federico abduction!

I worked closely with Harry Lynn for several weeks and arranged for him to meet and interview Mrs. Bennett and a number of other UFO witnesses in Rockland County and elsewhere. Most were willing to cooperate with NBC with one nearly universal reservation. Harry put it this way: "Usually, when I do a story, everybody seems eager to be on TV. But not here, not with UFOs. No one wants his name used, I had to shoot everyone so that their faces are not visible and so on. It's really strange. They want to tell their stories, they want the information out, but they are afraid of ridicule, afraid to be recognized." Only a few witnesses—Paul Federico and Mac McMahon among them—made no special effort to have their appearance concealed. If there is a consistent false impression abroad in this area, it is that UFO witnesses as a group are publicity-seekers. The opposite is more often the case.

It was a cold afternoon in January when Harry Lynn, his three-man camera crew, and I drove to Snake Hill Road above DeForest Lake to film a reconstruction of the Mac McMahon-Paul Federico encounter. It was also something of a reunion of friends since Mac and Paul had not seen each other in three years. Through Harry's growing familiarity with the UFO case material and his discussions with Ted and me, he was aware of a range of circumstances which indicate possible abductions. He knew, of course, of the two-hour period of missing time in this particular case, but another clue dramatically surfaced that afternoon during the filming. On the way up in the car, I had mentioned that sometimes dreams contained suggestions and even partial details of

forgotten abduction experiences. I had described the time in almost every abduction when the captive feels relaxed and calm,
even sometimes recalling, as we have seen, waves of warmth and
happiness. About a half-hour later, as we stood beside Mac
McMahon's car and looked out over the lake, I happened to ask
Paul Federico if he remembered ever dreaming about his experience. He said that he had, but the dream was peculiar and he felt
funny repeating it. I assured him that I took it very seriously, and
prevailed upon him to share it. Federico spoke slowly without a
trace of uncertainty or hesitation. Obviously, it had been a very
clear and vivid dream.

"I could see an object coming down ... landing ... staying
there for about fifteen or twenty minutes, and seeing a beam of
light come out, shine on the area, shine on me, and one thing I
could remember that seemed very strange—I was not scared at all.
I felt very relaxed, very calm, and very at ease, almost as if I was
in my mother's arms as a little baby." Paul is a bespectacled, schol-
arly-looking man in his late twenties, and is employed by a large
airline. His dream as he retold it was oddly touching and inge-
nuous.

By the end of that afternoon, the experience at DeForest Lake
had been revivified for Mac McMahon. Over the past several
weeks, he had spent hours reviewing the details for Harry and me,
going over his recollections, and thinking intensely about what
had happened that night. He saw the television program as it
finally appeared in three successive segments on the NBC "Six
O'Clock News," watching himself and Paul Federico standing at
the site. A few weeks later, I called Mac to ask how he was and to
inquire about his reaction to the documentary. More or less spon-
taneously, the wall of amnesia had begun to crumble. He told me
that he and his girlfriend were driving home late one evening,
when suddenly, in a rush, he said memories began flooding back.[3]
He remembered the UFO landing and the beam of light shining
on him exactly as Federico had "dreamed" it. He recalled being
inside the ship and being examined by small, frightening beings.
The television program had dealt extensively with the *idea* of abductions but without presenting any details of the UFO's interior
or the "examination" process. A drawing of UFO occupants had
been shown, but McMahon described his captives somewhat differently. There was no way anyone could connect his specific recall with what had been discussed or portrayed on the screen. The

emotion with which he described his experience was both familiar to me and unmistakably genuine. Many details of his account
will be familiar by now to the reader. Above all, it must be borne in
mind that McMahon reported these details to me in March of
1979—months *before* Steven Kilburn, Howard Rich, or David
Oldham described their "on-board" examinations. I asked Mac
McMahon if the table he was on had been metal.

MM. No. Formica sort of top, whitish top, rim around the outside,
     very similar to a counter, but it was in the center of
     the floor. It was either the center or my head was up
     against the wall . . . and my feet sticking into the middle
     of the floor . . . the wall across from my body, across from
     me, would have been roughly six feet from the end of the
     table. And I'm six feet tall, so I'd say the room was twelve
     feet across.
BH: How about height?
MM: How high was it? *(Pause)* No general impression of
     height.
BH: How was the light in the room?
MM: Light seemed to come from behind me and up above.
BH: Do you remember seeing a light source?
MM: No. The room was well lit. There was a light on me from
     behind and it was like a lamp . . . it felt like a lamp. The
     light was like a lightbulb behind me and up above.
BH: Though you couldn't see it?
MM: No. Forty-five degrees up from my belt. Light directly
     above my head.
BH: Though you never did actually see it, you just felt a source
     there.
MM: Yes, there was a source of light there.
BH: How was the room shaped?
MM: First impression is circular, but I doubt it.
BH: And these figures . . . you said there were three of them
     along the wall . . .
MM: Against a flat wall. That's why I say it was not circular.
BH: How far were they from the table?
MM: They were up against the wall, from my feet, six feet. One
     was right at my right hip, and bent and looked into my
     face.
BH: Any sense of the eyes?

MM: Yeah, Black eyes. Big eyes. Yeah. Very calm. Very, very calm.

BH: Any communication?

MM: No. There might have been, but I don't think so. There was none to me directly. I felt like I was being regarded as an animal.

BH: And you said they were just compassionless, just . . .

MM: No feelings. The doctor one . . . peered into my face. I mean, *peered*, stared intently. And I mean, the eyes were . . . he seemed to gauge emotion from eye contact. And it was much more steady, intent, I mean, very, very intense gaze. And it was right into my face, right into my eyes. And they were not hypnotic or anything like that, and I was able to look back and scour the face. And the drawing at the end of that show. That fits. That fits a lot of it together.

BH: You said the figures had this grayish skin . . .

MM: Yeah. Pale. Very pale.

BH: What about the texture of the skin? Did it look like our skin?

MM: Couldn't . . . I first thought plastic, but I doubt that. I really don't have any faith in that word. It's like trying to describe red to a blind man. Hard! Harder skin. The fingertips felt more firm than ours. And they were on my shoulder, I know that, just below my . . . no, I had a T-shirt on, and that would be ridiculous for that time of the year . . . and it would have been on the forearm where my tattoo is on my left arm, on the muscle itself, on the rear of the arm, the fingertips grabbed me there, I remember that.

BH: And you said you were struggling. Were you really struggling? Were you able to . . .

MM: It seemed like a dream sequence. That's what it seemed like. It seemed like a dream sequence. It didn't quite come out all together. It didn't register well, I know that.

BH: Any sense of clothing on these figures?

MM: Clothes? Yeah, they were dressed.

BH: You said that one guy had on a sort of medical outfit?

MM: That's what it reminded me of. Maybe that's because of the way he examined me. I'd say it was hard to describe. It would have been a snap high collar, like . . . you see on the old doctor shows.

BH: Sort of a turtleneck?

MM: Yeah. The other ones wore more of a coverall . . . grayish-green, darker than their skin, but along the same skin lines. More form-fitting. And they were built well. They were built powerfully. I remember that.

BH: They weren't weak-looking?

MM: No. They weren't weak-looking at all. They looked like miniature people, but there were no skinny arms and all that crap, they were built as normal as a person would be. That's what it seemed to me. They didn't seem extra-thin. They seemed normal, only five feet tall.

BH: But their faces were . . . how about the relation of head to body?

MM: The face seemed bigger and the head seemed more round, and maybe a little bit larger, but human.

BH: But they definitely had shoulders, and a build?

MM: Yeah, they had a build. Definitely a build, definitely a structure, and I would say skeletally they were similar to us.

BH: Incidentally, did these images come back from time to time or did they all come in a rush one time?

MM: That night they came in a rush. I was almost in tears. That was about two weeks ago. I told Theresa. I just started remembering a lot of stuff, and I started talking to her, and I almost went to tears, I almost went to pieces. I was driving the car and talking and everything was just flowing out, and I'm almost in tears, and I started to shake.

When I'm driving the car, I do a lot of things that are automatic, like driving home, especially at night. When I'm a little tired, I can drive and talk, and I'm in a different zone. I shut off everything except for that.

BH: Mac, would you mind if I talked to Theresa about this?

MM: No.

BH: You understand, I'd like to get her recollections of this . . .

MM: Sure. Definitely. Verification. You've got to have it.

BH: Do you remember any physical pain?

MM: No. A sense of numbness. That is definitely remembered. Except . . . there was no pain . . . I felt normal, except I don't remember the actual thing that happened. I do know something happened. It felt like I was being ripped to pieces, and put back together again, and I can tell you that, though there was no pain accompanying that memory.

So I'm saying that because of what I think was done to me would have caused pain in any other situation. I just had a hypodermic injection in the foot 'cause I've got calluses. I can't stand that. That drives me completely up the wall. My tolerance is low. But I did notice my reaction. I did take note of it in a part of my head that I wasn't conscious of until later. But when it started coming out, it started coming out in a panic, that things were happening, and as soon as I told them I was listening to myself, and accepted that, the panic was gone.

BH: Did you notice any communication between them, any sounds at all?

MM: I hate saying this—it seems as if they moved and talked without speaking, and that's one idea I just don't like, but they seemed to talk without speaking. Maybe they were talking, but I don't think so. I thought of hand signals. Enforced silence. They could talk if they wanted to, but they didn't choose to. You don't want a chimp to know that you can talk, so you don't talk in front of the chimp.

It wasn't an antihuman attitude, it was more of a "We're going to check you out, pup. Get up there on the table" sort of a deal. I get the same impression when I take a dog to the vet. Maybe that's what's bothering me, 'cause we used to own a kennel. That's the sort of impression I got from these people. "Hi, pup, get up on the table here, sit down nice, don't wet yourself."

Mac McMahon's account is rich in observations, both visual and psychological. His description of feeling like a dog on a veterinarian's table is remarkably similar to Barney Hill's remark that he felt exactly like a hunted rabbit he had once seen, motionless and terrified, falsely believing it could somehow escape.[4] "I felt like a worm on a hook," Mac McMahon said to me later. Other memories were equally specific. His sense of their behavior is exactly like that which Steven Kilburn reported months later: "They were as compassionless as possible. Their attitude was completely utilitarian. They did exactly what they had to."

Mac's description of their physical appearance is worth investigation. He had seen on the television documentary a drawing made from Steven Kilburn's description of his captives. McMahon said that though the head in this drawing reminded him very much of what he had seen, the bodies were different. "They were built well. They were built powerfully. . . . They weren't weak-looking at all. . . . There were no skinny arms. . . . They didn't seem extra-thin." The fact that McMahon accepted only the facial image of Kilburn's reconstruction and firmly rejected the skinny, attenuated body, is evidence that he was not unduly influenced by what he had seen on television. His description presents a variant on a standard humanoid type. Figure 5 in the illustration section is a sketch of one of Kilburn's abductors; Figure 6 is a drawing made by Betty Andreasson of one of her captors in a 1967 incident. Though the faces are similar, the bodies conform to the two different types. Her drawing had not been published when McMahon described virtually the same type. He also reported that the figures were four-and-a-half to four-and-three-quarters feet tall, though the "doctor" was taller—about five feet. Andreasson also described the leader in her encounter as being taller than the four-and-a-half feet average of the rest of the crew. There is another striking concordance between the two descriptions. The skin of his captors, Mac McMahon said, was like "plastic . . . Hard! Harder skin, the fingertips felt more firm than ours." These fingertips had seized him by the arm, so he had a vivid sense of their firmness. Steven Kilburn described the "perfect fingers" which touched him as he lay on the table as looking "like hard plastic, and it feels hard. I don't know how he could possibly feel anything with a hard finger like that." Each witness not only made the same visual and tactile observations but also reported them in identical language.

Harry Lynn had been interviewing witnesses until the last weeks of January, assembling videotape from NBC's archives, and searching for what he hoped would be the central image of his documentary—the filming of an abductee undergoing hypnosis. One can imagine that if only a small percentage of witnesses are willing to try hypnosis in the first place, how few of these would agree to do so on camera. The shooting could be arranged so that the witness's face would not be seen, Harry explained, but we all understood the difficulty of finding a willing subject.

Steven Kilburn had had, by this time, two hypnotic sessions—the first, with Dr. Franklin on May 11th, 1978, and the second with Dr. Clamar on December 1st. I asked him if he would consider the idea of a third session to be recorded by the NBC cameras, and he agreed to think it over. Soon thereafter he talked with Harry at his Rockefeller Center office, and was introduced to Chuck Scarborough, the newsman who would introduce and narrate the documentary. Within the week, after receiving Harry's firm assurances of anonymity, he agreed to the proposal.

On Thursday afternoon, February 1st, Dr. Clamar's apartment and office was invaded by camera, sound, and lighting technicians who transformed her living room into a mini-studio. For various reasons, everyone was a little nervous. Aphrodite, of course, was the only person whose identity would be known and she would also appear on camera. Shots of Steven would focus on his hands which lay folded on his chest; his face would remain in shadow. None of the technicians had ever filmed or observed anything remotely like what they saw that afternoon: a normal, intelligent man in a deep hypnotic trance reliving his capture by the occupants of a UFO.

What emerges from regressive hypnosis is always unpredictable, depending as it does on the subject's willingness to re-experience possibly traumatic events. Having committed his employer's resources rather formidably, Harry Lynn was more than merely looking forward to the afternoon's results. I myself am always uneasy at the beginning of a hypnotic session, as the reader will have gathered by now, so ironically the only person who appeared relatively calm was Steven Kilburn. Entering into a trance state meant that he was escaping from the pressures of current reality and traveling back into time, into those different pressures of a night in 1973.

Dr. Clamar set the scene, leading him slowly back to Maryland and the fifty-minute drive home from his girlfriend's house. She asks him to look at his watch: it is five minutes to three. He is sleepy, but he is afraid to stop and rest. "I don't want to do that. Don't stop me." His respiration quickens. "Something will happen if I stop." "Okay, then," Dr. Clamar says softly, "you keep right on driving." Steven's voice is tense, "I'm afraid to stop. I thought it would happen if I should stop." She asks him what he is going to do. "Get home . . . as fast as I can." His voice is suddenly urgent. "Something's in back of me! . . . It's in the sky in back of me, and it's low and I can see it in the rear-view mirror." There is a long pause. ". . . It's gone. I don't . . . I don't see it." Dr. Clamar asks him what happened. ". . . I'm afraid to . . . think about it. I don't know. It's just gone.

". . . It was really low, just above the trees . . . and I go fast. I hit the gas. I go even faster than I was before." After a long pause, Dr. Clamar asks Steven what's happening now. "I'm trying not to think about it. I'm just . . . just driving. Going home. The thing scared me, though. It kind of felt like . . . it's happening. It's happening and I knew it would. . . . I mean, I almost knew what to expect. I don't know why. . . . It scared me but I don't really think it surprised me." She asks if he has ever seen anything like this before. ". . . I don't think so. Not that I remember. It was quiet, I had the windows up, so maybe it made noise but I didn't hear anything. It just came up suddenly, really fast, with no noise, and then was gone. It's dark outside so I don't know . . . I don't know. . . ." After another long pause, Dr. Clamar asks again what's happening, and Steven says he's almost home. "It's almost light out . . . I'm kind of worried about whether I'm going to wake up my parents. I think it is light out! Yeah, it's pretty early in the morning." Again, she asks him to look at his watch, check the time, and he answers with the precision one encounters so often in hypnotic regression. "I didn't look at my watch. There's a clock . . . on top of my mother's refrigerator. And it's . . . seven after five!" The trip is supposed to have taken less than an hour. "I don't know what happened to all the time . . . so I tiptoed into my house and went to bed." Dr. Clamar says that he seems upset, and, she asks what's happening. "What am I going to do about the time? . . . It's . . . it's missing."

The existence of the one-to-two-hour time lapse leads Dr. Clamar to her next question. "Would you like to go over that ride again and see if something got left out?" Once more, Steven sets out from Frederick, Maryland, on U. S. Route 40. He sees the UFO approach and pass over. Then his car is suddenly pulled off the road. He is deeply frightened. He gets out and stands near the front door, watching two "dark things" crouched near the fence. "I'm afraid to look there. I'm really afraid to look there. . . . I don't have any weapons or anything . . . They're coming! I go to my glove compartment and it's . . . ah . . . a flashlight. Oh, a flashlight! . . . Maybe I can use that to hit something. (Agitated) And it's standing there, just looking at me! Not those things behind the fence . . . I can't do anything with the flashlight. My hands are still. I can't move! I can't take one little step! They know it, too. God, what is it? Jesus! There's . . . there's another one coming now. There are five of them, and they . . . they . . . ah . . . Jesus! Arms are really skinny. The head is really big, and the eyes are completely black, and they shine just a little bit from the reflection . . . there is a nose . . . like a tiny, little raised ridge and two little holes . . . like little pin holes. They're just checking

me out. I can't move, though. I'm on my feet, but I am relaxed . . . my hands are at my sides and I'm completely . . . can't move at all. Can't even turn around."

Steven continues with his description of the figures, until he
pauses and Dr. Clamar asks him if he is still paralyzed. "Not as
much. I can move my head. I can't move my arms, though, at all."
Then she asks: "What happened to your arms that they can't be
moved?" "There's just no strength in them . . . they don't hurt. I
just don't have any muscles. It's almost like I have no will to do the
things I want to do. I think I'd be almost afraid to move anyway,
though."

Next, Steven describes the clamp on his shoulder. ". . . It
hurts my back. It's twisting me. Jesus! Give me a break. I'll turn.
(Laughs nervously.) Just ask me to turn, I'll turn. . . . Oh! Oh no!
(Labored breathing) No! It's there! Next to my car. The thing I saw!
The thing I saw in my windshield . . . and it's just sitting
there . . . this thing . . . and the light coming from it. I think
they are spotlights or something. Really bright. I can hardly see it.
And this thing is extending from it, like a big . . . ah . . . like
a . . . like a boom. It's a tool or something to turn me around!
And it's locked on my shoulder . . . I still can't move, so I don't
know . . . why they had to do that. My back . . . it bends my
stomach out . . . and my shoulder back. . . . Back hurts from it.
Really hurts. Getting a little angry. They don't have to do that. I'm
thinking that I wouldn't hurt them—they shouldn't hurt me."
Shortly thereafter, we decided to bring the session to a close, so
Dr. Clamar made a new request. "Steven, suppose you get back
into the car. Can you do that?" "If I forget about them." "All right.
Let's just erase them from your mind, erase that scene from your
mind and get back into the car." "Okay." "You back in?" "I'm on
the road on my way home." "Good. Let yourself arrive at your
parents' home." *(With great relief in the voice)* "I'm already
there!"

Within a few moments, Dr. Clamar brought him out of the
trance and the filming ended. It was impossible to know, looking
from face to face, what the NBC technicians were thinking, but
there was no mystery so far as Harry Lynn was concerned. He
knew that he had captured many minutes of dramatic footage.

When the completed documentary was shown twelve days
later, its high points came during Steven's hour with Dr. Clamar.
The entire traumatic episode was covered by carefully selected

excerpts from the hypnotic session. The unsteadiness of Steven's voice, the irregularity of his breathing, and the fearful tension in his hands were all too obvious on the screen.

Harry Lynn had filmed another interview with Steven the day after his hypnosis. This time, he was alert and fully conscious as he expanded upon his recollections. "In a funny kind of way, I felt physically much larger than they. I felt like I weighed three times as much as these things. But I was far inferior. I just felt that. And I don't know why. It was just a feeling they gave me. I got the feeling that if they would have wanted to communicate with me, they could have easily. But they weren't really that interested. I think they were being very analytical. I think this is why I was afraid of them. Because I really felt that, if one of them had wanted to look inside my body, and they would have had to cut me open to do it, and it would have hurt me intensely, they would have done it. Not to hurt me, but just to do what they were trying to do. And if it had killed me, well . . . they weren't trying to be mean or vicious. I think they were just out to do their job and that was it." Steven continued: "What frightens me, and what *really* frightens me is that because I didn't remember this before I underwent hypnosis, and now remember it, this could have happened to you. I think this has happened to a lot of people. And I don't mean ten or twenty, I mean thousands . . ."

Steven's unsettling observation was followed by a bit of theoretical underpinning—astrophysicist Robert Jastrow on the subject of life outside our solar system:

"If I hold my hand up to the sky like that, it conceals a part of the universe, and behind that hand there lie no less than a thousand trillion stars and planets like the Earth, but within the visible universe I think it would be extremely egotistical to think that the only intelligent life in that vast universe is right here on Earth. We are teeming with life in this world, and in that world of life, man and his entire planet are newcomers, are recent arrivals, not at the summit of creation, but somewhere near the bottom of the heap."

Steven's words ended the program:

"If anything happened to me, it could happen to you—let me put it that way."

6

The Virginia Horton Case

A few days after the final NBC "News" segment on the UFO phenomenon, Aphrodite Clamar phoned to tell me about an interesting call she had received from a woman we shall refer to as Virginia Horton. They had been introduced through a mutual friend who had just described the television segment filmed in Dr. Clamar's office; it piqued Virginia's curiosity. Though she knew very little about UFO's, she had had a strange experience as a child which seemed to involve a time lapse, and she was interested in pursuing the matter through hypnosis. Dr. Clamar suggested she get in touch with me first for a preliminary interview, and on February 21 she called.

Virginia spoke quickly and directly, in a firm, young-sounding voice. She told me that her friend had recounted the filmed hypnotic session and mentioned the theory we had presented that many, many people may have had UFO abduction experiences without any conscious recall. "I told her I thought that was really unbelievable," she said. "I can't think of a single person who . . ." and then it had dawned on her. As the words came out, something connected in her mind, she said, something that had happened to her as a child. And later, she had remembered a second incident that also "fit the pattern," in that both incidents seemed to involve memory loss. She had been holding the first event in the back of her mind all these years—ever since she was six years old—thinking, "There's something odd about this and when I grow up I'm going to understand it."

Before giving me any details, she asked me about the UFO phenomenon, and about my role as an investigator. Clearly, she was concerned about protecting her anonymity. She is a lawyer with a major corporation whose management might not understand or tolerate her curiosity about such an exotic subject. She told her husband about her desire to explore this childhood mystery through hypnosis, and he was very supportive, but she insisted we not reveal her identity.

The incident that had remained so vividly in her mind had happened in the summer of 1950, a few months before Virginia's seventh birthday. She was living on her grandfather's farm in southern Manitoba near Lake Superior. She had been outside playing, and had then gone into the barn to gather eggs; there were only a few chickens, and this was one farm chore she enjoyed very much. Then, she said, "All of a sudden, I was in the yard and I didn't remember going from the barn into the yard towards the house. I had an itch on my leg, and I reached down to scratch it. I pulled up my blue jeans and when I scratched my leg I realized it was wet. I was covered with blood, from a cut on the back of my calf. It was a large and clean cut . . . no dirt or anything. It must have been at least a half-inch deep and an inch long. It was bleeding, but there was no pain."

Virginia explained that her reaction was odd because she and her family are all notoriously pain-sensitive; this cut didn't hurt despite all the blood pouring out. It was doubly strange because she had no idea whatsoever how she had cut herself, nor how she arrived in the yard. One second, she had been in the barn gathering eggs and, the next second, she was standing in the yard with a bleeding leg. On top of everything, as she was about to discover, there was no rip or tear in her blue jeans, despite the fact that the cut was far up her leg, near the place of her calf's maximum thickness. Every young girl probably manages sometime to cut the front of her leg—barked shins being a badge of childhood, like skinned knees—but a half-inch deep slit on the back of one's calf is a little harder to achieve.

"I went in the house," she continued, "and I showed my mother. 'Look at this cut I have. I have no idea where it came from.' My mother and my grandfather—I remember my father wasn't there—were alarmed, and my mother bandaged it very carefully. The funny thing was, even at that age I realized there was something very weird about the cut, and later I ripped the bandage off, thinking 'I want to remember this.' It left a very nice, straight scar . . . the only scar I have on my body.

"There were things in the barn that could have cut me, so we all went out and looked around, but they couldn't find anything. The only natural way I could have gotten cut required that I somehow catch myself on the jeans hard enough so that they would be pulled up, and then get cut on something different, or else my jeans would have been cut, too. Even at age six, I was clever enough to figure that out. The only sharp thing we could find was a roll of tin plate about six feet off the barn floor. There just didn't seem to be any explanation.

"We went back in and they told me not to worry about it. But, as I said, it never once hurt. It was clean. There wasn't any dirt in it. It wasn't ragged, and the kinds of things you can cut yourself on on a farm are ragged and dirty. And so I ripped the bandage off and I said to myself, 'I want to see this wound. There's something fascinating, completely fascinating about it.' Normally I didn't like to look at blood or anything like that and I always cried and carried on when I hurt myself."

I asked Virginia if she had read much about UFOs, which she assured me she hadn't, and then asked her about any prior interest in anything that might be related to the phenomenon.

"I've always wanted to fly in outer space; in fact, even as a teenager I wanted to be an astronaut."

I mentioned Allen Hynek to her and his name seemed vaguely familiar, but she really knew almost nothing about the UFO case material; her interest, instead, seemed focussed on NASA and the American space program, which she knew in detail. This entire childhood business had come up only because of the television program her friend had described to her.

"I called Dr. Clamar and told her that I wanted to be hypnotized. It was possible that this was somehow a figment of my imagination, but I really wanted to try to find out what actually happened. I called my mother to ask her what she remembered about it, but she didn't remember anything much, and thought the whole thing was a little weird.

"Then she said, 'But there was that time later on when we were at the picnic, remember, and you showed up out of the woods covered with blood.' I had forgotten all about it till she mentioned it. It happened when we were on a family picnic, and my father was taking movies of all the kids, and my brother and I came rushing out of the woods. I had been separated from my brother and I didn't remember where I had been, and I was talking when somebody said, 'You have blood on your blouse.' I was horrified and I started feeling the tip of my nose, if I had a bloody nose or something. There was nothing, no wound, but I had blood on my blouse from somewhere, as though I had been splattered.

"I said the only thing I could remember is that I saw a beautiful deer in the woods. It was almost like a mystical deer . . . it was very strange. It's all on film . . . me with blood on my blouse and feeling all horrified and kind of yucky. I've always hated that film because it looks so awful. But my mother just reminded me about it, because she said that was a time when I was missing and no one knew where I was. The first time, when I was six, I had been out all afternoon playing, so my mother had no idea if there was any kind of a missing time situation then. I just went on and on about that deer, though, this beautiful deer that I had seen."

I asked a few questions about the circumstances. Virginia had been sixteen at the time, and the picnic took place in Germany, near the Rhine valley, about thirty or forty miles from Frankfurt. My next question has become a regular one in cases which may have a time lapse or other clue which suggest a possible abduction. I asked Virginia if she had ever had any dreams which might bear on the subject. She had.

"I remember, when I was about thirteen, dreaming about traveling in outer space and going far, far away and meeting people that I knew like they were old friends, and I talked to them about things and they explained things to me and showed me things. I wanted to stay there, but they said no, I had to go back. They said I could share what I knew with my friends, but I couldn't stay."

I asked if she remembered how she traveled, if there was some kind of vehicle involved, and she answered that she couldn't remember a vehicle, though she frequently dreams of flying. Our conversation ended after I told her a bit more about the way we go about investigating a UFO sighting. I added that, so far as I knew, there was nothing in the UFO literature that served as a precedent for her accounts, and that it was highly possible that there was, in fact, no UFO involvement. I strongly cautioned her against reading anything about UFOs prior to her hypnotic sessions, and we made arrangements to get in touch with Dr. Clamar for the first appointment.

I must admit that I was curious about Virginia's strange story, even though it seemed basically unrelated to the UFO phenomenon. First of all, Virginia herself was an interesting and highly intelligent woman, apparently successful in all the important ways. She held, as I was to find out later, a very responsible position, and was considered by her colleagues to be quite brilliant. She was happily married and maintained a strong, continuing relationship with her parents.

In recounting her story to me, she was specific in her recall of details, and truly puzzled as to what had actually happened. A special tone came through in the telling, a tone which we have learned to respect when we hear it: people who have had encounters, and those who, through hypnosis, have recalled abduction experiences, have a particular objectivity which rarely contains what one might call "moral coloration." Despite the fact that part of this encounter, particularly the beginning, might have been quite terrifying, it is neither "The devils seized me," nor "I was singled out by God." Instead, as we have seen, the quality of the experience is more that of the laboratory, a nearly neutral situation in which the captors investigate and seemingly run tests in which the captive is immobilized and made to feel, so far as is possible under the circumstances, comfortable. A number of psychologists who have interviewed witnesses and read the hypnotic transcripts have told me that they detected neither paranoia nor delusions of grandeur. The witness's frame of mind is better described as perplexed, often fearful, yet apparently objective and curious as to what happened to them and why.

The second detail that linked Virginia's story to an aspect of the UFO phenomenon was the factor of a time lapse. Both times, on the farm as a child and on the picnic in France as a sixteen-year-old, Virginia herself was aware of time she could not account for. She told me later that, when she came out of the woods just before she discovered the blood on her blouse, her parents had asked her where she had been, and she told them she had been with her brother up until the last minute when she had seen the deer. Her brother insisted he had been searching for her and calling for at least a half hour. The discrepancy was immediately swept aside when Virginia's mother spotted the blood on her shirt, and their concern shifted to this new problem.

One of the arguments against mere psychological aberration as an adequate explanation for cases like Virginia's is that the witnesses are apparently normal people who have gone through, say, thirty-five years of life (Virginia's age) with no obvious signs of aberrant behavior—no hallucinations, no instances of amnesia, no paranoid behavior or whatever—yet one afternoon, at, say, age sixteen, something happened for a short time that the witness cannot recall. In the incident in the French woods, of course, we have as evidence for *something* strange, real, and non-hallucinatory, the film of Virginia discovering the blood on her blouse and the testimony of her family that she had been missing (and in retrospect, from various accounts, the missing time period seems to be somewhere from a half-hour to one hour long). The vast majority of encounters or abduction accounts are neither hallucinations nor hoaxes; indeed, in my investigations, I have never run into either. (This is not to deny that such things may have happened from time to time; they are simply very rare and usually obvious from the start.)

Inquiries into Virginia's case moved slowly since the investigating team in normal circumstances consisted of a nine-to-five computer expert, an overworked psychotherapist, and a professional painter—Bloecher, Dr. Clamar, and myself. I spent eight days as visiting artist at the University of Texas in Austin shortly after Virginia had first called me. Ultimately, several weeks elapsed between that call and her first hypnotic regression session with Dr. Clamar, a not untypical delay. In the meantime, we had spoken again by phone, and again I was struck by her obvious intelligence. This second conversation was more wide-ranging, involving as it did an extended discussion of hypnosis and its reliability as a method for uncovering the truth. Virginia grasped the issues instantly, choosing from an extensive, even technical vocabulary with speed and precision. It was as if her well-stocked verbal closets were always in perfect order; in a split second, she is able to lay her hand on whatever phrase she needs while the rest of us grope about on untidy shelves.

Her physical appearance is equally striking, and one feels she is the sort of woman who is inevitably noticed wherever she may be. She came, accompanied by her husband, Mark, for her first hypnotic session. I had arrived a few minutes before and was chatting with Dr. Clamar when the doorbell buzzed, and I answered it. Virginia stepped in, a tall, handsome woman wearing a tailored suit and carrying, as I recall, a thin attaché case. An instant half-memory flashed through my mind, a long forgotten image from a Fifties movie of Alexis Smith in a business suit hurrying through a revolving door, every inch the attractive, efficient career woman. Virginia's gaze, when she fixes it upon you, conveys a combination of feminine vulnerability and enormously clear-headed analytical skill. She is above average in height, perhaps five-feet-eight-inches or so, and has the kind of athletic proportions that suggest abundant physical health. One of the touching aspects of the subsequent hypnotic regressions was seeing Virginia relaxed upon the couch in a deep trance, a solid and fully mature businesswoman, speaking slowly with locutions proper to the little first-grader she was at that moment revivifying.

Mark, her husband, was rather quiet. This was Virginia's afternoon, and one can only guess what he was thinking about a subject so bizarre, which his wife was intent upon exploring. In any case, he seemed supportive of her desires in the matter, and, since the idea of hypnosis strikes fear into even well-educated hearts, perhaps his presence was necessary to steady both of them.

We entered Dr. Clamar's little office and took our usual positions: the subject reclining on the leather couch, the doctor about three feet away, sitting on her straight-backed wooden chair, and I on the floor near the head of the couch with my recorder and hand-held microphone at the ready. An extra chair had been brought into the room and Mark placed it at the other end of the couch. Occasionally, during the hour-long session, he would reach over to gently stroke Virginia's feet and ankles in a nice, calming gesture of physical support.

Dr. Clamar first induced a hypnotic trance in Virginia simply to let her experience the feeling of such deep relaxation for a few minutes before bringing her out of it. This is the "dry run" that prepares the subject for the next step, which is to introduce a deeper trance state, and then to move into regression. Aphrodite takes her time bringing the subject slowly down, down into a very deeply relaxed state. Then she sets the scene, describing the time, the place, and the circumstances to trigger specific recall.

The verbatim transcript of a hypnotic session is, in its cold, flat neutrality, quite misleading. Virginia was a very apt hypnotic subject and her memories developed with great ease, but the way in which words, phrases, and even sentences were inflected is crucial. Short of writing what would look like stage directions, there seems to be no satisfactory way to indicate these subtle shifts of emphasis.

One can detect at least three distinct levels of discourse. The simplest is when Virginia relives her long-ago experience in the present tense: "I walk up the hill, I say to my mother," and so on. In these cases, the language and phrasing is often quite childlike— what one would expect of a precocious six-year-old—and the sense of immediacy can be startlingly vivid.

The second level is when Virginia comments on her experiences, speaking more or less to Dr. Clamar about what she had just re-experienced. "I remember I always liked eggs, even when I was littler," etc., and often this kind of past-tense discourse flows quite directly out of the other. Usually the vocabulary in this mode is that which one would expect of Virginia at her current age.

A third level is more complex. Dr. Clamar would occasionally ask a question which would bring up a subject slightly outside what was being actively recalled. At these times, Virginia would slip into her six-year-old persona and try to remember, while analyzing the evidence with her present adult faculties. So several modes underlay the narrative, often sliding one into the other, and producing a rich psychological mix.

Dr. Clamar induces the trance, a process lasting about fifteen minutes. Virginia is provided with a safe "cloud" from which she can witness and re-experience a childhood event with complete freedom. She is taken back to a warm, sunny afternoon on her grandfather's farm in Manitoba . . . "You are playing outside in the yard. . . ." When she begins to speak, Virginia's speech is slightly slurred because of her very relaxed state. The sentences follow each other logically, but slowly, and she speaks in a somewhat childish idiom.

VH: I sit on the grass . . . the grass is very thick and green. I blow the dandelions. I always like them because they are so fluffy. I sit under a big oak tree that has a big swing in it, and I like to swing, and I like to look at all the plants and flowers, and I have my own little garden with things growing up although I was disappointed that they

didn't come out as neat as Mama's garden did. It's sort of
all mixed up and I can't actually tell exactly which were
the weeds and which were the flowers . . . but I expect the weeds to turn into flowers. I didn't pull out anything. That's my garden. It's supposed to grow . . . and
I walk around the yard, pick up the dirt—the dirt's moist.
I look at the pigs . . . I like to look at the little piglets,
and I walk up the hill. I look for some interesting stones
and sometimes I see lizards all around. They're scary,
but I kind of like them. They're like little rocks, but I
don't like to pick them up. I look for interesting rocks
and I look at the big piles of cow manure . . . they're
really huge . . . and I like the barn. We used to have
more animals. Now I think we just have a few chickens.
There is one horse or maybe two horses. I go in to get the
eggs. I remember the feeling of those nice, warm tummies and putting my hand under each tummy. They
don't always have eggs under them . . . and so I have
to feel around . . . they have fat tummies, so you sort of
have to poke around . . . and sometimes there are two
eggs. I don't think the eggs were gathered every day. So I
gather them. I think there are eight or nine of them and
they were brown.

I remember I always liked eggs, even when I was
littler. My grandmother had a porcelain egg for darning
and I was very attached to it and I got one for my birthday. I like it. I always like eggs. They had such a nice
feeling.

So I get all the eggs that I can and I go to the house
and I remember that my leg itched—itched, you know,
like it itches when you—if you accidentally sprinkled
water. . . . It's the sensation of having fluid on the surface . . . that kind of an itch—and I reached down to
scratch and it still itches, so I pull up my jeans and—I
wasn't looking at my leg, just reached my hand down
and my hand feels all wet, so then I look down and my
hand is all covered with blood and I see blood on my leg
and I'm really surprised because I'm afraid of blood and
being cut and how could I be covered with blood and I
thought, well, I wonder if it's something from a chicken
or something. I didn't think it was my blood at first. Then

I see that I have a cut and the cut's deep; it's bleeding and dripping down my leg into my sock . . . I have very dark blood and I'm kind of alarmed about it. But it's not even as though it's my blood. It's somebody else's blood; somebody else's cut . . . and so I go running into the house with the eggs. I'm careful not to drop them, and I say, 'Mom, look. I cut myself.' She said, 'What did you cut yourself on?' and I said, 'I don't know. I just have a cut.' She looked at it. She sees a lot of blood and she stops whatever she's doing and she looks at it. She says, 'Well, you must have felt it' . . . and I say, 'I don't know. All of a sudden there was blood. I don't know what it was from.'

(*Virginia uses a slightly different tone of voice when she repeats her mother's words.*)

Mother: Well, where were you?
VH: I just got the eggs out of the barn.
Mother: Well, didn't you feel it?'
VH: No, I didn't feel it. I don't know what I cut it on.
VH: And then my mother said something to my grandfather.
Mother: There's something sharp in the barn?
VH: Gramps said, 'Not that I know of. Why?'
Mother: 'Virginia cut herself.'
VH: And Gramp looked at it and he said, 'What did you cut it on?' and I said, 'I don't know. I just . . . suddenly it was bleeding. I don't know what I cut it on.'
Gramp: 'Does it hurt?'
VH: 'No, it doesn't hurt.'
Gramp: 'It's a deep cut.'
VH: And they wiped it off with a wet cloth and I'm just staring at it and I'm wondering why it doesn't hurt and Mom put a bandage on it. It takes her awhile. It doesn't stop bleeding, though. It's still bleeding, though not as much. It's itchy. It feels almost as though . . . it itches from the blood touching my skin but the wound itself doesn't have any feeling at all. Like it isn't even part of me. Like I'm looking at somebody else's leg.
AC: Ask your mind to help you recall how you got the cut.

VH: How do I ask it?
AC: Let yourself go into yourself.

(Further instructions from Dr. Clamar.)

VH: Well, I'm kind of afraid to watch myself get cut. That
           will bother me.

*(There follows a five-minute period in which **VH** discusses pain, her fear of it, and her fear of remembering this incident. It is clear to Dr. Clamar and to me that there is a definite resistance to further recall. After a pause, Virginia speaks again.)*

VH: I think my leg was cut with a scalpel. It was just really
           sharp and clean . . . as if somebody made a nice, clean
           quick incision . . . and I don't think that it hurt, but I
           think I expected it to hurt.

(And again, Virginia hesitates to recall more details, and gives further examples of her fear of pain. But then she resumes her narrative.)

VH: They took a little cut. They didn't mean to hurt me.
AC: Where were you when this . . . was taking place?
VH: I was just lying on the couch, a little couch like this. It
           was comfortable, you know, like a bed or almost like a
           medical thing, but it is . . . it does not have the quality
           of a doctor's office. It's not chromey and white and the
           light's bright. There's plenty of light but I think maybe—
           it might be pale gray or a real soft gray. It's pearly. Those
           kinds of colors. . . . There was a luxuriant feeling to it.
           Elegant and simple and rich. I'm trying to think if it had
           some smell. Clean. Really an ozone smell. That was the
           smell. Kind of a clean smell, but nothing very specific.
AC: How were you feeling?
VH: I was really relaxed and almost at home. Comfortable.
           Curious. Like you feel when you're a guest of somebody
           and you're glad to be there. I . . . ah . . . it seems that
           I was told about the cut, that it wouldn't hurt and that
           there was a reason for it, but I don't think the reason was
           one that was too clear to me . . . whatever the explana-
           tion, I didn't really understand.

AC: Who told you about the cut?
VH: Hmm. I'm trying to think. Who told me about the cut? I
        don't know. I just could say it was direct communication
        with my mind, but I wouldn't necessarily claim it was
        telepathic . . . but it seemed the trouble I had under-
        standing was not the words so much as just the idea was
        one that I didn't understand.
AC: You don't understand it conceptually?
VH: Yeah, the conceptual part I didn't understand, but I
        didn't have any trouble in communicating. Whatever I
        was told, the communication process wasn't a difficult
        one, whether it was direct mental communication or
        words or English . . . it was just that at that
        age . . . the communication was straightforward and I
        didn't even think about how it worked . . . and who it
        was. It was sort of like how my grandfather explained
        things to me—just explaining, a friendly person who was
        explaining things; explaining that we need a little, bitty
        piece of you for understanding . . . and it was as
        though they had a puzzle that they were working on and
        it was very important to them. And they asked my per-
        mission. I guess it was a they . . . it was as though
        somebody was doing the explaining and someone else
        was the one who did it (the cutting). I don't have a strong
        sense of how many somebodies. I don't have a visual
        image. I have a visual image of soft colors, pearl-grays
        with some blue or mauve . . . but a kind of a textured
        feel, like leather and velvet, you know those kinds of
        nice, smooth comfortable textures, but I don't
        have . . . it could be that somebody was in a different
        room and talking to me and I knew there was somebody
        talking to me but, um—it was as though I was in a room
        by myself and yet I knew I wasn't. It's as though they
        said, 'You can't see us because you wouldn't understand
        how we look. It would scare you.'
               No. They didn't say scare. It was as though you
        wouldn't understand, so it was easier to just talk. You
        know, I think it could be that I didn't see anybody at all.
        It could be that it was just all handled by automatic
        equipment, except that they explained to me what the
        equipment would do, you know, and how and why and
        did it in such a way that it was like an extension of some-

body that I was communicating with . . . not a face, not a hand, but there was a gentleness about it. It wasn't anything abrupt. Whoever it is, it's someone I'm very comfortable with. It's either somebody that I've known, except that I think it just reminds me of somebody I've known, like my grandfather . . . somebody who's older and whom I'm very comfortable around, like a very explaining type of person.

It's as though there are more people than one but I think I only talked to one. And I'm more curious about where I am and more curious about the room and the immediate environment I'm in than where they come from and what they mean or what they're about. The room doesn't have an alien feeling; it's just different than I've seen—fancy, modern—and it seems pretty big. It seems like the room is either spherical—no, the room is like a round room or half of a round room. I don't see behind me, but what I'm looking at is round, I think, and it's like the walls are round, too. Round. It has a quality like the TWA terminal at JFK—round, curved walls.

There are lots of things to catch my eyes: things that shine, they're sparkly, like crystals or like instrumentation or . . . but they're so pretty that they don't distinguish in my eyes between whether they are things, or art. Just pretty. Like pearls and like crystals and like metal . . . mostly silver. It doesn't seem to be gold-colored. It seems to be silver-colored. And it's big—it seems it's big—it seems, it seems—um—bigger than your (Dr. Clamar's) living room, it seems maybe bigger than my living room, but not quite as big as my whole apartment. It's a big space. But, of course, I was littler. And the light doesn't come from any one place and it isn't all the same color. It changed a little bit and there are colors in different places, but only soft.

AC: How did you get from the chicken coop to here?
VH: Hmm . . . you know, it could be that I went to the chicken coop afterwards . . . the chicken coop . . . I don't know. I don't know (puzzled hesitation). Let me see. How did I get there? I'm so overwhelmed by being in the place that I am that I don't even remember getting there. How did I get there? Gently. It wasn't rough.

AC: It wasn't rough?

VH: No, it was gentle. It was like I was playing and I was just doing something and then all of a sudden I'm somewhere else. Nothing rough about it. Not rough at all. I think, however, it is just that I get there or something, but I don't understand. Just, "here I am." Then I think it's all right. Quiet, too. There's not much sound . . . maybe a soft, soft, soft subdued hum or noise like a humidifier makes, but there's not a lot of noise. It's nothing like flashy or bright or noisy, or abrupt, like maybe I'm just in the yard and then I'm somewhere else gently, nothing noisy or flashy or abrupt about it. It's almost like it's a dream. (Long pause.) In fact, maybe I thought it was a dream except, except I'd never had a dream like that! (Emphatic.) Also there's a strong sense of person to the person I'm talking to. A very grandfatherly quality about him, a quality that reminds me of my grandfather, who is very loving and very patient . . . likes to explain and share things with me and he's fun. . . . The place is like a dream, except the person's not like a dream. The communication is very real.

What else did he tell me? I . . . think he explained things. Well, you know, it's almost as though it was somebody I knew. You know, like 'How are you? How are things here and how have you been?' It isn't necessarily somebody I specifically knew but it does have a quality to it. Like somebody I know. 'Hello, how are you? How are things?' 'They're fine. They're fine. This is such a nice place.'

And—umm—(long pause) I guess we did talk about the stars. It's like he says, 'You know, you look up at the sky. You see all those stars.' 'Yes, I have done that.' 'And each one of those stars is a place like the sun that has its own places, like your place. And all of those stars have their places. There are a lot of things there, a lot of different homes, and we're from a long way away, from one of those places,' and it seems that he spent some time explaining to me that there are different kinds of places, you know, some that are like where I live and some that are very different and some that are very nice and some that aren't and some that are modern and

some that aren't. And so it's a very big, exciting place to
explore. You would like to go and see a lot of different
places, what they're like. . . . Some of those people
know each other and some of them don't, and he knows
quite a lot of them. It's all sort of matter of fact. I
mean . . . it's just like somebody would describe visiting Europe to you, you know, that there are different
countries and they do different things in different countries, and you can travel between them like, pretty much
like explaining to a child about foreign places. And also
that the people that live there are all very different and
some of them know things and can do things that are a
lot different, mostly friendly, but not all. Kind of a long
description of the variousness of life, places that people
live and the adventures of visiting different places and
learning more about it. And I guess he explains why I
am there (*in the craft*) . . . ·that I am part of that adventure of discovering a new place and that it (*Earth*) seems
like a nice place, and I say, 'Yes, it is. It is a nice place.'
And I guess I ask him what his place is like, too, and,
umm, what did he say? He says his place is different,
that it would look strange to me, but not super-strange,
and, umm, he was very happy. He was very happy about
meeting me and about visiting, about talking to me. It's
like the whole thing is a big happiness for him, as though
he . . . you know, I have that sense that . . . it's a big
deal, happy thing for them just to be talking to me and
he's trying to share their excitement with me.

　　And I'm not so excited as I am just kind of happy
about it and—let's see—he's sort of . . . he doesn't tell
me too much about himself; it's like—umm—he has
hands, says he has hands, it's like his fingers are longer.
Well, I mean, maybe not longer, but it's like they're skin-
nier. He calls to mind . . . I don't know whether he
calls to mind or his description calls to mind . . . maybe
like tree frogs have, you know . . . and I don't remember if he says how many (*fingers*). However, how ever
many there are it isn't like they're a lot different . . . maybe four, maybe there's six. It isn't a lot different. And, umm, I think he says that they're a little
grayer than we are in color and he says that it would
take me quite a while to get used to how he looks.

I don't feel any overwhelming compulsive curiosity specifically about it. It's as if he's right there, just in the process of communicating. Umm, when I was a little kid, I always had a very easy rapport with older people, my grandparents and other people . . . he's just like another one of them. You know, like discovering another old friend. I have always had older people, friends, who explain things to me, and I accept it as just that kind of a thing.

And what else? . . . They have eyes. The eyes are different than ours. I don't remember exactly how. They might not have eyelids . . . and they might not have two eyes; they might have three or they might have two. I'm not sure about that, but they have eyes, and I think they stand; I think they have a body that stands up like ours does. Tall. Slim-type body. They can walk around . . . and the eyes are at the top. Let's see. Sort of going through the parts of him that are like the parts of us. Let's see if he says anything that's different. Ah . . . the skin's different. Bones are different. I guess he says his insides are arranged different, and I think he says something about the brain is a percentage of their total body . . . it's a bigger part of them. Hmm. Now what else did he say is different? I think hair. I don't remember whether they don't have any hair or whether the hair is different or whatever their surface is, it's somewhat different. Smoother, I think. Maybe like soft, pearly leather. It seems like their bones are different.

I don't think he said whether he was a man or a woman, but it seems like whatever it is it reminds me of a masculine thing, grandfatherly. Grandfatherly. He's old. Yes, he's definitely old and he doesn't tell me how old old is. He's just old. And that reminds me of my grandfather, too, who used to lie about his age, and he would say he was one hundred and three, which he wasn't, but he would just say it because he was telling me that he was old, and this person told me that he was very old, too, but he wouldn't tell me how old.

I think I just talked to one person. It seems like a long time. It seems like a whole afternoon, you know, a long, relaxed afternoon.

AC: (*Inaudible question about the incision.*)

VH: It's almost as though the couch has a thing on it which
        does that by itself, and I didn't see the person who does
        it. It's as though it's done remotely. You know, have you
        seen those things where you put your hands in when
        they handle radioactive material? Your hands go in and
        you handle instruments and then, at a remote location,
        something happens. It's like that. I don't think they have
        any direct contact with me, physically. It's as though
        wherever I am lying they're on that side of me behind
        the wall, or perhaps that's just where the sound comes
        from. It's as though I am talking to them over there in the
        next room. I guess it's because they tell me that, you
        know, I breathe my kind of air. I guess they breathe dif-
        ferent air. I'm not sure about that, but it's as though, well,
        whatever it is it's for my comfort. All this, it's just like
        you find it so natural. Matter of fact.

(Break is continuity where the tape was changed. **VH** discusses
wanting to see them again, but how can they find her?)

VH: It's an easy thing. It's almost as though he can identify
        me by . . . it's just like I stick out who I am, you know,
        like he can tell where I am.
AC: How can he tell who you are?
VH: Umm, like he can recognize a voice. It's like, he says, I
        can recognize your voice. It's sort of like recognizing
        brain waves, or something . . . it's like everybody has
        their own pattern, own trademark, so that he doesn't
        have any problem about that. When I think of it, I
        didn't . . . (explain?). It seems that I just accepted that.
        He said, 'It's like recognizing your voice.'
AC: Does the wound have any function in their ability to
        'recognize you'?
VH: I'm thinking (pause) . . . umm. They didn't talk about
        blood. They just said, 'Take a little, teeny piece of you
        home.' It's as though, the way they described it to me, it's
        like a combination of a souvenir. . . . Yeah, I guess it
        does . . . a combination of a souvenir and a way of get-
        ting to know me better. And they asked my permission
        and they said it's very important and it won't hurt. And I
        say, 'Fine.' So I don't watch. It's as though there's kind of

chromey stuff over there, you know. And so I don't
watch. I don't think—I don't think it feels anything more
than when you rub your fingernail on your skin
or . . . (pause) maybe, I don't know whether maybe it
hurt, and they told me it wouldn't hurt. Since I decided
to do this (undergo hypnosis) and I've been thinking
about it—it's like I could feel feeling in my leg. It's as
though maybe there was pain there, but I was told it
wouldn't (hurt) and then I didn't feel it. It was like the
pain was inside and the pain wanted to come out—um—
but I don't think it hurt at the time, and I think I asked
'Aren't you going to put a Band-Aid on it?' and they said,
'No, we'll just stop it from bleeding.' So whatever they
do, they do it, you know, like this, and then it just closes
itself and stops bleeding, like that's all part of what they
touch me with, you know, just like (pop) . . . but there's
no Band-Aid. O.K., so that's fine. Yeah, I guess they
leave it attached to me. I mean next to me as though it's
just holding it against me, and uh—yeah, it's against my
leg. Soft, like that, and (pause) he has to explain to me
that   in   a   while   that   I   can't   remember
him . . . yeah . . . and 'You won't be able to remember unless you see me again.' I have a hard time understanding why not. He says, you know, people will be
upset, and I say, 'Why?' He says because it's different
than what they do. It's one of those things . . . kids—
you know—why? Why? Why?' This is just nice, you
know. My mother won't be upset. I'm certain! They say,
'Well, that may be, but other people will be and you
don't want them to treat you like you're weird just because you visited me.'
    'No. Why would they do that?'
    'Because people just do.'
    'Now, I don't think so, I just don't think so.'
    'Yes, they do.'
    It's sort of like I don't believe him, but he tells me
that that is the way it is . . . because I don't have a
sense of weirdness about it, so I can't imagine why anybody else would.
    We laugh about some things. I can't remember
what. Some things are funny. Some kind of chuckley

things like—oh, it's funny. It seems like we laugh about chickens. I don't know. It's just that we do some laughing about how funny things were. I don't really know what.

Yeah, he just asked me if I would like to visit him at his home, and I said, 'Yes, I would.' And so that's another maybe. I ask him if it's nice, and he says, 'Yes, it is.' You feel a lot like the way it feels right now, and, um, he seems to enjoy how much I enjoy all the sparkly things. It doesn't mean that they have a lot of sparkly things at home.

AC: *(Inaudible question about the purpose of his visit.)*

VH: We had . . . it's the adventure of it. You know, it's the fun of it and the adventure of it. He explains about all those wonderful, interesting places to visit. How different life is in different places and . . . the different kinds of animals and plants and people and different ways of doing things, and that it's so interesting to see and learn about them. So he just explains it like an adventure.

It's funny. When I went to graduate school, I remember that people would ask me what I wanted to do. I said I wanted to be an adventuress, and I was very taken with the idea of adventure, and traveling around and seeing neat things and trying neat things, meeting interesting people. It sounded like a lot of fun, and he said it was a lot of fun, and that was why he had come to see me and that's why he would try to come back another time to see me again if he could.

Yes, he painted a *wonderful* picture of all there is to see. Beautiful things, unbelievable things . . . and no end to them. No matter how long you looked or how far you went, you'd never get to the end of them.

AC: Did he tell you how you could get to visit these places?

VH: Yes, he said he could take me there, but that it would take a while and that we didn't have time now. Maybe some other time he would. And, ah, you know, like, 'Your Mom would be upset if we went away for a while, you know.' A while didn't seem to be—didn't seem to be years, you know, it could have been months, but it would take a while, which seemed natural, of course, and, uh, yeah, he couldn't do that without asking my mother's permission. And I said I was sure she wouldn't care. I said I'd ask her. 'No, we couldn't do that just now.' He didn't say he would and he didn't say he wouldn't, but it was just something we couldn't do right then, so maybe we would do it another time.

AC: Has he done it for others? Has he taken others to his place?

VH: I don't think I asked him. I don't think—you know the light might have been very bright. It seems like my eyes hurt me. (Virginia was rubbing her eyes.) Maybe the light was very bright. Pretty, but bright. (Returns to the question.) Did he take others? Well when we talked about it, he didn't talk about it as though it was a new idea or something that was an odd question. It was like, you know, you'd ask your grandfather if he would take you to town to go to a movie, and it wasn't that it was a novel idea or anything. It was as if he felt like it, he could or would, and I don't think I asked about anybody else.

It seemed like—it seemed like it was just a special relationship with me, but you see that was true of the way I related to older people, so I don't know whether that was—I mean, I was especially close to my grandparents and especially close to aunts and uncles and it was always a very special relationship to me. They were closer to me—it was just that kind of a thing. We were good buddies and that just seemed very natural to me, but . . . he talked about the adventure of it as though he wasn't the only person who did it. People did it because it was a neat thing to learn, and a fun thing to look around, and it didn't seem it was unusual for more than one person to do it. The thing is, you know, it wasn't like I was talking to strangers—that's what made it so interesting. You would have thought, you know, when I first got there, I mean it wasn't an uncomfortable place, but you would have thought that, when I started to talk to somebody, it would have seemed like—it's almost like there wasn't much even in the way of introductions.

AC: As if you've known each other from somewhere or other from before?

VH: Either that we had known each other, or about each oth-

er, or were just the kind of people who found it easy to
get to know one another. It just wasn't—it wasn't like
when you meet a stranger.

We had reached a logical stopping place in what had turned
out to be a remarkable session. I signaled Dr. Clamar and she
nodded agreement. After a minute or so of instruction about how
relaxed she would feel, and how easy about what she had learned,
Virginia came out of the trance. She yawned, stretched, and
smiled and the tension broke; we all realized at that moment how
deep our concentration had been, and how intense our psychological involvement in her unfolding adventure.

It was well into the dinner hour, so we departed quickly. I
hardly knew what to say after the revelations of the past hour, but
I mumbled good-bye and thanked them for their time; then I
headed back to my place in Chelsea to mull over what we had
learned. So many things coincided with other abduction cases; in
fact, all during the hypnotic session, little bells of recall kept
sounding in my mind, as detail after familiar detail surfaced.
When I had time finally to re-examine some of the case material, I
found the specific parallels I was searching for in other accounts,
most of which are either completely unknown to the public, or at
least extremely obscure.

The general description of the circular walls and the even,
sourceless lighting of the examining room naturally fit the pattern.
But there was an interesting detail about the *color* of the light.
Virginia had said that it "might be pale gray, or a real soft
gray . . . pearly . . . those kinds of colors." "Gray" or "pearly"
seemed odd words to use to describe bright light, but in the 1976
Casey County, Kentucky, abduction of three women, Ms. Elaine
Thomas, under hypnosis, also described the examining room as
being lit by a gray light.[1] Barney Hill, under hypnosis in 1964,
described the room in which he underwent some kind of physical
examination as "being filled with this bluish light . . . which
didn't cast any shadows."[2] David Stephens, abducted with a companion in Maine in 1975, thought the curving walls of the examining room were gray and the floors shiny.[3] So we have a narrow
band of colors used to describe the atmosphere—pale, soft gray,
pearly, bluish—denoting a cool, specific range far away from either *white*, which one might expect, or a normal incandescent
range.

Virginia described this gray light as being very bright; in fact, she frequently rubbed her eyes during the hypnotic period. In her second session, she even complained that the subdued lighting in Dr. Clamar's office was too bright, and ultimately we had to switch off the lamps and continue almost in the dark. Carl Higdon,[4] who was abducted in Wyoming in 1974, complained later about the lights in the hospital room where he was taken after his ordeal. They were too bright, he said. His eyes were extremely bloodshot and teared constantly. Mona Stafford, another of the women in the Casey County case,[5] suffered a severe burning and tearing of the eyes. Her two companions also had trouble with their eyes, though Mrs. Stafford's problem was so severe that she consulted a doctor. Betty Hill,[6] describing her position on an examining table as she recalled it through hypnosis, said, ". . . the light is very very bright, so my eyes aren't always open. I'm a little scared, too. I'm not particularly interested in looking at them (the humanoids who are performing the examination)." Young Gerry Armstrong was abducted at the age of twelve from the grounds of the school he was attending in England. When he was found seven hours later, he remembers, there was something wrong with his eyes although he is not sure what the problem was; he feels he might have been told that his eyes were dilated.[7] This abduction of a twelve-year-old in 1953 creates an interesting additional parallel—the very early taking of a child—but through many of these encounters—the Wyoming, Kentucky, New Hampshire and English cases I have cited are only a random sample—eye reactions are extremely common.

Prior to her second hypnotic session—which turned out to be more startling even than her first—Virginia discussed with Dr. Clamar and me some further specific details which she had consciously recalled. Hypnosis is an odd process in that most frequently after the subject comes out of the trance he or she continues to remember things. It is a little like turning off the garden hose; the flow immediately slows, ebbs, and finally trickles to a stop—the turn of the valve does not produce instantaneous results. In a conversation which was, of course, recorded at the time, Virginia said this about the equipment which made the cut on her leg:

"It was something like dental equipment, but much smoother. It didn't look like something abrasive or scary; it was more like, maybe half the size of your torso . . . mostly smooth like a metal box with rectangular contours, but rounded, and with fixtures that might pull out, you know, to do things like dental equipment does. It's retractable but nothing so sharp and crude as that . . . more like soft contours, more like a tentacle. It was as though the thing that touched me was just like a massager, like those electric massagers, the long ones. Just something simple-looking, almost a tubular thing. It reached out and just laid against my leg. It looked to be all metal. No obvious cutting edges or anything like that. It didn't have any real evidences of fine instrumentation, you know, cutting edges or plucking edges or filing edges." Just a simple, tubular object which came out of a boxlike instrument on the end of a retractable arm. I asked if she noticed any sound.

"A soft vibration, maybe . . . I think I felt it, but I don't think I heard it."

David Stephens, whose 1975 abduction in Maine I have already mentioned, described lying on a table near a machine which "looked square, had lights on the left side of the front, and it had an arm coming out" with something on the end of it, "like some kind of X-ray machine or something."[8] Betty Hill described a device which was like a letter opener in shape which scraped over her arm.[9] One of the Kentucky abductees recalls an elongated bullet-shaped object about an inch-and-one-half in diameter being placed on her chest.[10] It seems to me these witnesses are trying to describe the same equipment through the use of various homely images, with varying degrees of success. Virginia's "elongated massager" image describes an object conventionally about six or seven inches long by about one-and-one-half inches in diameter, which accords nicely with Elaine Thomas's "bullet-shaped"—cylindrical—object "about one-and-one-half inches in diameter"; this silhouette, of course, is not unlike that of a letter opener. And most interesting is the persistent "neutrality" of the description—an object that seems efficient and totally unspectacular in appearance. It constitutes the exact opposite of the complicated *Star Wars* gadgetry so inescapable in pop culture. Virginia's "machine" gains validity to me by virtue of its plainness and simplicity.

When Ted Bloecher listened to the tape of Virginia's hypnotic session, we were able to discuss at length the new factors which it presented. First of all, as I've mentioned before, the Hill case of 1961, which surfaced only in 1964, was for many years the earliest abduction case which had been satisfactorily investigated and eventually accepted by most UFO investigators. But here we were with a case that preceded it by eleven years! A few other cases earlier than 1961 had come to light in the years following John Fuller's book on Betty and Barney Hill, and a few had been rather summarily studied, though very few had been explored through hypnosis. Here, we had an unfolding case with an eminently intelligent and credible witness, who bore a physical trace—Virginia's very noticeable scar. (see illustration section)

Even more important was our realization at that moment that Virginia, like Steven Kilburn, had no conscious recall of a UFO sighting. When these two cases which we had uncovered were seen in context with the "Patty Price" case of 1973[11] and the Judy Kendall case, we knew that there was a sub-group within the UFO abduction spectrum: cases in which people are abducted and all memory traces of a UFO sighting are subsequently suppressed. As Steven wondered aloud on NBC's UFO presentation, how many people may have had this experience without knowing it? And how many years has it been going on?

Ted Bloecher, drawing on his mental storage files, pointed out that a significant number of humanoid cases over the last decades involved sightings by children, and many of these took place in rural settings. In dozens of instances, children reported that, while they were outside playing, one or two small men wearing strange silvery or gray costumes approached them and then departed as suddenly as they had appeared. How many of these cases, we wondered, might have involved time lapses that a six-year-old girl or a ten-year-old boy, playing alone in the afternoon, would never have noticed? What were the dimensions of the problem? It was as if our classic type of abduction case—the automobile being stopped at night as a glowing object descends—may represent only a narrow aspect of the phenomenon.

And what were "they" doing with a six-year-old child, and why did they need to take a "little, bitty piece" of her? What was the problem or "puzzle" they were working on? Most of the abduction cases on record involved some kind of sample taking during the examination, if that last term is indeed even remotely accurate; skin samples, blood samples, hair samples,[12] almost everything one could imagine, but this seemed somehow more serious—a piece of her flesh, a deep incision across many layers of skin and muscle.

One of the differences between Virginia's encounter and the other abduction reports we have been considering is her apparent lack of any fear. It is important, first of all, to remember that her story begins when she is already inside the examining room of the UFO. The reader will recall that the most consistently frightening time is at the outset of the experience when the abductee is simultaneously paralyzed and approached by the captors. Even after her second hypnotic session (the subject of chapter 8), Virginia still had not remembered in detail that section of her encounter, so one can assume her unconscious mind effectively censored out the "bad part." The six-year-old child who underwent this extraordinary adventure probably handled it differently than many adults—and also might have been treated differently by her captors. Obviously, these two sets of variables exist in each abduction experience.

The Betty and Barney Hill case of 1961[13] presents a classic illustration of variations in both treatment by the UFO occupants and reactions on the part of the captives. The Hills were driving through New Hampshire's White Mountains, returning from a vacation, when they saw a moving light which seemed to be slowly following them. Eventually, they are "lured" off the main highway. They stop their car and are approached by a group of men. Betty is led to the landed UFO by her captors; as she walks, she sees Barney behind her, being assisted by his captors. His eyes are closed and he appears to be asleep. "I turn around and I say, 'Barney! Wake up! Barney! Why don't you wake up?' And he doesn't pay attention." Under hypnosis, Barney said he felt as if he were floating. He did not remember Betty calling him. He noticed the next morning that the tops of his shoes were scuffed, and the probable cause emerged, again through hypnosis; he recalled being dragged up the ramp and into the UFO.

In microcosm, two different modes of treatment by the UFO occupants are visible here: Barney Hill, a large, well-built male, is rendered almost senseless and is more or less dragged aboard the ship. Betty Hill, smaller and female, is walked aboard and remains quite conscious throughout. The patterns of treatment continue inside. Barney is only vaguely conscious during the examination itself. Betty, on the other hand, is not only fully awake, but communicates at length with one of the occupants. As we shall see, she is asked some of the same questions that Virginia Horton is asked in a colloquy that appears to be more intelligence-testing than information-gathering.

The Hills' subsequent reactions were as different as their experiences had been. After the terror she felt at the beginning of her kidnapping, Betty handled herself with equanimity, even going so far as to question her captors about their origin, and to ask for an artifact to prove the experience really happened.[14] In the following months, before her experience was recalled through hypnosis, Betty's life was relatively untroubled. But, for Barney, the buried memories of his encounter had drastic results. Nightmares, insomnia, and a recurring ulcer led him to seek psychiatric help, and it was this decision which resulted in his trying hypnosis in the first place.

Applying these patterns to the cases we have been examining, one can see that Virginia Horton's treatment by her abductors, as well as her reactions to them, resemble Betty Hill's, while Steven Kilburn, Howard Rich, Mac McMahon, and David Oldham are handled—and respond—more like Barney Hill. A possibly pertinent analogy comes to mind from the human context. When zoologists tranquilize, capture, and tag moose or elk or deer to facilitate the study of their migratory habits and other behavior, slightly different dosages and procedures are followed for an aggressive buck than for the smaller, less-dangerous does and fawns. One can easily imagine how "zoologists" from outside our world might also devise different methods of handling their various human specimen. Virginia Horton's experience, then, so different in tone from Steven's or Howard's or Mac's experience, is perhaps more due to her sex and age than it is to any basic differences in the attitudes or purposes of her abductors.

7

PITTSBURGH AND THE MOUNTAINTOP

Abrupt and rather drastic reversals of theory have occurred from time to time among UFO investigators and researchers. It was once generally thought that, if a person reporting a UFO encounter had a prior interest in the subject, that person's report should be automatically discounted. Prior interest meant contamination and therefore unreliability. Although there is a rationale for that inference, the validity of the opposite proposition eluded investigators for years. Psychological theory finally alerted us to the fact that someone with a hidden, traumatic UFO experience might later on be unconsciously drawn to the subject. Indeed, a particular kind of intense and inward curiosity about the UFO phenomenon might be motivated by a forgotten but real abduction experience.

During the five years I've been actively involved in UFO investigations and research, I've met four people whose solitary and rather obsessive interest in the subject, coupled with a few other indications, suggested to me that they might very well be harboring unconscious memories of UFO encounters. I met one of these, a man whom I'll call Philip Osborne, through his profession; he works in the news media and in 1978 was doing a piece on UFOs. I noticed that his interest in the subject had a particular edge to it. It was almost as if he accepted too much, too easily. He seemed comfortable with what, to others, was very strange case material. I vividly remember my own skepticism in 1965 when I first heard details of the Betty and Barney Hill case. It seemed grotesque and

inconceivable. It wasn't until the abduction pattern began to repeat itself that I swallowed my nervous pre-judgment and looked
at the evidence more objectively. I mentioned this case and my
original reaction to Philip, and he said, "I remember when I first
heard about it, too. It seemed perfectly logical to me. I didn't doubt
for a second that the Hills had been abducted."

Philip Osborne is thirty-seven years old and lives not too far
from me in New York's Greenwich Village. He is a practical,
tough professional in a highly competitive field. He is not the kind
of man who is easily taken in, and, in fact, his profession demands
skeptical hardheadedness. Over the years, I have helped a number of other people who were doing articles on the UFO phenomenon by supplying information on current investigations. Most
have been curious but detached in a way that implies: "This material is interesting, but I can't really get involved in something so
controversial and strange. I'll take what I need, write it up, and try
to forget about it." Philip was decidedly different. He seemed at
home with it, even to the point of drawing inferences and noticing
subtle details and correspondences that I had missed.

I hadn't been in touch with Philip for perhaps a month or so
after the NBC UFO documentary had been aired, but then one
day he called me. He had seen the program and wanted to talk
about it. The thing that had most struck him, he said, was Steven
Kilburn's remark that, if this UFO encounter had happened to
him, it could have happened to anyone. Philip said he'd been
searching his memory for any event in his past that might indicate
a similar forgotten experience. Something had happened very recently that made him remember an odd experience he had years
before in college. A few weeks after the NBC program, he had
awakened in his apartment in the middle of the night absolutely
paralyzed. He could not move, could not turn his head, could not
even call out for help. This terrifying state lasted a minute or so
and only gradually did he regain control of his body.

Almost immediately, he recalled the earlier, very similar, experience. It happened when he was attending Carnegie Tech in
Pittsburgh, probably in 1964. He was living in a small third-floor
room in a house on Fifth Avenue. He awakened one night and
found himself totally paralyzed. He had not been dreaming; there
was nothing to prepare him for this total usurpation of control. He
could not call for help. Worst of all, he sensed someone or some-

thing—a presence—in the room with him. His fear lessened as the paralysis ebbed away, but so frightened was he still that he got up, put on his clothes, and went outside to take a walk.

There was more. He recalled one other odd experience, and this from his early childhood.

This is something else that I keep coming back to. When I was a child my parents took me on a vacation to the Smoky Mountains in Tennessee. I think it was my brother who left his coat behind at a mountaintop picnic site where we had had lunch, and we didn't miss it until later. I remember we had to drive back up after dark to look for it, and for some reason it was very frightening. I just have the feeling that something might have happened to me then. There's really nothing specific, but I've just always remembered that time as being very strange and very frightening. Maybe it was just the drive up the mountain in the dark, but my mind keeps coming back to that time for some reason.

These incidents, taken together, seem to be not much weightier than the indications that we had in the Steven Kilburn case. Superficially, this case appeared hardly worth pursuing, yet Philip came equipped with that other clue I've mentioned—a very definite and resonant prior interest in the UFO subject. He mentioned an interesting detail about the very recent paralysis incident in his New York apartment. As he struggled to call for help, he thought of his older brother and wanted to call his name. He said he had not seen his brother for years, and that they had never been particularly close. It registered in my mind, though, that he and his brother had been together in the Tennessee episode, and that a very old memory linking the two incidents was perhaps trying to surface. We talked about pursuing these incidents through hypnosis, and he agreed.

A few days later, Ted and I met Philip at my studio. Our goal was to get down the consciously remembered details of what were now three distinct events: the childhood experience on the mountaintop, the 1964 Pittsburgh paralysis incident with a "presence" sensed in the room, and, finally, in 1979, the New York paralysis incident. It was necessary to have specific information for Dr. Clamar to use in setting the scene during the hypnotic regression. Also, we had to decide which incidents we would go into during the first session and which would be postponed until later. The three of us sat around the dining room table, Ted and I with pads and pencils at the ready, as Philip supplied us with whatever details he could recall. And then, in his calm, even voice he added one new element—a bombshell. "Do you think," he asked, "there is any reason to go into the question of my scar?"

"What scar?" Ted and I asked with one voice.

"I've always had this scar since childhood," he explained, "and no one can remember how I got it. My mother can't remember and neither can I. It just seems that one day, there it was." The scar was about three inches long and perfectly straight. It was located at the outer juncture of his thigh and hip, but other than this difference in the location of the cut, the situation eerily brought to mind the Virginia Horton case.

Philip thought that his unsettling trip to the Great Smokies took place when he was either six or seven years old. Since he was born in 1943—the same year as Virginia—and the vacation most likely occurred in the summer, it is very possible that he received his "scar of unknown origin" exactly the same summer as Virginia received hers! By this time, I was fairly sure that Virginia Horton's second peculiar adventure—her disappearance at a family picnic in France and her reappearance sometime later, her blouse stained with "blood of unknown origin"—would turn out to be another abduction. She was scheduled for her second hypnotic session on May 16. So another disturbing parallel presented itself, the possibility that Virginia and Philip were each abducted at age six in the summer of 1950, and then reabducted as young adults at ages sixteen and twenty respectively. The coincidences involved if this thesis turned out to be correct seemed incredible.

On April 28, 1979, Ted Bloecher, Philip, and I gathered at Dr. Clamar's office for Philip's first hypnotic session. We had decided to concentrate on the original childhood experience in the mountains of Tennessee. Dr. Clamar went through her preliminary interview and "dry run" session, after which Philip decided that he wanted to continue directly into his memories of that 1949 or 1950 summer vacation. It was during this session that I really saw how differently people can react under hypnosis. Philip was silent for long, long periods. The small muscles in his face worked, his eyes seemed to be active behind their lids, and he appeared to be very reluctant to share what he was experiencing. He was obviously undergoing a great deal of fear, but it was internalized, and not allowed to break into the open. Characteristically, he would, un-

der questioning, begin to describe an image. Then he would fall
silent, his closed eyes moving in agitation, his hands trembling.
His breathing would become irregular and minutes would pass
without a word. Then he would say, "I think I want to forget
what's happening and think of something different." It was as if an
intensely vivid narrative had passed through his mind; we had
read the results in his face and body, but we had been denied the
facts. Occasionally, he would describe what was happening, but
more often, he experienced his memories in nervous, agitated silence. Though the transcript of his first session will be presented
in isolated sections, a classic abduction scenario did emerge.

   Dr. Clamar puts Philip under hypnosis, and returns him to
"that early period in your life when you were at the Smoky Mountain National Park with your family, your brother, and your sister.
You're all there together as a family having fun . . ."

   Philip's observations come after a few minutes of silence and
half-phrases.

PO: I'm not . . . I'm not experiencing any scenes. I just see
      something that looks like the . . . like the upper part of a
      geodesic dome. (Very long pause. Quiet, continuous agita-
      tion.)
AC: What are you feeling as you see this scene?
PO: Uh . . . nothing. That I'd just as soon calm my-
      self . . . I'll think of something else.
            My eyes seem to be jumping around a lot. It's . . . when
      I think about that that my eyes jump around a lot.
AC: Is there a light there that makes them jump around?
PO: Yes. It's just bright and it's in sections like a geodesic dome.
      (Long pause. Agitation.)
AC: What's happening?
PO: I'm trying to uh . . . uh . . . forget about it. I'm just trying
      to relax.
AC: Would you like a minute out to rest a moment?
PO: Yes.

(Dr. Clamar allows two or three minutes to pass. Philip seems
calm and relaxed. After another long pause, she resumes her
questioning.)

                          *   *   *

AC: Tell me what's happening now.
PO: (Agitated, restless) I don't know . . . (whispers). I don't know.
(After another long unsettling period with only a few exchanges, Philip speaks again.)
PO: I would just like to relax more. I would like to relax more deeply.
AC: You would like for me to relax you more deeply?
PO: Yes, I would like for you to do that.
(Dr. Clumar induces a deeper trance.)
PO: I'd just like to lie in the sun.
AC: Let yourself sink . . . visualize yourself on a nice sunny beach, wide, sandy beach. You lie on a towel feeling very, very peaceful. Relaxed, peaceful. Peaceful and relaxed. (Long, long pause ensues.)
PO: (Whispering) I want some rest. I saw that dome again.
AC: Would you like to tell me what you saw, or do you want to keep it to yourself?
PO: Yes, ah, I saw it as a . . . sphere . . . and then all of a sudden I'm just really going towards it very fast, and it just sort of consumes me all around. There's light all around. And then I felt like I was traveling very fast. (Pause) I feel like I'm inside.
AC: How are you feeling?
PO: It's not as if I'm standing. I'm just sort of being, that's all.
        I feel that there is a dome overhead and that one-fourth of it is hinged and it lifts up so that there is a wedge open. That's all . . . everything just seems very amorphous and things just sort of floating past . . . that's all. (Pause)
        But I do think of that scar. I feel like I shouldn't, but I do.
AC: Would you like to talk to your scar?
PO: (Nervously) No.
AC: Why don't you ask it anything you want to?
PO: (Whispering) I . . . don't think so. . . .
AC: How do you feel about the scar?
PO: Well, I . . . it just seems so silly, but I see something like a . . . I almost . . . I see a hand. It's very shiny. But I don't, ah . . . see it really.

*   *   *

(Again, Dr, Clamar suggests he relax more deeply, and if he wishes to, dream for a few minutes)

PO: *(After a few moments.)* I don't really have a dream exactly . . . just a feeling, that's all. It's not just . . . . just a feeling, that's all. I have the feeling that it just sort of goes back together by itself. *(Pause)* But I do have light all around. I feel better than I did.

AC: What makes you feel better?

PO: I don't know. I just feel ah . . . not as frightened as before. There were all kinds of things zooming past me. I'm more relaxed now. I just feel like I'm lying there.

(After a few more exchanges, long pauses, and subtle agitation on Philip's part, Dr. Clamar brings him out of the trance. Her instructions are worth quoting.)

AC: You are going to feel very, very deeply relaxed. Whatever thoughts or feelings you have in your mind or expressed in your body through tension, will sort themselves out in the ensuing days and increasingly, with each passing day, you are going to feel much, much more deeply peaceful. Whatever confusing thoughts, disordered thoughts, whatever thoughts you have running around in your head that are also reflected in how you hold your body, how your body feels in terms of relaxation or tension, are going to sort themselves out, so that, in the ensuing days and weeks, you are going to find yourself feeling much, much more deeply relaxed, much more peaceful. In the future, should I hypnotize you again and ask you to relieve these experiences, you are going to find it considerably easier because they will have sorted themselves out into a much, much more orderly, organized fashion, and you are going to be feeling very comfortable in looking at them, addressing them, re-experiencing them, knowing that they are free from any emotion, tension, or anxiety. In the future, should you address yourself to these experiences, you will feel comfortable with the world around you, comfortable with your thoughts, your experiences, your feelings . . . comfortable with the world around you in every way. I will count from

one to five . . . (and her final instructions returned Philip
to consciousness).

Philip appeared somewhat drained of energy when he came
out of the trance. I felt that very large struggles had taken place in
silence, and that we had been given only occasional glimpses of
their causes. But as Ted and I questioned him, at least one of the
reasons for Philip's strained responses became clear—he had
more or less refused to describe imagery or events that seemed
"too pat," too close to what he and we might have expected in a
UFO enounter. It was an odd kind of self-censoring about which
Philip was ultimately as ambivalent as we.

"I was very conscious through most of it of the whole purpose
of the thing, and I felt like the things therefore that I was seeing
were probably just imaginary."

Ted asked, "Then, essentially, were you editorializing what
you were actually experiencing?"

"Right. In other words, I would see something and I would
say to myself in effect, 'Well, that's what I'm supposed to see." So
therefore . . . probably this is just the process of imagination. But
I felt like I was sort of hurtling through space actually, and it was
just . . . I was trying to put the brakes on."

Ted wanted clarification. "Do you mean space literally, or
through a particular space?"

"Well, I did see things like stars, etc., again, which in my mind
I just said, you know, 'That's too appropriate.' But once I got into
this illuminated sort of thing, all around it was as if the one end
just sort of vanished and I was just hurtling very quickly in one
direction . . ."

Ted asked, "Did the movement follow the experience of feeling like you were inside of it?"

"First of all, I could feel that I was outside of it and I was
looking at a dome which was almost like a nuclear reactor or
something, that it was divided up into triangles like a geodesic
dome, and that it was illuminated, and I started zooming towards it
very quickly and then just sort of penetrated it and was inside of it,
and then it was as if I was inside of this brightly illuminated thing,
and then that just sort of broke away at one end and I was just kind
of hurtling through space. . . . The whole thing was very abstract, but I saw the parking lot. I mean, I imagined that I went to

the parking lot first and then that (the domed object) was sort of what appeared. I'm not saying . . . I'm not saying that it was in the parking lot, but I'm just saying that that's the next thing my mind went to."

A few questions and answers passed back and forth, and then Philip continued.

"I was looking at the bottom side of it which was quite dark and the impression was darkness all around, only that (*the bottom*) was even darker than the darkness. And then, at one point, I sort of sensed the dome on top of it, again, which is very bad (*chuckles*) but which was incredibly brilliant metallically . . . you know, a very polished surface. . . . It's as if I had the power to mentally turn the disk over, I would be able to see a dome that was very brightly reflective. . . . Anyhow, the predominant impression was that it was very shiny and metallic and against a very dark nothing background."

I brought up a different issue. "You mentioned being afraid . . ."

"That was because I was hurtling through space and . . . I just had the feeling I wanted to put the brakes on. I just wanted to withdraw from that because . . . I don't know why. . . . It was just that the initial impression of it was . . ."

Dr. Clamar asks, "Feeling out of control?"

"Yes. Right, right!"

Shortly thereafter, we left Dr. Clamar's office and walked down Lexington Avenue to a luncheonette. In weighing the overall situation, we had an ambiguous factor to evaluate—Philip's strong hesitancy about accepting the imagery and events his mind called up during hypnosis. And yet in almost every similar hypnotic session I could remember, the subject at some point said something like "This can't be happening," or "This must be a dream"—exactly what each of us would say in real life if one night we found ourselves in a deserted parking lot on a dark mountaintop, and encountered a large, domed, metallic craft of some sort. Clearly, more sessions would be required if Philip was to overcome his block about reporting what he was experiencing. In the meantime, however, certain signs were unmistakable. His fear was obvious to all of us, as was the sense he conveyed of living through a distinct and disturbing series of events which he did not wish to describe. Philip's account of traveling through the air and merging with the object through an open triangular panel was a new one to me, but Dr. Clamar sensed that his fear of the headlong

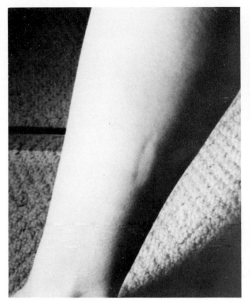

Fig. 1
Photograph of the scar on Virginia Horton's calf. See Chapter 6.

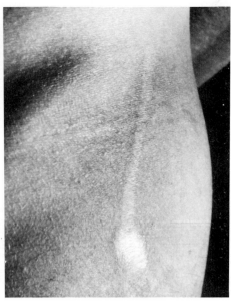

Fig. 2
Closeup of the scar on Philip Osborne's hip. See Chapter 7.

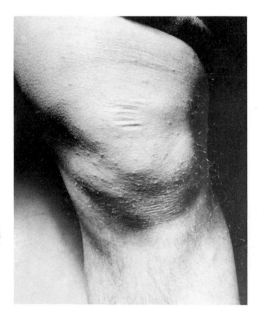

Fig. 3
Closeup photograph of the scar on Dr. Geis's upper leg, just above the kneecap. His was the only one of the three which required stitches, since it had pulled open during play. Each of these three scars was photographed in 1981, some thirty years after the incisions were made. See Chapter 10.

Fig. 4
Photographs of the North Hudson Park site of the 1975 UFO landing. Stonehenge Apartments is in the background, and the actual landing took place on this side of the tree on the left. In the distance is the upper West Side of New York City. *Photo courtesy Fred McDarrah.*

Fig. 5
Below left: Artist's reconstruction of one of Steven Kilburn's abductors.

Fig. 6
Below: Drawing by Betty Andreasson of one of her abductors. The incident occurred in January 1968, in South Ashburnham, Mass. Note the similarity of head shapes, neck and shoulders, and the differences in torso and limbs.

flight was basically a fear of losing control; in other words, more metaphorical, possibly, than literal. His description of the UFO as resembling the upper part of a geodesic dome is actually quite similar to a description given by six witnesses in a 1975 Snowflake, Arizona, close encounter.[1]

Philip's second hypnotic session took place the following week. Once more, his behavior in the trance state was quite different from that of most subjects I had observed. Long pauses occurred frequently, some lasting for five minutes or more. Characteristically, Philip would say something like, "I see a machine above me which has a kind of large eye . . ." Silence would then ensue lasting minutes while we observed nervous eye movements behind his closed lids, and agitation in both his hands and his breathing. Then he would say something like, "I'm not sure I see it . . . I think it's my imagination. . . . It's gone now." And then he would appear calmer, more relaxed. The transcript which follows is my attempt to include what seemed to be firm observation and to drop out the frequent hesitations and semidenials. It is more important at this point to see if these observations form a coherent and specific whole which is consistent from session to session than it is to worry over his frequent uncertainties. I leave to the reader's intuitive skill the task of sorting out the uncomfortable mix of Philip's imagination, his overscrupulousness, and the possibility of a strong, externally imposed fear.

The trance is induced, and Dr. Clamar asks Philip to concentrate upon the image of his leg. She asks if he can see the scar.

PO: Well, I see sort of an open cut maybe, or maybe a scab. . . . As I touch it, I don't feel any pain. (*Long pause.*) It's just I can't remember how I got that scar.

AC: Why don't you let yourself just dream about how you might have gotten that scar—where it came from.

PO: (*Long pause*) Well, I don't really know. I just sort of see, ah, it isn't as if I actually see it happen . . . I sort of felt more as if I don't really remember an accident . . . I just sort of felt as if perhaps it was cut open, and then I see a sort of a representation of just being opened up very cleanly and something taken out and then just put right back together, and I did have sort of a sensation of lying on a table, but I can't see it too well, but it looks like—I just think that it's a hospital.

AC: What does it look like it might be?

PO: Well, I just sort of see whiteness . . . I get sort of the im-
     pression of being carried somewhere else . . . like on a
     stretcher . . . (*long pause*).

(*Dr. Clamar asks what's happening.*)

PO: Well, I sort of saw that hand, that metallic hand that I saw
     last week only that is not really what it looks like. For a
     moment, I sort of thought I had a glimpse of it, but I didn't.
     Couldn't really see it . . . I saw it as at first a sort of me-
     chanical hand of the type that you see in, ah, robot hands
     and for handling nuclear materials and that sort of thing.
     But I don't think that's it, exactly. The one thing
     that . . . the sensation that I think is right about that first
     hand is the fact that there is something that's very, very bril-
     liant, very polished. A metallic suface, and I had the im-
     pression of light reflecting off it, and then I did have the
     impression of a very bright light shining on me. But I don't
     think it was from . . . Well, at least at one point, it is more
     to the side . . . I'm not sure if there is a light shining on me
     from that table. (*Long pause.*)
        I see that same thing I saw before . . . very
     round . . . the thing, a large, illuminated, round spherical
     thing (*the UFO*). I'm not quite as much aware of the divi-
     sions, and, ah, for some reason, it's not putting down as
     much light. (*Pause*) . . . It's not putting out as much light,
     but I don't know why, but when I see it, I just sort of move
     and glide towards it and just dissolve into it. (*Pause.*) I'm
     trying to figure out if it's supported from the ground or if it's
     just in the air. I have the impression of vertical supports
     from the ground . . . and there are times when it seems
     quite gigantic. (*Long pause.*)
        Above me, I just have the feeling of some sort of me-
     chanical apparatus, but I can't see anything very clearly. It's
     just an impression.
        I do see some abstract images that I just couldn't de-
     scribe. (*Long pause.*) I feel like, if I approach it in the right
     way, it can have a great calming effect, but I don't really
     know how. Because it can be either very calming or very,
     ah, well sort of an unpleasant thing. It can have . . . some-
     times I feel like there is a great calming effect. . . . (*Pause.*)
     I just find myself sort of relaxing and letting it alone.

AC: At the count of three, you are going to find it much, much easier to see . . . one . . . two . . . three.

PO: Well, ah, I had seen something that was sort of, kind of a wall arrangement as if it was decorated with some kind of painting and there was something on that and there was a kind of ah, an, um, an eye motif on that, but it was not just a shape, just the almond shape, but when you counted to three, it turned to a large eye that was staring at me. The eye is either disembodied or else there is a person's face is blackened so that just the eye is apparent. . . . It's just very intense and piercing.

AC: How does it make you feel?

PO: At first, it wasn't very pleasant. I saw it more clearly at first. But I don't see it so much now.

(Dr. Clamar asks Philip how old he is as this is happening.)

PO: I can't see myself but the . . . number eight pops into my mind. *(Pause)* I can see a seven too.

(She asks what he is wearing.)

PO: Well . . . I see sort of a plaid from a shirt and maybe short pants.

AC: Do you remember wearing a jacket?

PO: Well, I didn't, but I can imagine myself in a coat. *(Pause)* I guess it's a leather jacket *(long pause)*.

AC: You said that you could imagine yourself in that coat. . . . Which coat? Can you tell me a little bit more about the jacket?

PO: It looks sort of like a brown leather jacket, a short waist-length jacket. It's kind of, ah, beat up a little bit.

AC: Do you like that jacket?

PO: I don't know. I didn't even know I had a jacket like that. . . .

The session continued, but shifted its focus to the later Pittsburgh incident, which we will consider in a moment. Meanwhile, so many fascinating parallels between Philip's and Virginia Horton's accounts had surfaced that they bear immediate consideration. I asked Philip afterwards if the hand that he remembered—the one with the metallic fingers—was a different image from the

robot arm which he apparently associated with the cutting of his
leg, and he answered affirmatively.

"They weren't versions of each other?" I asked.

"No, it's as if they both are images. They come into my mind;
they are suggesting some other image like the hand is more or less
like a glove from a piece of medieval armor, only much more
shiny."

"Medieval armor, of course, is jointed," I continued. "Was
this jointed?"

"Right. In other words, you have the feeling that each of the
separate fingers had separate little sections . . ."

So there were two distinct images—a jointed metal hand, and
a less-articulated robotlike arm which seems to have done the
actual cutting. His description under hypnosis was of "a sort of
mechanical hand of the type that you see in robot hands and for
handling nuclear materials and that sort of thing." Virginia Horton
had described the way she was cut in this way: "It's as though it's
done remotely. . . . Have you seen those things where you put
your hands in when they handle radioactive material? Your hands
go in and you handle instruments and then, in a remote location,
something happens. It's like that. I don't think they have any direct
contact with me physically." Again, two witnesses who had never
met or spoken to each other use the same metaphor to describe a
particular aspect of their UFO experiences. And apart from Philip's recollection of a metallic hand and Virginia's sense of disembodied communication, neither recalled any UFO occupants. Virginia described the moment of the incision this way: "They said,
'. . . we'll just stop it from bleeding.' So whatever they do, they do
it, you know, like this, and then it just closes itself and stops bleeding." Earlier, she said they told her that they needed a "little bitty
piece of her" for "understanding." Philip put it this way: "I just
sort of felt as if perhaps it was cut open, and then I see a sort of
representation of just being opened up very cleanly and something taken out, and then just put right back together." The rooms
in which the operations took place are also described similarly.
Virginia said, "There are lots of things to catch my eyes: things that
shine, they're sparkly, like crystals or like instrumentation—but
they're so pretty that they don't distinguish in my eyes between
whether they are things or art." Philip said that he had seen something, "Kind of a wall arrangement, as if it was decorated with
some kind of painting and there was something on that and there

was kind of an eye motif on that . . ." I have listened to many hypnotic sessions and read many transcripts; the only two people who ever mentioned the words "art" and "painting" were, again, Virginia and Philip. One could almost believe that the ship or ships in use in 1950, the physical operation itself—removing a section of flesh, and the methods of the UFO occupants were identical, as were the ages of the abductees and the time of their abductions. So far, the concordances were amazing. Even the way I had heard of their cases was identical—as a result of the NBC broadcast.

Over the years, I have tried to train myself to discount the calm tone of voice a witness will often use to make an odd or illogical statement seem the most natural thing in the world. If the case involves a time lapse, and therefore a degree of memory control, witnesses will often describe their strange behavior as eminently logical. Philip awoke in his Pittsburgh bedroom paralyzed and sensing a "presence" in the room. So terrified had he been, he said, that he got up, got dressed, and went outside. So natural was the way he recounted it that it took me awhile to realize that his behavior was, on the face of it, most unusual. I tried to think what I would have done had I been in his place. First, I would have turned all the lights on, perhaps put on the radio or TV, and if I had been *really* terrified, I would have gone to awaken someone else in the house just to talk the fear out of my system. The very *last* thing I would have done would have been to go for a walk at three A.M. outside in the dark, where the "presence" might be lurking. Prior to this hypnotic regression, I asked Philip if he remembered where he walked to that night. Had there been an all-night delicatessen nearby or a bar or someplace where he could rub elbows with other humans?

I offer the following transcript as illustration of the way external control of the subject's memory can not only block out actual events, but also somehow "fill in" with explanations which ultimately make no sense. One can feel Philip's uncertainty growing as he talks about the experience.

PO: I probably just walked around the block, that's all. . . . The immediate vicinity was a residential area, and if you walked about four or five blocks, you came to a commercial area. I really don't remember where I walked.

BH: It is, when you think about it, unusual that you would, in being frightened, that you would actually get up and go outside.

PO: (*Laughs*) Well, that's unusual but, you know, this room—this was quite a small room, and it would tend to get rather claustrophobic at times, and if something like that happened in this little room, you know, all of a sudden, well, I don't know, I . . . I was not in the habit of getting out and walking around blocks at night certainly, but . . . it just seemed like the thing to do at the time.

BH: Well, I just think that . . . the only reason to ask questions about it is that it was an event you had singled out as being unusual to you at the time.

PO: It was.

BH: And in thinking it over, it seemed unusual that . . . well in my situation, if I were frightened, I would turn on the lights . . . and I wouldn't think of going outside . . . where, theoretically, the thing is that is frightening me, whatever it may be.

PO: That's true unless I associated the thing with the room . . . but it's strange because I just don't know . . . I think it was just that I figured that I needed the cool air. . . . Probably I was awakened at that point and couldn't just lie back down and go to sleep right away so that was something to do.

BH: And especially in a very small room.

PO: Yeah. Well, I had never thought of it, to be honest. I had certainly never thought of that, but I, uh . . . who knows? I don't.

BH: What we've got to do is try to run down all the possibilities.

PO: I never thought of that. That's interesting (*chuckles*) to be honest with you. Now that you mention it. I never did think about that, of course. Well, I don't know. I certainly don't have any recollection of anything happening.

BH: I'm not necessarily convinced about any one particular incident here. The only reason I even ask these questions is I was curious what the physical layout was to see if it would have been even remotely a natural thing for you to get up and run down the street to get coffee.

PO: Well, now, I wouldn't . . . I certainly don't think I've any recollection of doing that. I probably would . . . I have a recollection of . . . or it seems to me . . . I must have gone, oh, let me see. . . . If you were to go more or less in the direction of the back of the house, there was a road that sloped up this same hillside and, up on top of that area, there are a number of . . . three or four large mansions, with fairly large grounds that are unoccupied or were unoccupied at the time. One was the old Heinz mansion.

BH: But you probably walked the other direction. You wouldn't have gone up the hill.

PO: No, I don't think I would have gone up there. That was the route I would pick in walking to school, but I don't think I would have then.

BH: Not at night.

PO: No, I don't think I would have done that in the middle of the night.

Philip's rationalizations for his unusual behavior were coming slowly unraveled. All of the reasons for his three A.M. stroll, which he delivered in such a natural tone of voice, began to seem absurd to both of us. His final recollection was of the hill behind his house, where several deserted mansions sat on rambling grounds, a memory which I realized was potentially significant. If Philip, like Howard Rich, had been visited in his bedroom by some kind of controlling force and then "led" up the hill to the grounds of the deserted Heinz mansion, an abduction could have been physically carried out with little chance of interruption.

The latter part of Philip's second hypnotic session was taken up with the Pittsburgh incident.

AC: Let yourself relax. At the count of three, you are going to find yourself back in college. You are feeling very relaxed. One . . . two . . . three.

PO: (*Long pause*) I can see that room a little bit more clearly.

AC: Would you please describe it?

PO: It's small and I see a face in the window. The bed was on the left. There was a sloping wall because of the roof, and there was a projection out toward where the window was, and it was painted a different sort of dull yellow there for some reason, and the rest were painted white. And there were old-fashioned bookcases with glass covers that lift up high on either side of the window against the wall. And I was just very curious about that presence at the window. But I can't exactly put myself back into that . . . I can't exactly experience that event, though.

AC: Let yourself drift deeper and deeper. Your mind and the images will become much more available to you than they ever have been before.

PO: (*Very long pause*) I see it as I saw it then . . . I do think that I must have sensed that light, like I just sensed now . . . but at the time, I was only aware of a sort of a silhouette and just now I really did become more aware of a figure. . . . It did change. As I look at it . . . it really sort of eludes my efforts to look at it. . . . But I did have the impression that this head was kind of embryolike-shaped. These eyes were really sort of tucked into the forehead. A big forehead, but the eyes are metallic . . . (*whispers inaudibly*). Something's strange . . . but anyhow I just associate this with the window and this light that's coming through. . . . But it's not a very big window . . . two small windows, actually. Green window shades. The old-fashioned kind. (*Long pause*.) But I do . . . I sort of have the impression of someone saying that it's O.K. now (*pause*). I don't know why, originally, it was dark in the room, but I do have an impression of light . . . (*long pause*). I think that it is possible for me to go much deeper.

Despite his request and Dr. Clamar's effort to induce a deeper trance, nothing resulted. In a few moments, after more periods of silence, we ended the session and Philip was brought out of the hypnotic state. Immediately afterwards, I brought up the matter of the "big eye" that he had seen. I asked about its size—was it like a normal eye or was it larger?

PO: Well, I had the impression at one point that it was quite huge.

BH: How large?

PO: Well, that was maybe the initial impression—a couple of feet. I don't know. If it was maybe ten feet up in the air, it was maybe larger than that. I don't know.

BH: Yes. But you had a feeling it was above you? In other words,

rather than on a vertical plane, that it was suspended somehow?

PO: Yes.

BH: And it had like a pupil type of thing? We are assuming it
was not a real eye.

PO: It did, but it would sort of, you know, keep changing. . . . I
never have just a stationary image, but I get a sort of initial
quick impression and then it starts degrading into all other
kinds of things.

BH: Do you have the feeling that it was moving or that it was
stationary?

PO: Well, it's hard to answer what you say because neither in a
sense. You know, you have the general impression of being
there and then, and then I see, you know, various different
kinds of . . . I probably saw more than one eye at one particular time and then the pupils sort of . . . the pupils
started changing and being different . . .

A large, evidently moving and changing eyelike device was
suspended over him. Charlie Hickson,[2] abducted in Pascagoula,
Mississippi, in 1973, reported that there had been a large machine
hanging overhead. "It looked like an eye. Like a *big* eye. It had
some kind of an attachment to it. It moved. It looked like a *big* eye.
And it went all over my body. Up and down." Betty Andreasson,
abducted in South Asburnham, Massachusetts, in January, 1967
described a very similar piece of equipment suspended over her,
and she later made a drawing of it. This object seems different
from that which Steven Kilburn described, though its location
seems the same. As I have pointed out many times, the UFO
abduction phenomenon breaks down not into just one absolute
pattern, but rather into several closely related, parallel patterns.
Hickson, Andreasson, and Philip Osborne all faced a similar eyelike apparatus, though, in other respects, Philip's case diverges
from theirs. This complexity is more or less what one might expect
if the phenomenon is as advanced as it seems to be, and as relatively unfathomable. Imagine two medieval serfs comparing notes
after having been rushed through differing batteries of tests in a
modern hospital. I offer the example not so much as an explanation of anything, but as a means of keeping our ideological doors
slightly ajar.

On June 7, 1979, Philip Osborne had his third appointment with Dr. Clamar and he concentrated on the Pittsburgh incident. I was not present for this hypnotic session, having already moved to my Wellfleet studio for the summer, but Ted Bloecher attended. This time, as with each of his sessions, a few more details emerged, each of which was consistent with what we already knew. There were many periods of silence, some of which lasted five minutes or so. The transcript which follows has been edited to eliminate false starts and irrelevant material.

PO: I can imagine myself lying in the bed, but . . . I don't know, if I tried, maybe I could just allow myself to recreate it.

AC: Why don't you take just a few minutes now to recreate it if you wish, or do anything else that you want to.

PO: (After a pause of nearly five minutes) Well, I can just sense that I would like to be able to yell out, but I can't, and I see a very terrified expression on my face, but that's just imagined, of course.

AC: It might not be imagined, it might be real.

PO: (After a pause of two minutes) And I . . . I can see myself finally being able to say, 'Help, help, help' and I'm being . . . ah . . . sweating. (Long pause.)

AC: What's happening in your body, Philip?

PO: I'm just sort of drifting into another sort of level of consciousness.

AC: Just let yourself drift into that other level of consciousness now. The energy is flowing freely and easily within your body and mind.

(After five minutes, Philip begins breathing more rapidly and shows signs of moderate distress. This lasts for about a minute and then subsides. He sighs deeply several times. There follows another silence of ten minutes, broken several times by deep sighs.)

PO: I can sort of recreate things in my mind up to a certain point, but I can't seem to go any further than that.

AC: That's all right. You don't have to go any further. You can do it another time, or not at all. It's really up to you.

PO: I could just feel myself lying in the bed and . . . I have that sensation of my jaw locking, and so I would try to move it, but I couldn't and . . . once the whole thing was over with, I could see myself leaving, going down the stairs and leaving. And I think . . . I'm pretty sure I left by the front door, which I don't usually do . . . I think I left by the front door, which is a big, metal, ornamental iron door, with glass, and I think . . . I really wasn't sure . . . first, where I went. But the only thing that really comes to mind is going . . . oh . . . to the . . . ah . . . a short distance away, there's a roadway that goes up a hill, just a short residential drive, and I . . . I remember the stone wall . . . where that roadway goes up, and I see myself going to the Heinz mansion. This is directly to the top. That's the first turn-off to the left from that roadway, and it is perched up on top of the hill, and it is . . . nobody live there. And I just can't . . . I'm not sure, but I just sort of sense a commotion going on, not in the house, but outside of the house. I don't know, I just can't get a clear image of what I . . . except that I seem to be very curious. I don't seem to be particularly tense any more.

Very little else emerged. After a long period of silence, Dr. Clamar brought Philip out of the trance, but the story had been advanced further than before. Philip later told Ted that the commotion he saw as he walked up the driveway to the Heinz mansion was occurring at the back of the house. It seemed to him to involve a number of figures, but he could not make out any details. One of the more puzzling recollections from Philip's previous hypnotic session was his description of a figure in the window of his third-floor room. The basic problem was that the window was *behind* his head and he was, in his paralyzed state, unable to turn around. How had he managed to see this strange personage? His description of it was quite precise, as if he had observed it close up. I questioned him about it after he had been brought out of the trance.

BH: You say this face had this fetuslike look look?
PO: Yes. First of all, I saw it from more or less of a profile, and it was, I guess the face would have been facing the right. . . . Yes, either it was sort of turned away or somehow or other the features of the face were not apparent to me, but the initial impression was this large cranium, you

know, sort of like an embryo . . . . and also, I did have the
impression of blood vessels or something. Like some sort of,
ah, well, I guess blood vessels or something or other. Some
sort of a texture. And then as the head revolved around, you
know, you had the impression of this great forehead with
these large eyes. . . . Well, no, not exactly like that drawing that Steven did . . . the eyes were somewhat similar in
proportion, but it was more . . .

BH: It was rounder, perhaps?
PO: Well, (the head in Steven's drawing) was more or less egg-
shaped without so much the sensation of a forehead, but I
had more or less a feeling of a forehead, and his eyes were
more or less contained under there. . . .

The eyes . . . Well, I had the impression of their being solid . . . but then I think that this feeling of the
metallic . . . that it was almost like a metallic plate, or
something. Nobody sees that, do they?

BH: No. And that's even though you had the feeling of blood
vessels?
PO: Yes.
BH: Because that seems like kind of a funny mix.
PO: Well, it is a funny mix. Yes, no question about it. I did not
get the impression of a grayish skin. If anything, light, but, if
anything, maybe with some sort of a fleshy or a pink cast,
not a gray or a gray-gray.

(He began to describe his feelings at the time.)

PO: At a certain point, there is a transition that seems to take
place. Sometimes . . . it has a much more calming effect.
BH: Yes, I suspect that that is something that actually happens in
the experience, that there is the frightening aspect and then
there is a tranquilizing aspect.
PO: Well, I suspect that that is really what was going through my
mind, on this judgmental level, I was saying, 'I wonder if I
have been tranquilized or something.' Now that was almost
as if I was experiencing that . . . that suddenly I felt much
more calm. And then usually I drift from that state, I drift
away from the thing altogether, and, you know, I start thinking about something else, and it just becomes unimpor-
tant.

BH: You said that it was as if you were getting a sense of being
       told 'Everything is going to be all right,' or something like
       that.
PO: Oh, yes. I heard that everything will be all right.

*(The conversation ended with Philip's characteristically careful
disclaimer.)*

PO: I was just trying this time to tell you whatever just sort of
       popped into my mind. It was very much just kind of a
       collage of impressions . . . There was not any kind of se-
       quential thing. . . . There was not any involvement, real-
       ly, or the feeling that I was reliving anything . . . rather,
       that I was acting as an observer.

This statement has, I believe, a specific importance, which I
will come to in a moment. Meanwhile, the first thing to be considered is the figure as Philip described it. He was careful to distinguish the shape of his head from a shape he had seen on the NBC
documentary, drawn from Steven Kilburn's recollection. The
large cranium with the eyes tucked underneath recalled drawings
of humanoids reported in the Travis Walton[3] and Sergeant
Moody[4] cases. (See Figures 9 and 10.) The main similarity to the
face in Steven's drawing, he felt, lay in the proportionate size of
the eyes and the size of the head. His description of metallic eyes
on apparently semitransparent skin which showed the blood vessels underneath, was indeed, as he said, a funny mix, and one that
I had never precisely heard of before.

Now we come to the crucial question—how did he see all this
while lying paralyzed in bed, facing away from the window? The
answer is clear from a close reading of the transcripts. As Dr. Clamar asks him to describe the little third-floor room, he says, "I see
a face in the window. . . . I was just very curious about
that . . . presence at the window." As the episode comes to light,
he continues. "*At the time*, I was only aware of a sort of silhouette . . . and *just now*, I really did become more aware of a
figure. . . . It did change." (*Emphasis mine*.) I believe that Philip,
in his scrupulous manner, is trying to differentiate between a
vague image, "a sort of silhouette," that he recalls in connection
with the window and the fuller image of a humanoid, which
seems to be tied up with later events. This more complete figure,

which had a specific "fleshy or pink caste . . . not a gray or gray-gray skin," apparently was seen close up and in decent light, so one can assume that it was encountered *after* the incident in the bedroom, and in another place. In fact, when I asked Philip if this more detailed figure was inside the window glass or outside, he answered this way: "It was neither. It was just associated with the glass, with this window . . . I was not seeing this from the viewpoint that I was in at the time. I was seeing it from the viewpoint of the here and now, it standing there and looking at me." One is left with the unmistakable sense that Philip is recalling two different times that he saw the humanoid, and so his final remark takes on special meaning. "I was just trying . . . to tell you whatever just sort of popped in my mind. . . . There was not any kind of sequential thing. . . ." His description of the events of that long ago night in Pittsburgh was, in his words, very much a "collage of impressions." Images were recovered, but not in any precise order.

When one puts together the narrative sequence it closely resembles Howard Rich's experience. First, Philip awakes in his room, absolutely paralyzed, and sensing a presence, a vague silhouette behind him. A strange light fills the room. He gets up, dresses, and goes outside, up the hill to the grounds of the deserted Heinz mansion. There, he finds himself drawn toward a group of figures standing behind the building, and the abduction is consummated. His abductors have large, bulging craniums, and metallic-looking eyes. More was to be revealed in his fourth hypnotic session, and much of what we already knew was to be confirmed.

For a number of reasons, there was a delay of almost a year between his third and fourth hypnotic sessions. The ebbing and flowing of Philip's hypnotic recall was a frustrating problem that bothered him more than it did Ted and me. We were also busy with our own work, and with a number of other UFO cases, but when the investigation did resume, we were very pleased by the results. As I pointed out in the Steven Kilburn case, long pauses between hypnotic regressions have one distinct advantage, and that is the sense one has of consistently recalled events. Fantasies can wander promiscuously from month to month, and deliberate inventions are hard to keep straight. If, ten months later, a hypnotically recalled narrative confirms in both outline and specific detail what was recalled ten months previously, then we are probably dealing with an actual, historical event.

On April 12, 1980, Philip, Ted, and I gathered in Dr. Clamar's office to resume our inquiry. Again, the transcript which follows has been edited somewhat to eliminate much of what one could designate the Philip Osborne system of backing and filling, claiming and disclaiming.

AC: Your memory goes back to that night in college, that night we have been talking about. . . . (*Hypnosis is induced.*)

PO: (*After a long pause*) My dominant impression is of some sort of a presence at the window. That's what all of my attention is focused towards and it's as if there's a black, ah, blot or something that's obscuring whatever may be there from my vision. . . .

    The thing that is strange is that my impression of the room is it's very bright, and, ah, there is light although I know that is not the case. It was not a bright room, and, ah, I don't recall any brightness at all, but that's the image that my mind is creating now. (*Pause*) I do feel like there is something there to be seen, not necessarily in this room, but, you know, something that I'm linking to it . . .

AC: If you were to see in that window, what do you imagine would be there?

PO: Well, it isn't just now that it's in front of the window, but it's sort of in the middle of my field of vision and that's what I am trying to, ah, lift, but it does not happen. Ah, as to what I would imagine to be there, the only thing that I notice is that I sense a kind of presence there. (*Long pause.*)

    I can imagine myself in another environment, almost, as if I am in another place or another enclosure, and it isn't so much being able to see it, as just sensing it. (*Long pause.*) And I do have a sort of a sense of reclining and of being kind of enveloped in a sort of, hazy, kind of state. For some reason, it seems as if I'm sort of aware of two small balls or spheres that are illuminated from within. Ah, they're sort of either, on either side of my head, or I'm not sure that they stay there in that position, but there is a feeling almost as if I am encased in a kind of dome, but it has that impression. (*Long pause.*) There's confusion concerning those things that I am describing as balls. Ah, I can almost have the impression that they are eyes . . . ah, but there definitely is a state of calmness associated with this image. It is as if one suddenly makes that transition—and I do recall that from earlier sessions here—that there is a definite transition where all of a sudden calmness seems to prevail (*pause*). I almost have the sensation that I could be floating in a reclining position, or at least not aware of whatever may be supporting me, but there is just a kind of energy field surrounding me, or a kind of hazy kind of quality. I could imagine that there is some presence there. . . . It's almost as if, you know, I can sense that someone is around, but I do not see anybody. (*Long pause.*)

I have the sense of something uncanny, and, ah, you know, like the Tin Man in *The Wizard of Oz* . . . but then I did go back to that, ah, sense of paralysis. The strange thing is that my attention is drawn to a telephone at the head of the bed, and I do recall at that time I had the sensation that I should reach for the telephone and call for help, but there wasn't any telephone there. I don't know why I would think of a telephone. There was no telephone there. That was one thing that was very illogical.

AC: Could you describe this "*Wizard of Oz*" figure?

PO: It was . . . the *Wizard of Oz* character. . . . It wasn't . . . I'm sure it wasn't anything that I saw. It was just an association.

I'm trying to imagine leaving the house and, for some reason, I see myself leaving by the front door, which I don't think I would have normally done. . . . I'm just trying to imagine what possible way I did go when I left the house. For some reason, I do just feel drawn to that spot, the (*Heinz*) house. I see kind of an aerial map and all of the lines are pointing in that direction. . . . It, ah, it's as if I'm sort of tracing through it without so much experiencing it, but I can imagine myself going up a driveway which is relatively close to the house and, ah, there's almost an arrow that points over to the, to my left, which would be on the opposite end of the house, and, ah, almost a kind of a sense of inquisitiveness on my part—not a fear or anything. And I think that, at another time, I have said that I sensed a sort of activity there. Now, it isn't so much as if there is an activity, but it's almost as if there are people standing there, almost in a line. I don't see them precisely as people, but you just have the impression of figures, and, ah, there's nothing more to see there. It's all very dark. It's more of an impression. (*Long pause.*)

I hesitate to say it, but (*I have*) almost a sense of a flying saucer there and I'm just trying to imagine what might have happened next. (*Long pause.*) I don't see any light around at all. Of course, it may have been, I mean, whatever might have been there, there may have been a starlit sky, a moon-lit sky, with the lights from the surrounding houses reflected in the sky, but there isn't any light there, and I do recall before that there was a sense of activity or something. Someone moving around and doing something in the dark-ness, but I don't know exactly how that connects with the Impression now.

After another long pause, Dr. Clamar brought Philip out of the trance. Ted and I began to question him both about the new details he had recalled and his calmer behavior in the hypnotic state. I commented upon the fact that he had not seemed so ner-vous this time, and he agreed, saying that he had definitely felt more detached.

BH: Now, you said, the two spheres that seemed to be illumi-nated appeared to be small. You said they were on either side of you, close to the face.

PO: Yes. And then I sort of have the feeling that, well, you know, you have these kind of dreamlike impressions that are very difficult to describe, of course, that they could have moved above me. As I say, I could almost sense that they were eyes at some point, but initially, I mean, in dreams sometimes one thing can sometimes transpose itself into something else, and these are just the kinds of impressions that I have.

BH: The big eye, you see, we've talked about before. The big eye—you saw the single eye. Close to you.

PO: Yes. Well, I wasn't aware—I frankly don't remember what I said about that, but I wasn't aware of a single eye close to me.

BH: Yes. That was more an earlier experience anyway.

PO: Yes.

BH: Associating that with the Tennessee experience . . .

TB: Philip, on the association of place with these two spheres, do you get the sense of being in your room at Carnegie Tech?

PO: No, no, no. This was where I had sort of been dis-

BH: placed to. . . . Gone beyond that into another . . .
BH: Another area. Enclosure. I think you used the word "enclosure."
PO: Yes. I had the sense that, you know, there was a kind of space all around me and that I was more or less in the middle of it.
BH: One other thing that you mentioned now that I don't recall your having mentioned before (*This is an incorrect memory*—**BH**) was a brightness in your room. You didn't think this was ordinary to the room.
PO: No. And I don't recall it, either. That's one I certainly—you know, I don't recall it from anything. I don't know why that suddenly presented itself. But I had somewhat the feeling that maybe that was something I was inventing to counteract the unpleasantness of that occasion. You know, suddenly I was feeling the room as bright and a more cheerful kind of place.
BH: You said this thing about feeling very relaxed and calm, and that there was a transition where you passed something that had not been very calm, and went into a calm state. You did mention that actually at an earlier session, too.
PO: Yes, and I recall that. You know, there are certain things when you are coming to, that you suddenly do remember, something that you had experienced previously.

We adjourned shortly thereafter to a delicatessen for more conversation and a bit of lunch. In response to a question, Philip elaborated on one of the details he had obliquely, and rather unclearly, mentioned when he was in the trance state, and this was the matter of the "hazy kind of state." He said that around the table on which he lay—or floated—the atmosphere itself seemed hazy, or "glarey," as if the air was not absolutely transparent. Immediately, I remembered Steven's words: "I almost want to say that the air in the room is white also. . . . Everything is kind of milky or misty or something. It doesn't shine, but everything has almost that metallic kind of glow to it . . . including me." Virginia Horton, the reader will recall, described the color of the light as being "pale gray, or a real soft gray . . . pearly . . . those kinds of colors." When I see the adjective "pearly," I picture not so much a specific hue as a particular kind of delicate reflectiveness in which the light *in front of* an object appears to be intangibly colored. I do not want to force my definition upon the reader, but my guess is that Virginia is using a different metaphor for the same conditions that Steven and Philip are describing. In the preceding chapter, I gave other examples from the case literature of this kind of observation. A recently published book, *The Tujunga Canyon Contacts*,[5] includes an interesting double confirmation. A young female abductee who is called Lorie in the book describes the light inside the UFO as being "misty." But she also describes small, round lights like Philip's glowing spheres which moved over her body. "I felt like being on an operating table and being inspected. . . . Those lights going over me . . . (were) like scanner lights. . . . I was being inspected in a relatively painless manner by some sort of light. It wasn't threatening to me." Philip had been quick to explain that the large eye he had earlier described was not connected with the Pittsburgh encounter. This time, the scanning—if that is what the function is—was carried out by the small moving spheres of light. The mechanical man for which he invoked the calming and charming image of the Tin Man in *The Wizard of Oz* is a full-scale version of what in earlier sessions had been merely an armored hand. He described the benign (and, sadly, heart-less) film character not as "anything that I saw. It was just an association." Jack Haley standing in, as it were, for something that in actuality was probably far more unsettling; again, the unconscious mind seems to be avoiding, or at least softening, the clear, fearful edges of remembered reality.

Putting together all of Philip's basic images and superimposing them upon the narrative as it presented itself, this is what we can safely surmise: In 1950, at the age of seven, or possibly the following summer, Philip and his family traveled back up the Tennessee mountaintop after dark to retrieve his brother's lost jacket. In some as-yet-unknown fashion, Philip was apparently separated from his family and pulled swiftly into a UFO resembling a geodesic dome, which hovered in a deserted parking lot. (His physical capture and abduction without abductors is similar in its degree of vagueness to Virginia Horton's.) Inside the UFO, as Philip lay on a table in a hospital-like environment, a "robot arm" made an incision, removed something from his leg, and then closed the wound. Above him hung a large eyelike apparatus which at first frightened him, but then calmed him. The method of his return to his family in their automobile is as yet unclear.

About thirteen or fourteen years later—it was probably

1964—Philip awoke in his third-floor room near Pittsburgh's Carnegie Tech to find himself totally paralyzed. He sensed a presence, a silhouette, at the window behind his head. Light suffused the room. In moments, the paralysis left him. He dressed and went outside. Following mental directions, like a "roadmap in his mind," he ascended the hill behind his house to the grounds of the deserted Heinz mansion. Feeling inquisitive and without fear, he approached a line of figures standing behind the house. Nearby, there was a "flying saucer" and, in some way, he next found himself reclining inside a domed room filled with hazy light. Two small glowing balls or spheres hovered on either side of his head, which again calmed him. Two types of figures are associated with this experience: a pinkish, flesh-colored humanoid with "metallic eyes" and translucent skin, and a metallic, very shiny, robotlike figure with jointed, armored hands. Exactly what else happened, how Philip returned to his room, is still unclear.

A particularly striking indication of the accuracy and tenacity of Philip's hypnotic recall came to light through an innocent error of Ted Bloecher's. Immediately after the fourth hypnotic session in April of 1980, Ted mentioned that the line of figures Philip reported in front of the Heinz mansion was seen *this* time in general darkness; ten months earlier, Ted thought, Philip had described them moving in front of a bright light. Philip immediately disagreed. "I don't think I said that. I guess I may have because I never remember everything I have said before, but I really don't think I ever saw them against any bright light." We checked a transcript of that June 1979 session and Philip was right—he had never reported seeing the figures against light. It was a simple mis-recollection of Ted's, but it offered a test both of Philip's suggestibility and the tenacity of his remembered imagery. We were all pleased that the error had occurred.

The spectrum of human response to the abduction experience is indeed a wide one, yet the varieties of human behavior and recall under hypnotic regression are vastly larger. The transcripts I have presented vividly illustrate these problems. But it is my belief that what we have here is not a wide, irregular collection of various UFO abduction accounts, each equipped with its own degree of credibility. Instead, we are seeing a wide variety of *human response* to the same basic, unearthly experience. And later, to the still different and unsettling act of recalling this experience through hypnosis. The abductees vary more than the abduction process itself. Philip Osborne's and Virginia Horton's accounts show this perhaps more clearly than any other pair of cases I have studied. In neither instance, we must remember, was there any prior conscious memory of a UFO sighting or anything else that would indicate a possible abduction.

By the middle of May 1979, we had uncovered many of the aforementioned details of Philip's second—his Pittsburgh—abduction, but by a fortuitous coincidence, I was able, a few months later, to visit the site where we believed it had happened.

In September of 1979, I received an invitation to lecture at the Carnegie Institute's Museum of Art on the occasion of Willem de Kooning's retrospective exhibition. In a nicely unorthodox decision, the museum staff had decided to ask a painter who had known and admired de Kooning and his work for many years, rather than an art historian—a colleague rather than a critic. Philip gave me the location of the house he had lived in, and when I arrived in Pittsburgh on December 10, a sculptor acquaintance of mine drove me to the spot. After my lecture later that night, I revisited the area to try to judge its plausibility as a UFO landing site.

The Heinz mansion is the largest of several houses and outbuildings spread over perhaps fifteen acres. It is occupied today by a religious order, and by eleven-thirty in the evening, everything was quite dark. Knowing what I knew from Philip's account, the place took on an eerie, slumbering quality as I walked across the silent lawn. A few lights from some neighboring houses and the distant sounds of traffic coming from down below barely touched the dark, isolated calm. The hilltop was flat except for a large, roughly ten foot deep, bowl-like depression, the remains, I guessed, of a pond which must have been drained many years before.

Everything about the place reinforced its plausibility as the location of a UFO landing site. Everything about its desolate mood underlined the idea that Philip, after the fright he'd experienced in his room, would only have walked up this hill if he had had absolutely no choice in the matter.

8

THE ALSATIAN DEER

At the time of Virginia Horton's first hypnotic session, Aphrodite Clamar made a telling observation. She pointed out that, when a young child receives a deep gash which bleeds copiously, the event invariably becomes part of the family oral history, the "day Suzie slipped on the rock and cut her leg open and it bled so badly." For example, I have a small scar on my scalp where I was hit by a sharp tin can. The accident happened around 1937. My older brother and his friends were playing kick-the-can, and Jimmy Gilliland's foot sent the can hard against me. Forty-three years later, the details are still vivid to my mother and my brother. Evidently I bled dramatically, and another childhood accident entered the family chronicles.

It is against everything we would normally expect that, though Virginia's parents remember their daughter's deep childhood wound, they have no idea at all of its origin. And in 1979, when Philip Osborne first asked his mother about the source of his scar, she could not remember anything about it, either. A few weeks later, she told him that she thought she remembered something about his falling off a tricycle and cutting himself, but she wasn't sure. I called her in May of 1979, and this time she said she thought he had cut himself on the sharp edge of a toy. I asked if she remembered actually witnessing the accident or if she recalled what kind of a toy it had been and she answered no to both questions. Though her recollections were admittedly—and strangely—vague, she was certain of one thing: the accident had happened in the evening when there was no way to get Philip to a doctor. His wound, she said, was treated at home.

Under hypnosis, Philip described the environment where the incision was made as being "hospital-like" with a stretcherlike table. His mother's statement that he definitely had not been taken to a doctor's office or to a hospital's emergency room is therefore significant. It eliminates the possibility that Philip could be confusing his incision's "white environment" with a real hospital since he had not been taken to one in the first place.

Nothing is more vivid than blood. A childhood accident which causes a wound deep enough to leave a noticeable scar thirty years later should have become a dramatic event in family history. The details of this kind of traumatic episode should have become deeply etched in parental memory, yet neither Philip's nor Virginia's mother seems to recall very much at all about what happened to her child. Beyond recollecting that the accidents happened when their children were very young, everything is hazy.

If the causes of their wounds were as Virginia and Philip recall them through hypnosis—incisions made by remote-control, robotlike machinery inside a UFO—then everything falls into place. The parents remember very little for two and possibly three reasons. First, none of the parents actually witnessed their child's accident, so they could have no idea, first-hand, of its cause. Second, neither child had any conscious memory of how the injuries occurred, either, and so neither was able to explain anything at all to the parents. There were no details to remember, except the fact of the wound itself. And third, there is very possibly a degree of control by the UFO occupants of the parents' memories as well as those of the children. As we have seen in the David Oldham case, for example, and as I have noticed in numerous other cases, the particular person or persons who were abducted are not the only people involved whose recollections have been tampered with. One should expect, with such distinct scars as those Virginia and Philip bear ("The only mark on my body," Virginia said), that the parents definitely should remember more about these "accidents" than they do . . . unless, of course, more than a mere dollop of forgetfulness was stirred in from the outside.

When Virginia first called her mother in 1979 to ask about the original 1950 farmyard incident, her mother was slow to remember—but she was quick to recall the time Virginia emerged from the French woods and discovered blood on her blouse. Virginia, herself, had almost forgotten this second episode, but a moment's reflection offers a possible reason for their varying degrees of recollection. The difference is caused by the movie Virginia's father took of the picnic. Virginia's mother had seen the film a number of times, so the image of her daughter's blood-bespattered blouse would have burned into her memory. Virginia told me that she, herself, hated the movie because of the stains—again, the unnerving vividness of blood. The physical reality of the film image was something she actively tried to put out of her mind. It was unpleasantly graphic, and it had, after all, happened to her. For her mother, however, the film record of the 1960 incident may have successfully counteracted the memory control exerted *that* time by Virginia's abductors. Obviously, this is speculation, but it does present a plausible explanation of what seem to be arbitrary differences in the two women's degree of recall.

Virginia and I met ten weeks after her first session for her second hypnotic session. Our main goal was to explore her 1960 experience in France, but there were also a number of loose ends left dangling from the 1957 abduction recall. Central was the issue of how she got inside the UFO in the first place. We talked about this problem before hypnosis began, and Virginia said she had a vague sense of having been physically picked up and carried by someone, though the details were unclear.

"It was just as though somebody was carrying me over to the couch and setting me down. I don't think I was picked up by a machine . . . or by a vacuum . . . nothing like that. It was like a humanoid type person picking me up and carrying me. I haven't had any vivid memories about it."

I brought the conversation around to the subject at hand.

BH: That incident in France at the picnic. Have you thought much about it?

VH: Well, I just thought about it, but nothing came back to me, except to remember again the sense of wonder that I had at the time at the beautiful, beautiful deer that I saw. You know, it was as though I had walked out of the woods and claimed that I saw a unicorn. There was that sense of excitement and wonder. And when I think about the visual memories that I had, there wasn't anything unusual about the deer, except that it was looking at me . . . and it was looking at me in a very conscious kind of way, but it could just as easily have been that I was hypnotized and thought I saw a deer to make it easy to have a story to tell.

AC: Yes, it could have been suggested.

BH: You mentioned that to me, in fact, the very first time we talked about it.

VH: Yes, right.

BH: As a matter of fact, you said something to the effect that, the more you talked about the deer to your parents, the less you were sure you had even seen a deer. You said it was like . . . like you were high on the idea of having seen the deer and yet you weren't sure how real it was.

VH: No, it was a very real experience, but I was just speculating to you that maybe it wasn't a real deer. Maybe it was something else I was suggested to remember as a deer. . . . I don't have any doubts that I saw something that moved me. Something real. It wasn't a product of my imagination. It may have had a hypnotic cover, but it looked like a deer to my memory. . . .

(Dr. Clamar begins the induction of hypnosis and takes Virginia back to the age of six in her grandfather's farmyard.)

VH: I'm just looking around the yard, remembering the way it was. I was a lot more connected to the grounds then than I am now. I used to notice, you know, how the dirt was different on rainy days than on dry days, and how the plants changed every day. The dandelions turned fluffy, you know, when they make their seeds. This was something that I was connected to every day which I'm not any-more . . . to the animals and to the yard.

AC: Would you like to re-experience that connectedness?

VH: Yes, I would.

AC: At the count of three, you will find yourself reliving and re-experiencing and revivifying the connectedness that you felt. The earth, your environment, and yourself . . . one . . . two . . . three.

VH: (Long pause) Rocks, too. Every day I would go out to play and I would talk to the plants and the animals in the yard and the chickens and all these things. I think that's one of the things I told my friend on the ship. I told him about the different kinds of animals. I guess that's how we got to talking about chickens. I think from that, that's when he suggested that I go gather the eggs and bring them in. I don't think my mother had told me to gather the eggs. I think when I explained to him about it, he just told me to go do that. Just to go about my business.

He probably knew that I had a cut and that would be a good way to cover it. But I think I told him a lot about animals and plants, 'cause he was interested in that, what they look like and what they feel like, how they live and eat. How big they are.

AC: Did you draw any pictures for your friend?

VH: I think I described them verbally, but he could understand them. He might have had pictures that he showed me and I would say, 'Yes, they look like that. No, they don't look like that.' And I would describe them texturely, too. What they felt like, what their fur felt like or their feathers or the leaves or whatever. I don't think I drew. I think I just described them. How many legs they had, you know. What kind of mouths they had. What kind of ears, what kind of eyes. I told him about lizards. There were lizards that lived down in the barn that were kind of cute and I told him about those.

AC: What was your friend like?

VH: Curious. And a good listener. Had a sense of humor. And very patient. And very old and mature. I mentioned last time that when I asked how old he was he just said, 'Very old,' which reminds me of my grandfather, but I had the sense that he didn't think I could understand how old he was.

AC: How tall was he?

VH: Ah, I think he was about as tall as my uncle. A little bit shorter. My uncle is short, probably five-feet-five-inches or -six- inches. He was probably somewhere between five feet and five-feet-five-inches. And I think he was taller than the others, but only by an inch or two. Maybe a little bit more. The perspective of the kid . . . the person who carried me was shorter than an adult. Sort of the size of a big kid.

And I think the impression that I have that I told you about the last time, about what the skin was like and stuff, I think now that that was the clothing they wore. I think they wore something to cover their skin, which I thought was them, but was really what they were wearing, like a soft, supple gray, almost suedelike space suits, to cover them.

Not like the ones we wear—ones that were as smooth and close-fitting as their skin. And that I thought was them, but it wasn't. It was what they wore outside to protect themselves. Skin-fitting, and it was fairly thick but very soft and the texture of really fine leather, you know, like nice French leather shoes, really soft leather. Not suede, but soft kid. Gray and ah . . . body temperature was not different than mine. Well, maybe it was different, but not so much that I felt cold or hot. You know, like you were touching a cold-blooded animal . . . of course, it was a warm day and it may have adjusted to our temperature but it felt like something that wasn't cold. . . .

And, ah, the head was simplified, as though the thing he wore over his face didn't have very many openings. I guess it had, I think, two eyes, but I think what I thought was like big eyes were probably just like glass surfaces or bubble surfaces to protect the eyes. I didn't think I saw them without their costumes on or what they really looked like. I think they just had little protective bubbles that let them see peripherally, but screened out the excess radiation or whatever they didn't want. And they were dark and I thought they had big, dark eyes, but I don't know that that's true. I think it was that it reflected a lot of sun. It seems to me our light was very bright for them, but on the other hand, inside their spaceship was very bright. So maybe it was just a different spectrum.

The person that talked to me later from remote was the one I assumed carried me, but it might not have been. The one that carried me was the taller one. I don't remember . . . I think there were three people in all, but I'm not sure. Maybe two of them were outside. I think that's what it was. Two of them were outside and I think I saw them when I got carried in, but I think they wanted to take off their costumes, so they went into a different part of the ship that they could talk to me from behind the wall. I do think I saw them before they did that. . . . Explain that to me. Ummm . . . there was so much gray and their costumes were gray. But either they are gray or it has something to do with their spectrum. Maybe they're not color-sensitive . . . or . . . um . . . it seemed like the gray had a meaning to it, but either that was the color of the skin or it

was a soothing color to their eyes, or something. The gray
wasn't an accident or just somebody's color judgment.

This is Virginia's first extensive description of the figures who
carried her aboard the UFO. The details of their small size and
gray color closely echo the other descriptions we have heard, but
one of her observations stands out as particularly subtle—she felt
that her abductors' outer layer was not skin, but instead was some
kind of gray, skin-like fabric. It was "as smooth and close-fitting as
their skin . . . it was fairly thick but very soft, and the texture of
really fine leather." Sergeant Charles Moody[1]; the reader will recall, said also that his captor's skin was whitish-gray and the face
was "*almost like a mask.*" (*Emphasis mine.*)

Even more to the point, Steven Kilburn described what one of
his abductors looked like from behind: "I see the back of his head
now . . . it's perfectly round. Ugly little thing. And I think there's
a line. I don't know if that's skin on his head. A very, very faint
line like a ripple . . . like a seam. Right down the middle. I can't
tell if it's skin or something he has over head. It fits well,
though."

The correspondences between Virginia's description of her
captors' eyes and the other accounts are equally subtle. She said
that their dark eyes were "probably just like glass surfaces, or bubble surfaces to protect the eyes . . . I thought they had big, dark
eyes but I don't think that's true." Steven described the way the
eyes of his captor shone in the light from the landed UFO: "I see
the reflection . . . there's something really shiny coming off this
character's eyes. It's almost like they're black and endless . . ."
Philip Osborne referred to his captor's eyes this way: "I had the
impression of their being solid . . . that it was almost a metallic
plate or something."

As Virginia's narrative resumes, she begins to speculate about
her abductor's status and role. Even within the hypnotic trance,
she is conscious that her impressions are intuitive guesses.

VH: The feeling that I have about it was that this person was
       someone senior enough in his own society to have quasi-
       official status. . . . It would almost be like a retired *emer-
       itus* professor who was doing research that *he* liked for his
       own interest . . . that he'd gotten someone to sponsor, so it
       was on an official basis. But it was almost like I was in a
       private yacht or a . . . it was definitely not like a military

vehicle or a, ah, like our space shuttle. It had a private quality about it that was very much his stamp rather than kind of
an official government or an official diplomatic something. . . . It was like he was indulging his personal inter-
ests and they were also being indulged for him by the society, and this is more the feeling that I have now when I try to
think back about how I felt, rather than necessarily something that I was aware of then.

The things that he explained were like, 'This is a very
interesting thing that I do,' the way you'd explain your moti-
vation to do basic research to a child.

AC: What did you call him? Were you able to name him?

VH: What did I call him? Um, it seems like he used "I" and "we"
but, um, names . . . what did he call himself? I'll think
about that. I don't remember . . . I think it was just
"you."

AC: How did you get his attention if you wanted to ask him
something or say something?

VH: Oh, the feeling that I had was that they were listening with
bated breath to every word that I said and every thought
that I thought. You know, the communication process was
completely absorbing them, so I didn't need to get their attention. I had it constantly.

AC: Was there anything else about this experience that you
would like to tell me about?

VH: I'll think about it. It seems like there is. I think he asked how
long we lived. I'm thinking more about the tone of the question that he asked me, the things he asked me
about. . . . He asked how long we lived and how long
these different animals lived. And I told him that they
had . . . how many offspring the chickens have, and I explained about eggs versus having your own babies, and how
many people have, and how many different kinds of animals do, and I think I also explained to him about warm-
blooded and cold-blooded animals, which I knew
about . . . and I think I explained about nursing and how
long animals live and plants, too. He was interested in
plants . . . and, ah, I think he asked me what plants eat
and I told him they didn't eat anything, that they just lived in
the air. And I think I explained to him about the seasons,
and he asked about weather, too, and I don't think I knew
very much about weather. I mean, I explained how it got

cold and froze things, but I don't think I had very much
sophisticated information about weather to tell him
. . . about the seasons and how hot it got in the summer
and how cold it got in the winter. I told him it got cold
enough in the winter that you could pour a glass of water
out into the snow and it would freeze by the time it hit the
ground. So I guess he could have figured out from that how
cold it was.

AC: Did he show you anything in return for all this information
you gave him? Did he share anything with you?

VH: He told me a lot. He explained a lot. I guess, when we
talked about animals, he told me about different kinds of
animals and different places. They are very different in different places.

AC: Did he describe them to you?

VH: I think that when he asked me about animals and I said,
'Well, you know how animals are,' and he'd say, 'No,' and
he'd explain to me patiently that they're not a certain way
everywhere and that was why he was asking, because
they're different in different places. I think he showed me
something like slides as though, you know, like windows, so
that there were different pictures that would . . . mostly
they were pictures of star maps, you know, they would say,
'This is the star . . .' I don't think I was able to follow
exactly where things were in relationship. But I remember
later on I started to look up at the stars. It was just at that
time that I began to look up the stars and try to get a sense of
distances and relationships . . . So he'd explain them to
me, but I didn't really understand. I think most of the pictures he was trying to show me were where he came from
and where he visited and where we were with relationship
to that and, um, I don't know . . . I'll toy with that and
maybe I can remember it, but maybe if I had studied astronomy it would have been familiar, but I haven't studied astronomy. I've always avoided astronomy because I knew
that our astronomy doesn't reach far enough to where things
are for it to be . . . somehow, I guess he's from a long ways
away or I wouldn't have this very distinct impression that
I'm not going to find it in our astronomy. And yet he was
trying to relate to me. . . . He did tell me about the Milky
Way, you know, and tried to make a picture of how they
were with relationship to our Milky Way, and I think that

he was, like, from a different Milky Way, which means that he must have been from a very, very, very long way away because that's a whole galaxy. So we were dealing in distances of galaxies, not just stars.

AC: Did his maps look like the maps that we have now?

VH: They did look like star maps, yes, they looked like pictures of stars at night. They looked like slides of the heavens that you might show to somebody, but they had colors. I think they were color-coded for different kinds of stars . . . they had green, and mostly white and blue. Quite a bit of blue, and some red and orange. Yellow. The green was unusual. Mostly white and blue. Some orangey-red ones.

What else did he show me that I might remember? I think he showed me so much that I can't . . . that I couldn't. . . . There are places that have these kinds of animals and there were a whole lot of slides of things that would remind us of dinosaurs and then slides of other kinds of animals. There are a lot of different winged animals and different places. So I guess he was especially interested in the chickens because they are warm and have feathers, which is unusual. Birds were very interesting to him. There were all kinds of winged creatures and some of them were quite large. They must have different kinds of atmospheres. They're almost like . . . they almost look like fish. Big round kinds of like blowfish or something that go through the air. They must live in a very dense atmosphere. And, um, I guess snakes, too. Those weren't so common. I don't, oh, there were soft fuzzies, too. There were soft fuzzies like rodents, bunnies. Large ones. And he did say, too, that they were all different sizes.

Most of the pictures he showed me were plants and animals. A lot of different flowers of different kinds . . . almost like underwater creatures. You know how different they look. It seemed like he was showing me pictures of all the different kinds of things there are.

There were so many I couldn't soak them all up. I don't . . . I have to think if any of them really stick out to me. I think the creature that went through the air that was like a blowfish captivated my imagination. And some of the flowers because they were so exotic and beautiful. And fish. I remembered when I studied biology and looked at exotic fish, I had that same feeling. I think I saw a lot of exotic fish, but there were so many. It's as though he showed me a matter of hundreds, but I don't remember any of them very vividly. Such diversity. He kept talking about diversity, which was something that he was very interested in. Diversity. About how important biological diversity is.

It's very interesting that he said that over and over again. I think that was a message for me when I grew up, because preserving diversity is the reason that we protect the endangered species, so it was like a reassuring message from him, that he, like, he would be a scientist, and from a scientist's point of view, they cherished the diversity and therefore they would protect it from any kind of, um, ecological disturbance. Like from any other kind of species coming in. There was a sense of a protective quality about that, like if somebody else wanted to come here and colonize, they would protect us from having our life-forms threatened because they cherish biological diversity. . . .

He talked about it with a tone of voice that it was obviously something that he was not only interested in, but something he really cherished. You know, a very deep kind of a sense of wonder, and respect about it. Almost a religious quality, too.

AC: Do you have a feeling that he's still around?

VH: That he's still alive? Yes. I have the feeling that, if he wanted to come visit me, he certainly could. Yes. I have the feeling that he's old and that they live a long time and that therefore he's unlikely to be very much different from what he was then. . . .

AC: Do you feel that there is some way that you could get in touch with him?

VH: That idea has been crossing my mind lately that I would just try. I would just assume that I could, and go about it as though I was just thinking about someone, like you do when you want somebody to call you. And I thought I would work on that, maybe . . . the interesting thing is, you know, the speed at which you travel. I definitely have the feeling that they could travel fast. By fast I meant fast enough . . . he talked about it as though going from galaxy to galaxy were the kind of thing we'd talk about going from state to state or country to country. And the distances between galaxies are such that they must travel . . . either they travel faster than the speed of light, or they live for tens of thousands of years. Because the distances . . . sometimes galaxies are millions of light years away, so they have to be able to travel faster than the speed of light or they wouldn't be able to do it in one lifetime. Unless they're literally billions of years old. Hmm. I don't know. It's just that he's very old, and such a tone of voice . . . It's obvious he thought I couldn't understand how old was old.

AC: Did he ask you how old you were?

VH: Yes. I told him how old I was. I told him that I just started school and that I like school a lot. I liked learning new things and I remember that he picked that up and explained a lot of what he was doing in the same way: he was trying to learn new things about what our world was like.

At this point, there is a short interruption as the tape is changed. When the recording resumes, Dr. Clamar has shifted the subject to Virginia's experience in France. She describes the weather of that day, nearly twenty years earlier.

VH: It was a day like today. About this temperature, and overcast. It wasn't raining, but you wondered if it were going to.

It was cool. And, um, fresh out. It must have been . . . spring or early summer, maybe June. Umm. The same time of year. (*As the 1950 incident* —**BH**) And I think it was Sunday. We had all gone for a family picnic and my brother and I took off to look at the fields, the woods and stuff. We were wandering around in the woods. And, ah, oh yeah, I guess they had been looking for me. They were calling to me, and when I finally came back, I was telling them about the deer and they said, 'Where were you? We were calling you.' And I said, 'I didn't hear you.' I said, 'I was with my brother,' and he said, 'No, you were for awhile and then you weren't,' and he didn't know where I was, and I said, 'Yes, you were right with me.'

He was claiming that no, he couldn't find me. I said I was right there. I wasn't far away and I was chastising him for being so thick, but of course I was much more interested in talking about the deer than I was in telling him where I was because, of course, I was just down there in the woods. And I described this deer. And the way I remember it is that the deer was looking at me and saying good-bye. The deer was saying good-bye telepathically to me. I have that as a conscious memory—the part where I am looking at the deer and the deer is about the size of a small deer. Medium-sized deer. I don't remember the name of the species of the same size, but I would suppose it was my height to the top of my head, and I was already grown up. I was five-feet-seven-inches then, so maybe it was a little shorter, but it was about that tall, and it just looked at me, and it had this nice, bright . . . the same quality, big, dark . . . big, bright, dark eyes shining. And it was gray, too. The deer was gray. Gray-brown. It was looking at me. The deer was looking into my eyes and saying good-bye to me. I was all excited about having been able to communicate with this deer. But when I described it, I don't think . . . I think I just said it was a pretty deer and I didn't know how to describe the experience. But it was as though the memory that I had—it was a conscious memory—of having the feeling that I was communicating with the deer. That I was in touch with it. And that it was saying good-bye to me. It was as though I was talking to it and saying, 'Well, don't leave yet,' and then it just sort of dematerialized, disappeared.

AC: Had you ever seen this deer before?

VH: No, I hadn't. I'd seen deer before, but not this one.

AC: Had you ever had any experience that reminded you of this one?

VH: Well, as I was saying, it was as though the big eyes reminded me a little bit of the big eyes of . . . that the other people had. And I had a sense of a personality about this deer, but the personality was a younger personality, it seemed to me, than the older man that I was dealing with the first time. It didn't seem like the same person. I don't have a feeling about whether they were related or knew each other or . . . I mean, I had a sense of personality about this deer. There was a person inside this deer. That's what I knew. I had a strong sense of what the personality was like, and that it wasn't the same one. It's as though there's quite a big block to remember before that farewell scene . . . just kind of an emotional one to me. It was as though I had a friend and I didn't want it to leave, and it said it had to go. Good-bye. But it wasn't a final good-bye. It was like an 'I'll-see-you-again' good-bye.

AC: You keep covering your eyes, especially your right eye,
      touching it. How do they feel?
VH: This last time, too, they felt very sensitive, as though, you
      know, there are very bright lights in a spaceship. I remem-
      ber them as being extremely bright. The light must not have
      been ideal for my eyes. I don't remember it being painful,
      but just very bright. As though you want to shield your eyes
      from that bright light.

     Dr. Clamar and I have frequently observed this physical reac-
tion during the trance states of other abductees. Many times she
had had to switch off the single, low-wattage bulb she usually has
burning while her subjects are undergoing hypnosis. And now,
just as Virginia is attempting to break through her memory block to
recall what happened before she parted from the deer, her narrative takes a sudden jog back to the 1950 incident. The episode she
describes must be dealt with even though it sounds, on the face of
it, outrageous.

VH: As you were telling me about shifting from that one to the
      other one (*moving from the 1950 farmyard experience to
      the 1960 encounter with the deer* —**BH**), it seemed as
      though I had a memory that I finally did talk him into taking
      me for a ride, but he said he would just take me up and let
      me look at the Earth. So I did that and looked at the ground.
      I'm trying to remember what I looked at. I think I looked at
      where I lived. You know, North America from outer space,
      and it didn't look too much like a map, you know. It was
      fully covered with clouds . . . it wasn't so clear as the
      globes. I expected it to look like a globe, and of course it
      didn't because of all the clouds, but I did look at it and I was
      high enough that I could see the water at the edges, and the
      Great Lakes. We were high.
AC: What was the motion like?
VH: Smooth. Like a smooth elevator. Fast. Like as though it took
      only about as long as it takes you to get to the top of the
      Empire State Building. Not over a few minutes to get high
      enough to see. Except it seemed to me that it wasn't black
      out there. . . . Most of what I was looking at was light

blue, but then there was black around the edges. . . . I
don't know how high up that is. I don't know that I could see
the ocean. I remember that I could see the Great Lakes,
though. You could see the water and a lot of clouds. It was
pretty. . . . So he humored me that much, to see what it
looked like.

Though this episode is difficult to accept as literally true, we
must remember that so did each new detail of each UFO report
when it first came to light. In fact, in the UFO literature we do
have other accounts of abductees being taken on short flights.[2]
Logically, there is no way to reject one aspect of a report out of
hand simply because it strains our credulity more than other aspects of the same report.

Was Virginia's trip the recollection of an actual event or was
it, perhaps, something else—an interpolated dream or an artificially induced image like the nonexistent deer? Arguing for its
being an interpolated fantasy, there is the particular moment
when Virginia brought it up. Immediately before, she had been
trying to break through a memory block about what happened
prior to saying good-bye to the beautiful deer. In this and her previous session, Virginia went into long digressions just before each
breakthrough, as if the imposed amnesia were struggling to main-
tain itself. Her account of the ride she "talked her friend into" just
might be one of these digressions.

On the other hand, her description of the trip is subtly precise.
In the phrases of a six-year-old, Virginia said, "I looked at where I
lived . . . and it didn't look too much like a map . . ." A child
would naturally expect it to "look like a globe," and to find it did
not, though "it was pretty." There is not only a tone of authenticity,
but also a surprising accuracy to her description. It sounds to me
very much like what a precocious six-year-old might report if she
had, in fact, had the experience she claims.

Throughout the mass of UFO cases which have been collected over the years, there are literally thousands of instances in
which the occupants on the craft almost seem to be showing off,
demonstrating their capabilities before the astonished eyes of
fighter pilots, radar operators, civilian motorists, and even astron-
omers.[3] A certain theatricality flavors this behavior, and I have
alluded earlier to the theory that they may be slowly, methodical-
ly, "raising our consciousness" about their very existence. Perhaps
Virginia's trip, which, according to her, took mere seconds, was

more than just a favor granted a cooperative and intelligent six-year-old. It may have been just one more technological demonstration, but one that was tucked away for thirty years until its revelation through hypnosis. As the reader must know by now, the patterns of UFO behavior are a great deal clearer than their meaning.

And now, after another digression on the subject of her myopia, Virginia returns to the incident in the Alsatian woods.

VH: The deer. That pretty deer that I was so fond of. It was like my best, long-lost friend. I didn't want him to go away. He said he had to. I think he said he'd see me again. He had to leave. It was a person. It was a friend, and I don't, ah, I'm describing it as though it was a mystical experience, but it didn't feel that way. It felt like it was a good, good friend that I didn't want not to see any more. How I found him and how the communication happened I can't remember. There's a block-out. . . .
      I can think better when I cover my eyes because the light is . . . I can see it through my eyelids.

(At this point, the session is interrupted so Aphrodite can switch off the single office light.)

VH: Umm. The deer. Where does the deer come from? I don't know. Maybe I can just sort of walk around in my mind and get around it. It's as though I can't remember how I found the deer except I sure knew him and I sure communicated with him, and I sure didn't want him to leave, and it wasn't a sad thing. It was like such an excitement! It was as though you bump into a friend you haven't seen for a long time whom you really like, and you've lost their address, and you were so glad you found them. . . . I do remember my parents had been calling me. And, in fact, that is what the deer said—'Your parents are calling you,' and I said, 'Well,' you know, 'that's all right.'
      I didn't have a sense of lapsed time, but my parents said that I had been gone a while, but a while was probably no more than an hour. It might have only been a half-hour . . . it's that order of magnitude. But that's why he had to go because my parents were calling me. (Whispers.) 'Virginia . . . Virginia!' 'Well, you've got to go back and

have your picnic,' and I said, 'There's no rush!' So it's as though when they really started to look for me, that's when he had to leave.

(After a pause) I don't think it was a deer. I mean, the mental image of a deer is there, the visual image, but the inner experience of it is not of a deer but of a person. Very definitely a human kind of a person. I mean, I really like animals like my cat, and I know the difference between the person-heart of a cat and the person-heart of a people, and it was a person-people kind of thing.

We were talking about . . . I don't know what. About how beautiful something was. The woods or something like that. And yet when I got back, I had this blood on my blouse. Just a little. Just where you would if you had a nosebleed.

AC: At the count of three, let yourself go back to that period between leaving the deer and discovering the blood on your blouse.

VH: (Whispers) O.K.

AC: One . . . two . . . three.

VH: Yes. My parents were calling me, and the deer . . . I was looking for the deer. It was as though I was looking at him and talking to him and he said he had to go away, and I heard my parents call and I turned my head to answer them to say something like 'I'm here!' and when I turned back, the deer was gone.

But I didn't want to go back there because I was busy looking for the deer. I didn't think he was gone. He just disappeared all of a sudden. It wasn't like he'd walked away. But we were in the woods, so it was as though, well, maybe he stepped behind the trees or something. I mean I didn't have the sensation that it was (snaps her fingers) instantly gone except that it was in the time that I turned my head to talk to my parents. You know, 'I'm here!' In that period of time, the deer was gone, and I didn't know whether it had run away into the woods, but it was just completely gone. And so I spent a little while walking in that direction as though to follow it and find it because I didn't want to leave it, and all the time they were calling me, so finally I went bouncing back and all I could talk about was the deer. And they'd say, 'Where have you been?' And I said, 'In the woods with Roger' (her brother).

'Well, Roger's been here. He was looking for you.'

'Well, I went down there with him and I was with him the whole time.'

'Well, he just came back. He couldn't find you.'

'Well, I was right down there,' you know, which wasn't very far. 'I was right down there and he must have wandered off and got himself confused.' I was dismissing him as having lost me, and so they didn't pursue that anymore. There I was, and I had just come back from there since I answered them, but all I could talk about was the deer, and they were the ones—I guess it was my mother—who said, 'You have blood on your shirt.' And I looked and it was fresh. It was fresh, fresh blood. It was fresh as when you just cut yourself. It hadn't begun to dry at all, and so I looked on my hands, and no blood, and my neck, felt my face, no blood, and felt my nose, if I had a bloody nose. No bloody nose. And all of that is on film. I haven't seen it since we talked, but I have that on film because my father was filming all of us at the picnic. And so that distracted me and I was all of a sudden preoccupied, like where did the blood come from? I never made the connection between that incident and the other one until I called my mother to ask about the scar, and she didn't remember much about that except that it happened and that we never figured out what it was from, and she was the one who reminded me about the unexpected blood she remembered from this other incident, and having it right on my blouse, my white blouse.

I remember being very frustrated. They had been hollering at me. I mean, I remember thinking if they hadn't been hollering at me, I would still have been talking to the deer, and that upset me a lot. So I remember being grumpy about that. It's as though somehow I lost track of the deer because of that, and feeling very frustrated and disappointed and also as though I had lost something. Like if you're in a carnival with a friend and there are so many people and you turn to look at something and you let go of somebody's hand and it isn't as though they're permanently lost but you're separated and you know that there isn't any way that you can find each other for a while. It's a loss like being sort of yanked out of that transaction before it was over with. I have a big blank about what happened before that. Because the part I remember with that deer was the *end* of the conversation. But I remember it wasn't just I saw the deer that was pretty—it was the ending of a transaction.

It's as though there's a big blank spot in the middle, and I don't know why that's blank. Because the ending is so vivid. Let me think about that. Why would I have a blank? I guess they had to give me, you know, a forget-it thing, because of my parents and family and stuff.

AC: Amnesia?

VH: Yes. Because if I told them I was doing this, that, or the other thing, it was still at that age that they would have, of course, they wouldn't necessarily believe me. It's interesting when I was talking with my parents about it a couple of weeks ago, my mother had all kinds of other possibilities of how I had cut myself which were the ones she had had at the time, none of which made any more sense now than they had then, but my father had absolutely no doubt at all that it might have been exactly the way I remembered it. . . . He had a very high, well so did my mother, a very high confidence in our veracity. I mean we weren't lying kids and we didn't make up stories. But I think it *(the amnesia—BH)* was for our protection just in general. I probably would have told my friends in school and they probably would have given me a hard time.

At this point, Virginia goes into a fairly long digression on the subject of her need to keep this experience, and obviously her identity, confidential. It seemed to me at the time to exemplify the struggle between an externally induced block and Virginia's desire to remember.

VH: It's as though I have that kind of block about it and, uh, how can I give my mind a way around the corner of the block?

AC: Amnesia can be lifted. So let yourself just relax. Stay very, very comfortable . . . protected . . . as you sink deeper and deeper into this marvelous, protected relaxation. You will remember things which lie underneath which you have forgotten because you were told to forget. They're going to emerge now. You're an adult. You're among friends who will accept your experience. You may have been given amnesia for a time because you were a child, a young girl who didn't know quite what to do with that information. Now you're an adult. You can lift your forgetfulness and look beneath and see what you're forgetting. Forgetting is a defense. We all use it for things that we don't know what to do with, or are uncomfortable with. We forget, but it is not permanent. It can be recalled. Now you are going to let yourself recall what is underneath.

(Another fairly long digression ensues before Virginia finally breaks through her block.)

VH: I'm walking through the woods. There's a very bright light. There's a ship just like they have in the movies. It's round. It's top-shaped roughly, but I can't tell exactly. . . . There's so much light you can't really see clearly. It's interesting—here I go again with this feeling in my eyes. They're getting very tender. A very bright light. Pretty. Bright light. . . . There was some pink in it. And blue. Bright light. And then I hear almost like a whisper, 'Virginia . . . Virginia,' and I think it was in my head that they were calling me, so they knew my name or they knew how to call me in my head, so it was like my name was being called. And I realized that ever since I was a little kid I had this memory of being . . . it must have happened the first time, too . . . of having my name called, sometimes having my name called in my head. It's like I'm remembering somebody calling me. I don't ever confuse it that someone's actually calling me, except that, once in a while, I think that maybe somebody is thinking about me and I am hearing him call my name, but I don't have any confusions about what's outside and what's inside.
But I heard them call my name like a whisper. Not that it was quiet. It wasn't outside, it was inside. *(Whispers)* 'Virginia . . . Virginia.' So I recognized the call. It was like somebody I knew, and I went over to it and I went inside. It was like there was a bright column of light. I don't remember whether I went up stairs or whether there was a lift. I think it was like a ramp that I walked up. No, it was like a conveyor belt ramp. I stood on it and it lifted, and there was a celebration. They were visiting because they were celebrating something. It was as though they had finished a re-

search project and whatever the outcome was, whether to discover something, whether the research project or whatever—there was an accomplishment that they were very pleased about and very proud of, and they were celebrating. It was as though, you know, maybe like maybe he'd gotten a Nobel Prize for extraterrestrial biology—that kind of something or other. And he was—everybody on the ship was happy. Everybody was—it seems there were more this time than the three. And there was someone who became the deer later, was like a younger person, more like my age. Or it had the feeling of being more like a contemporary and it was a female feeling, like a friend. But I have that feeling about it and yet the deer didn't have it—it's as though it were the same person and yet when I think about the deer, the deer didn't necessarily feel like a female deer as opposed to a male deer.

AC: Androgynous?

VH: No. Maybe it was just a level we were communicating was one where you were oblivious to which sex it is, but there was definitely sort of a female friend on the ship, and also at least two of the original people who had been on the first trip. Maybe she was their daughter or their granddaughter or umptee-umpth granddaughter or whatever. It seems like it was a relative that got to come along to meet me and it was a party.

They were celebrating and they said they wanted to share it with me because my research or their research was—interesting, I have a twitch in my leg now (at her scar—**BH**)—their research used their visit with me so they wanted to share it with me because my contributions had been really helpful for them.

And so we were having a party and they were telling me about—they were having a hard time explaining to me why it was so exciting, except that the older man who had done the research was really beside himself with excitement. As though he had accomplished something that he was really proud of. It was really neat. And, uh, it had to do with research and it had to do with the study, but it seemed like its significance was greater. I mean, it was obviously very deep to him. It was something more than abstract research. It was something either that had changed their

whole understanding of the way life is in different places—
I mean, it was something of heavy, heavy significance to
him on a deeper level than just what we think of as a
research project. As I said, it had almost a religious quality
the way he felt about the research that he was doing. It was
like his own mission. Something that he wanted to prove or
something that he wanted to discover, something that he
wanted to accomplish with his research, and he had succeeded in doing that. And, uh, I guess they wanted a sample
of me to see how I was different. Because I told them I was
grown up. I said, 'I'm a mature'—you know, like I explained
to them I've done all my growing now. 'When you saw me, I
was a child, and I have done as much growing as I am going
to do.' And I guess they wanted to know how I was different. And I think they did take some blood from the inside of
my nose. I think I told them about the last time and I think
they didn't want to leave a mark on me. So I think that's
what happened. They did do that.

AC: Who did that?

VH: Umm. Who did that? It wasn't him and it wasn't the woman,
who—the girl, who was sort of my age. It was—oh, I think it
was his sidekick from the original trip. They used the same
instrument. It was like it had a handle that could just come
out. It was like a touch on the inside. A sort of hum, you
know, sort of like a—I'm searching for the right image that it
looked like, that it will remind you of. It was a nice smooth
texture. A microphone. Not the kind that is like an ice
cream cone, but just—this is one of the small ones, a little
one. Little hand mike. Right. But it was all smooth. It didn't
have texture to it. It was like, I guess it didn't have a groove.
It must have been—I think they use sonar energy. It must
have been. Focused. I think it was sonar because it had a
little hum like you held it and it would go *Hmmm* and then
that was all there was to it. And, since I remembered it happening the first time, I hardly even paid any attention to it.

AC: Was it put into the left or right nostril?

VH: I've been going like this *(touching the left nostril)*, so I think
it must have been here. I wonder why I was so annoyed to
find the blood on my blouse? The first time, I was glad to
have a visible, physical evidence of it. The second time, it
was just sort of annoying. So they did that, and it was just a

party. There was a lot of talking and a good feeling and they were playing, um, playing light inside. . . . There were lights flickering on.

AC: Were there any refreshments?

VH: I was trying to remember seeing if they had any refreshments, and I don't think they were able to give me anything. I don't think that they had anything that they gave me. Umm . . . I think they were playing music, too. And I think their music is more like what we think is like electronic, but not piercing and jarring. . . . It was patterned, highly sophisticated, stylized and patterned. . . . It was sounds that remind you of the sound of the wind going through the valley, for they were—you know, they were mellow sounds—they weren't piercing sounds or cacaphonous or anything. And, uh, there was some sound. . . . It was like it was quiet in the background because everybody was busy talking. They were talking to themselves, too. They were thinking at me, but they were talking to themselves and that had a sound—it was a little clicky, a little . . . it was like a voice was speaking, but a little bit more like smacking. You know, like *(she smacks her palms)* some of that stuff in it, in the talking. And at a higher pitch than we talk. More like, a pitch up here somewhere *(she raises the pitch of her voice)*, somewhere up here, that kind of pitch.

But I could hear it. And they were obviously excited. And they were trying to explain to me what they had accomplished, too. *(Chuckles)* It seems as though they—I don't think they put it that way—but I think they succeeded into talking somebody into considering us as an endangered species, *(more chuckles)* or something equivalent to that. Not endangered. No, I guess it wouldn't be that. Umm . . . it was like a precious species, kind of a classification. But it was more than that, too. It didn't have so much just to do with Earth, it had to do with . . . I guess maybe establishing the principle of noninterference, something like that. One of those things people like to deal with in science fiction themes. The kind of moral code they like to imagine intergalactic travelers have about not mucking up or interfering with indigenous cultures.

AC: Can you focus on the woman now? What was she like?

VH: Well, she looked like them. Except it seemed to me she was a lighter color. It's as though the older you got the darker gray you were. But it could be—as I said, they were wearing these things—I think they were their protective costumes and it might have just been that, the more senior you were, the darker it was. It might have been that. It seemed like hers was lighter, more creamy-colored. And it just felt like a younger person. Like a bouncier quality. It wasn't so deliberate, the way they expressed themselves; hers was more bubbly, more bouncy. And, uh, she wanted to hear about, you know, what the place (Earth—BH) was like. She hadn't been there and it was obviously a big treat for her to be there. I don't think she was really my age, but I think that, whatever she was, it was analogous to being my age. Then she was trying to tell me about the kinds of schools she went to. She was still a schoolgirl or whatever . . . how long it takes them to get through school. And, ah, I guess they have a mating process, too, because it was as though she was trying to explain about dating or whatever they do according to what would be analogous . . . what they do in their spare time. We were trying to discuss what young people do in their spare time. And, ah, she wanted to be a bioanthropologist like her father or grandfather, whoever he was. She was interested in that field. It was as though it was a very big deal for her to be there seeing me. (Brief interruption while the tape is changed.)

I think that the blood sample was . . . she was going to have a chance to examine it, study it, too. It was, you know, sort of like collecting moon rocks . . . she'd get a piece of it. Umm. Maybe they took a tissue sample. I don't know. Interesting. So she was really excited about that. It's sort of like my souvenir for her, and there were more people along. And some of them were more junior to him, considerably, and they kept quiet. It was like they stood respectfully off a little bit, but they were very—it was sort of like the whole thing was very awesome to them. It wasn't so much that they were considered lowly creatures as that they were just standing there kind of being awed, you know, seeing a strange person and being at the party. The whole thing was really, um, a heavy trip for them.

Well over an hour and a half had passed since Virginia entered the trance state. I signaled Dr. Clamar and, within a few

moments, we ended what had been, for all three of us, an extraordinary session.

As the reader must know by now, the UFO phenomenon is
fraught with disturbingly bizarre, even absurd accounts. The trouble is that, imbedded within this mass of nearly unbelievable material, there is a core of solid detail which we find repeated time
and time again. The overall shape of Virginia's scenario does not
differ in any basic way from the other abduction accounts we have
been examining. Despite its science fiction aspects, Virginia's narrative is supported by internal evidence. First, there is the detail of
the blood on her blouse. Its presence is confirmed by her family,
and it was even recorded on film. The blood was the result of a
probe of some kind inserted into her left nostril to take blood and
tissue samples. In another case, Betty Andreasson[4] was abducted
in 1967, though the encounter was not investigated for a decade.
Under hypnosis, Betty recalled being on the examining table:

BA: I feel shaky. He's taking an instrument and . . . ah! Ow!
       Wow! *(Deep fast breathing)* Why do you have to put that up
       my nose. Oh! He's putting that thing in my nose, and it's
       going up and it's breaking through something. I don't like it.
       Oh, and I can't move. It's hurting! He had that thing up in
       my head!

Sandy Larson,[5] abducted in August of 1975, described her ordeal. In a hypnotic trance, she revealed what happened inside the
UFO.

SL: It was like somebody took the knife and made the inside of
       my nose sore.
Q: Made the inside of your nose sore?
SL: Scraped it.
Q: Did you see anybody touching your nose?
SL: Uh huh.
Q: Could you see hands?
SL: No.
Q: Could you see an instrument of some kind?
SL: Yeah.
Q: Can you describe it?
SL: I would say like a little knife or like a cotton swab.

Q: Not very big, but something that was placed inside your
      nose?
SL: Uh huh.

A cotton swab, of course, is round, while a knife is thin and
flat. Though a volumetric object is not necessarily implied by her
description, what is called to mind is a small, elongated instrument
of some kind, and the pain that she associated with it. Virginia
made a drawing of the "thin, hand microphone" type of object she
recalled being placed in her nostril and it is compared in Figure 14
to a similar drawing made by Betty Andreasson. We are dealing
here, I believe, not with three different women's magical fantasies, but rather with three memories of what may well have been
an identical "medical" instrument. And an identical, unpleasant
operation.

The conversation that Virginia reported from her first—
1950—abduction has many parallels. She was asked about the life-
span of humans and various animals. She was shown star maps
which apparently were color-coded, and which were "like
slides . . . you know, like windows . . ." This last detail, to me,
is a six-year-old child's attempt to suggest the effect of a holo-
graph, since a window encloses a three-dimensional space rather
than framing a flat surface.

Betty Hill,[6] in her 1961 abduction, also was shown what was
apparently a three dimensional, holographlike star map. She, too,
was questioned about astronomy and had very little more information on the subject than had Virginia: "I asked where he was
from. Because I knew he wasn't from the earth, and I wanted to
know where he came from. And he asked me if I knew anything
about the universe . . . he said he wished I knew more about
this, and I said, 'I wish I did, too'. . . . He said, 'If you don't know
where you are (on the star map—**BH**), then there isn't any point of
my telling where I am from.' "

Betty Hill also was asked about life-spans and her conception
of time, though some questions were more specific and less philosophical. In an interrogation that again suggests to me more intelligence-testing than information-gathering, Betty continues, "So
then he asked me, well, what did we eat? And I said, we ate meat,
potatoes, vegetables, milk. And so he asked me, 'What are vegetables?' and I said that this is a broad term and could cover a great

variety of certain kinds of foods we eat. But I couldn't just explain
what vegetables are, there were too many. And he said was there
one kind I liked? I said that I ate a great many, but my favorite is
squash. So he said, 'Tell me about squash.' So I said it was yellow,
usually, in color. And he said, 'What is yellow?' " One thinks of
little six-year-old Virginia trying to describe to her abductors what
plants eat, and explaining that they eat nothing, they simply exist
in the air.

The ease one has following Virginia's account is hampered
somewhat by its three different levels of discourse. In the beginning, she speaks much of the time as a little girl who is not quite
seven years old, and her locutions are often charmingly childlike:
"My friend on the ship," "The cute lizards," "The soft fuzzies like
rodents and bunnies." But later on, as she recalls the French episode, her phrasing is frequently that of a Sixties teenager: the party
on board is "really neat." She scolds her brother "for being thick."
The female tried "to explain about dating," and the celebration
was "really a heavy trip."

A third level in her hypnotic account is the present-day, thir-
ty-five-year-old Virginia's use of contemporary language. She frequently speculates upon what she is recalling so the reader must
carefully separate "objective" memory from after-the-fact interpretation. This latter problem exists in almost all hypnotic recall,
but is particularly obtrusive here, since Virginia has a sharply inquiring and speculative mind. Her apparent lack of fear during
both experiences allows her a little imaginative elbow room. It is
as if she were sitting in a sparsely filled theater near an exit, noticing wisps of smoke, and having plenty of time on the way out to
wonder what is going on and why; this as opposed to being suddenly caught up in panic.

A close reading of the transcript reveals the differences between memory and speculation. Virginia carefully says that her
account of the leader's "research mission" is "more the feeling
that I have now when I try to think back about how I felt, rather
than necessarily something that I was aware of then." She states as
an accurate memory the fact that the inside of the UFO was very
bright, and then adds that maybe the light there "was from a different spectrum." She recalls that her eyes were quite dry and
irritated, but then speculates that "maybe they didn't humidify the
atmosphere. Maybe they just put in plain oxygen or nitrogen, but it
was very dry." The instrument inserted in her nostril "had a little
hum, like you held it and it would go *hmmm* and that was all there

was to it." But then she cannot resist guessing about a power source, and adds that it must operate by sonar energy.

When she describes her idea of the accomplishments that are being celebrated, her language clearly implies a guess, an approximation that is metaphorical rather than literal. "They were having a hard time explaining to me why it was so exciting. . . . It was as though, you know, maybe like he'd gotten a Nobel Prize for extraterrestrial biology—that sort of something or other." Obviously, what is most reliable in Virginia's account is what she presents as specific, objective recollection. Less reliable is what she frankly presents as honest, after-the-fact speculation. Being a lucid and verbal woman, Virginia searches for images and useful metaphors to flesh out the tone of particular memories.

Taking an overview of the Alsatian episode in the light of other abduction cases we know, and treating it as a transaction between Virginia and her captors, this is what one sees: an adolescent girl who had been abducted ten years earlier is somehow lured away from her family and into the woods. Telepathically, she is called by name. She goes towards the landed UFO and is taken inside. She is made to feel happy, part of a "celebration in her honor," but the main event is like the former—Virginia provides the gift. Blood and tissue samples are extracted from inside her nose. She is then taken into the woods and given post-hypnotic suggestions that she will forget everything except the fact that she saw a beautiful deer. She returns to her family only to discover that an odd time lapse has occurred, and that there is fresh blood on her blouse. Nineteen years later, after hypnosis, she remembers that she somehow had contributed to the success of whatever it was the UFO crew had been up to. In an apparent one-way transaction, they got from her what they needed, and she was left with a bloody shirt and a confused memory.

The situation of abductees being made to feel special, loved, members of the "select," occasionally occurs in abduction cases. The reasons for their having been singled out are almost always vague, but the abductees feel gratified and less frightened, though not necessarily less confused. An interesting parallel presents itself in the accounts of former followers of the Reverend Sun Myung Moon's Unification Church.[7] At the beginning of their recruitment, an overpowering sense of being needed and wanted is systematically instilled in them by Moonie operatives. Lonely college students are visited in their dormitory rooms, fed milk and cookies, invited to love-drenched weekend retreats, and slowly

won over before specific issues and ideology or dogma are even
mentioned. This love technique is so thoroughly overwhelming
that, when articles of religious belief are finally introduced, the
subject feels like an ingrate to reject them. Bestowing importance
and showering love upon the potential convert weakens his oppo-
sition and sets him up for whatever unusual demands are to be
made of him.

This potent method seems to have happened in a number of
UFO abductions. For example, under hypnosis, David Oldham
recounted the following dialogue. Standing terrified and unable to
move before his abductor, he says:

He wants . . . to hug me . . . says . . . says, 'Why are you
scared?'
'I . . . I've never seen something like this . . .'
'. . . Someone   loves   you . . . very   deeply . . . and
they . . . want to see you. Close your eyes . . . and be still.'
(These soothing words are immediately followed by a painful
operation of some kind.)
'What are you . . . what are you . . . putting me in? What?
It   hurts . . . Oh!   Can't   see . . . can't   see . . . can't
breathe . . . '
(David is told by his captor to relax.)
'O.K. . . O.K. . . .O.K. . . . I'm relaxed. I'M RELAXED!
Help! Help!'
(Dr. Clamar tries to calm him, and then, seconds later:)
Hands . . . in cramps . . . in cramps . . . in cramps! My
arms . . . Oh . . . my body is . . . vibrating. . . . I'm just
standing here . . . I can't see. . . .Something is above
me . . . and it makes me vibrate. . . .
(Again, after all the pain and fright caused by this new process, David is cajoled by soothing—and flattering—words.)
'Now' . . . he says, . . . 'We are working . . . with your
mind. We know . . . you have very strong mental abili-
ties. . . .'

It is difficult to avoid the impression that David is being loved
and used, loved and used. The bestowing of affection and importance upon a sixteen-year-old boy helps immensely in reducing
his resistance to whatever complex and hurtful procedures are
central to his abduction. The inference is the same that I made in

Virginia's abduction—the reality is the physical operation and its attendant pain, while the sense of happiness and love is an enforced illusion. (It should be added that Virginia insists the good feelings of the celebratory party were just as real as the blood and tissue samples taken from her, so my reactions are frankly personal and speculative.)

The use of calming, even deliberately misleading words before administering a degree of unavoidable pain is a familiar method to tens of thousands of doctors and pediatricians. In fact, as I watched David lying agitated and tearful on Dr. Clamar's couch, a particular image sprang into my mind. It was that of a little boy being rolled out of the hospital recovery room, his semi-anesthetized mind aswirl with pain and the surgeon's half-remembered words of encouragement.

This medical situation provides a helpful model for evaluating what actually may be taking place in UFO abductions. Consider the complexity of a not-uncommon Earthly event—surgery to remove a diseased appendix. At least three major aspects of the experience can be isolated. First, there is a series of what the patient experiences as physical acts. He lies in a particular hospital room. He is "prepped" for the operation, and perhaps then receives a tranquilizing injection. He is rolled down to the operating room, and there he receives a general anesthetic. Though he does not actually feel it, an incision in the abdomen is made, the appendix is located and removed, and the wound is closed. Eventually, the patient awakens in the recovery room, and usually then experiences some pain.

But second, and opposed to these physical facts, there are psychic aspects to his experience. The patient is naturally uneasy when he enters the hospital. The tranquilizing drug renders his perceptions vague and softly passive. The general anesthetic may provide him with seconds of dreamlike near-hallucination at each end of a period of unconsciousness. Recovery to full awareness is gradual and full of rambling, out-of-focus sensations. Afterwards, no one—least of all the patient—can absolutely sort out which perceptions are accurate, specific memories of his experience and which have been colored by the drugs and the general psychological context.

A third aspect of this common medical procedure is the way a patient integrates this experience into his life—whether he dreams about it, more or less forgets about it, whether or not it lingers as a traumatic event, etc. Obviously, individual idiosyncracies will provide a wide range of subsequent reactions.

If we were to select at random ten people who had undergone appendectomies, and then were to subject them one at a time to regressive hypnosis, we should expect a fairly wide range of response. Hospital procedures might differ, pain thresholds vary, and the ages of the ten might lead to different reactions, yet beneath these variations in detail and emphasis there would remain a unifying core of description. It would be clear that all ten shared the same basic experience.

And so it is, I believe, with Virginia Horton, Philip Osborne, Steven Kilburn, and the others whose accounts we have been examining in these pages. Three simple descriptions quoted earlier nicely encapsulate the range of response to one particular operation—the apparent taking of blood and tissue from inside the nostril:

The withdrawn and laconic Sandy Larson—"It was like somebody took the knife and made the inside of my nose sore."

Betty Andreasson, frightened and vividly susceptible to pain—"He's putting that thing in my nose. . . . It's breaking through something. . . . It's hurting!"

Virginia Horton, calmly comparing it to the earlier time when a similar sample was taken from her leg—"Since I remembered it happening the first time, I hardly even paid any attention to it."

During her hypnotic recall, Virginia made many quick observations—remarks almost tossed away—which have their echoes in other UFO abduction cases. She described her captors as "having a hard time explaining to me why it was so exciting, except that the older man, who had done the research, was really beside himself with excitement." Also under hypnosis, Betty Hill[8] said of the "tests" she was undergoing, "I don't know what they're doing, but they seem to be so happy about whatever they're doing."

Virginia recalled that, while she was in the woods, she heard her name being called "in my head . . . so they knew my name. . . . They knew how to call me. . . ."After his abduction in 1975, Sergeant Charles Moody[9] said that his captors "knew who I was and called me by my proper name—Charles. They did not use my nickname, Chuck. It was like they could read my mind and I believe they did because the elder or leader would speak sometimes before I would ask something." Barney Hill,[10] trying to find the proper phrase, said, "He did not speak by word. I was told what to do by his thoughts making my thoughts understand." Sandy Larson[11] was asked to describe the telepathic communication she experienced and she answered that it was "like a thought between two people, when you know what the other person's gonna say."

Virginia emerged from the Alsatian woods remembering only the excitement of her experience with the deer. She was annoyed by her family's insistence that she had been missing, because their hectoring questions interfered with her euphoric mood. "I remember thinking if they hadn't been hollering at me, I would still have been talking to the deer. . . . It was as though I had walked out of the woods and claimed that I saw a unicorn. There was that sense of excitement and wonder." This euphoria at the end of a UFO abduction is commonly reported despite the initial terror. It seems to me to be an artificially induced emotion, perhaps some sort of powerful post-hypnotic suggestion. Despite the fear Barney and Betty Hill experienced when they were first taken, Barney described the denouement this way: "I see Betty coming down the road, and she gets into her car, and I am grinning at her and she is grinning back at me. And we both seem so elated and we are really happy. And I'm thinking it isn't too bad. How funny. . . . I laugh and say, 'Well, there it goes.' And I'm happy."[12]

If Virginia's memories seem weighted toward the euphoric and devoid of anything specifically frightening, the reader will remember that she still has not recalled the moment when, as a little girl, she first encountered the approaching gray-clad figures. Even her very earliest recollection—the sensation of being carried toward the UFO—is imperfectly remembered. In every hypnotically retrieved narrative I have witnessed so far, there are a few missing parts, as if there were either periods of actual unconsciousness or some moments which have been especially deeply repressed. Despite this omission, the long, detailed accounts of Virginia Horton's two abduction experiences both fold neatly into the overall pattern. The descriptions—Virginia's and others'—cohere, and buried within them all are subtle clues to the possible meaning of these disturbing encounters.

9

SPECULATIONS

BOTH GRIM AND HOPEFUL

I

On its spectacular surface, a UFO abduction appears to be an encounter in which extraterrestrials capture and examine human specimens in some kind of anthropological-biological quest for information. But the questions Virginia Horton, Betty Hill, and other abductees remember being asked are the kinds of questions for which answers are easily obtainable: how long people live, what they eat, and so forth. To acquire this kind of information, along with basic anatomical data, a handful of human subjects should suffice; in fact, the typical abductee initially believes that he or she is one of the very few people ever to undergo such an experience. Yet so far—and despite all the obstacles I described earlier—roughly five hundred individual abduction experiences have come to light.[1] Surely hundreds, perhaps thousands of other such abductions must still lie buried in the silence of enforced amnesia.

Why have the UFO occupants taken so many, and why, apparently, do they attempt to conceal the nature and magnitude of their operations? Basic information-gathering on the species simply cannot explain all these separate events. Two other related possibilities suggest themselves, however: either the UFO crew members are taking something besides information, or they are leaving something behind with their captives.

When Betty Andreasson underwent hypnosis to explore her 1967 abduction, some evidence surfaced suggesting that she had also had an earlier childhood abduction. More significantly, she recalled that, during her 1967 encounter, when the instrument was removed from her nostril, there was a tiny spherical object on its very tip. This tiny ball had spiny projections around its surface, and she was certain that it had not been there when the probe was first pressed up into her nose.[2] Was this some kind of an implant that had been put in place in an earlier childhood abduction? We know, of course, that Virginia Horton had a lengthy encounter at the age of six, and that during her second experience a probe of some sort was inserted in her nostril and caused some bleeding when it was removed. She remembers "not paying much attention to it." Being somewhat squeamish myself, I also try not to pay too much attention when I receive an injection or have a blood test performed, so I can easily sympathize with her attitude. The possibility remains that there was, in her case, too, something on the end of the nasal probe when it came out that was not there earlier, and which Virginia did not happen to notice.

Dr. James Harder, professor of engineering at the University of California at Berkeley, is a distinguished UFO investigator and director of research for the Aerial Phenomena Research Organization (APRO). In the course of his investigations across the United States, he has worked with over one hundred people who, while under hypnosis, recalled abduction experiences. The majority of these, Harder believes, show evidence of having been abducted before, as children, often when they were six or seven years old.[3] Like Virginia, a number of them recall seeing the same captors both times.

One inescapable inference to be drawn from this pattern is that a very long-term, in-depth study is being made of a relatively large sample of humans, and that this study may involve mechanical implants of some sort. Perhaps Virginia Horton, Betty Andreasson, and others as children had tiny monitoring devices installed high in their nasal cavities, much as terrestrial ecologists and zoologists install implants to monitor wildlife. A neurosurgeon informed me that certain brain operations—tissue biopsies, for example—can be carried out by entering the brain from below, through this convenient channel. If such a long-term monitoring system is going on, it would help explain the decades of surreptitious UFO behavior and the absence of direct communication.

Dr. Robert Jastrow once said something to the effect that any extraterrestrials who have the technology to travel from their planet to Earth must be vastly ahead of us scientifically and intellectually; their behavior, then, would inevitably be somewhat incomprehensible. He added that if we understand everything "they" (and here he meant any UFO occupants)[4] are doing, then "they" are probably not extraterrestrial in origin. It's a neat, clean way to state our own anthropomorphic limitations. Our astronauts on the moon conducted a number of investigatory experiments across a wide scientific range. An advanced culture visiting Earth would probably also conduct many simultaneous investigations across an even wider scientific range, with the crucial difference that we could probably not understand all of them—either their purposes or their technology.

Virginia Horton's account is thoroughly consonant with Jastrow's dictum. "They were having a hard time explaining . . . why (their research) was so exciting." It is irrelevant to raise the kind of objection that goes like this: "If extraterrestrials are really here, why do they bother with six-year-old children when they can land publicly and talk to our presidents and our scientists?" As if Ronald Reagan or Jimmy Carter, or, for that matter, Carl Sagan or Robert Jastrow, must inevitably be central to *their* concerns. Maybe yes, but equally conceivable, maybe no. Perhaps their kind of *preliminary* investigation requires monitoring a wide range of people over their entire lifetimes, an idea no less implausible than many others I have heard. To oppose the hypnotically retrieved abduction accounts solely because of one's personal notion of how "real" extraterrestrials should behave is unbounded arrogance. These hundreds of similar, highly specific recollections are the core of the problem. They represent data, which we must deal with, one way or another.

There is another possible explanation for the apparently large number of individual abductions, one which does not necessarily involve either implants or a long-term study of the human species. What if the UFO occupants are *taking* something from their captives? Many people assume, again anthropomorphically, that if alien beings could travel across distances ranging upwards from four light-years (the distance of the nearest star, Alpha Centauri, from Earth) then they must indeed be supermen, and the idea is therefore ludicrous that they might need anything we possess. Even more outrageous, they add, is the idea that extraterrestrials might be afraid of us, or vulnerable in any way. But why assume any of these things? We may indeed possess something—a natural resource, an element, a genetic structure—that an alien culture might desire to use, for example, as experimental raw material.

The evidence for a particular kind of sample taking is very strong. In the introduction, I alluded to an encounter that took place in the Catskill Forest Preserve on November 8, 1975, and which Ted Bloecher and I later investigated.[5] Two young men on a camping trip were awakened by noises close to their tent. Fearing the possibility of a scavenging bear, they went outside, flashlights in hand, and noticed back in the woods what they thought at first was a large Airstream trailer. Realizing there was no road where this vehicle rested, they investigated further and found that it was, instead, some sort of peculiar, oval, semiluminous craft. Their flashlight beam then picked up a standing, silent, robotlike figure, and then another, and then still others. The two young men returned to their tent and built up their campfire after they discovered that the light of their flashlight, when held on one of the robotlike figures, immobilized it.

A kind of psychological siege followed, with the creatures approaching and withdrawing, approaching and withdrawing, coming as close as fifteen feet to the terrified campers. The men stood, hatchets in hand, behind a barricade of upturned picnic tables and benches. One of them later described his feelings to me this way: "You know, you're petrified . . . you're too scared to run . . . I felt that I was going to die there, that's what I really felt like, and I had to defend myself. . . ."

When the figures withdrew for a moment or so, the two campers made a dash for their car. The motor started and then suddenly died for no apparent reason. Its owner is a devoted car buff and he insists his vehicle was in top mechanical condition. It is at this point, I believe, that the two young men were abducted. Though neither has yet agreed to undergo hypnosis, our investigation establishes that there is roughly one hour missing from their account of that night's events; other evidence supports this theory.[6]

The point of all this is quite specific. About a week after their ordeal, one of the men noticed a small, round sore near his navel. Shortly thereafter, a second, and then a third appeared close to the first. Within a month long, straight, raised welts appeared running from these round sores downwards toward his groin in a converging pattern. Eventually, he entered a hospital for diagnosis, though he told no one about his experience in the woods. (His companion also was marked, but by two diagonal cuts near the base of his spine.)

Three doctors attended him—a kidney specialist, a dermatologist, and his own family physician. A kidney tumor was suspected, but the tests for it were all negative. An exploratory operation was proposed and rejected. A week later, the young man left the hospital and the marks gradually faded away.

Betty Hill recalled[7] that, during her abduction, a long needle was inserted in her navel. She was told that this painful operation was a "pregnancy test." Barney Hill, meanwhile, lay helplessly on another table as one of the UFO crewmembers pressed a cuplike device to his groin.[8] Judy Kendall[9] felt that she was being "catheterized." But these are just a few of the many abduction cases on record in which the medical operations involve the frequently painful use of a needle or other device in the groin or the lower abdominal region.

I asked a genito-urinary specialist his opinion as to what may be surmised from this recurrent pattern, and his answer was succinct.

"If someone is interested in taking sperm and ova samples, it can be done this way, by going in through the abdominal wall. You can get both kinds of samples this way. My guess is that the raised welts on the fellow from the camping trip indicate that a foreign object of some kind, like a hollow needle, made a channel under the skin that later became irritated and inflamed, and possibly infected. The straight lines and their convergence toward the groin would support this idea."

Like many other abductees, both male and female, Betty Andreasson recalled that a long, thin instrument of some kind was inserted in her navel. Under hypnosis, this dialogue ensued:[10]

Q: Did they tell you what the purpose was for the penetration of your navel? What was the examination for?
BA: Something about *creation*, but they said there were some parts missing.
Q: Can you explain to us what was meant?
BA: It was because I had a hysterectomy, I guess.

In a somewhat related account, a Wyoming man named Carl Higdon[11] was abducted on October 24, 1974, while on a hunting trip. At one point, he was told to stand behind a glassy screen of some kind for three or four minutes, where he was apparently scrutinized. Immediately afterwards, he was told that he was not what they needed, and a short time later he was returned to his parked camper.[12] Higdon, in fact, is sterile, having had a vasectomy.

These incidents support the unsettling theory that extraterrestrials need something from humans—possibly a certain kind of genetic structure—so presumably they must check through a large number of people to find what they want.

"Diversity. He kept talking about diversity, which he was very interested in . . . about how important biological diversity is." Virginia Horton's recollection of her captor's words further underlines the point, and leads to another startling possibility.

"It was as though they had a puzzle that they were working on and it was important to them . . . . 'We need a little bitty piece of you . . . (to) take a little, teeny piece of you home.' "

Philip Osborne's memory of his childhood cut:

"I see a sort of a representation of just being opened up very cleanly and something taken out and then just put right back together."

Virginia Horton's second episode, ten years after the first:

"It was as though they had finished a research project. . . . They wanted to share it with me because . . . this research used their visit with me . . . my contribution had been really helpful for them . . . . It was something more than abstract research."

A central difference for Virginia during this second abduction was the presence of ". . . someone . . . like a younger person, more like my age. . . . It had the feeling of being more like a contemporary, and it was a female feeling, like a friend. . . . There was sort of a female friend on the ship. . . . It seems like she was a relative that got to come along and meet me."

Virginia said the female's covering was lighter, more creamy-colored, and that she "felt like a younger person. Like a bouncier quality . . . more bubbly. . . . I didn't think she was really my age . . . she was still a schoolgirl or whatever."

Blonde, clean-complexioned, sixteen-year-old Virginia obviously identified with this creamy, bouncy near-contemporary who appeared fully-formed aboard the UFO ten years after a deep layer of cells was removed from Virginia's leg. The obvious and disturbing connection between these circumstances had gone through my mind as I sat observing the hypnotic session in Dr. Clamar's office on that May afternoon in 1979. As Virginia relived the experience, however, it seemed to me that she, herself, had not grasped its implication.

Can an advanced technology, whose home base is outside Earth, be experimenting, Luther Burbank-fashion, with various human genetic combinations? Our own present-day science has successfully mated sperm and ovum in a test tube, implanted the fertilized egg in a female body, and brought the fetus to term. Cloning is a much talked about area of current experimentation, moving slowly from lower animal forms towards man himself. There is no way to estimate what a radically advanced technology might be capable of, though Virginia's experience suggests an answer.

Having speculated thus far, I must now reiterate my discomfort with the act of theorizing itself, particularly in the context of the UFO phenomenon. I deliberately refrained from extensive speculation earlier on, in the hope that the reader will also concentrate, as I have, on data and not theory. The data, however, does suggest certain conditions that any theory must take into account, particularly, as I have said, the decades-long period of UFO activity and the large number of individuals who have been taken for the one or two hours these procedures seem to require. The theory of alien experimentation with human genetic structures satisfies these conditions.

In some UFO abductions—the Virginia Horton and Betty Hill cases are examples—extended telepathic "conversations" have taken place between the abductors and their captives. Occasional messages and even warnings, often pertaining to our misuse of the environment, have been reported. In a few other abduction cases, captives have somehow been shown cryptic, perhaps holographic images, again often bearing on ecological themes. (The Betty Andreasson affair, as detailed by Raymond Fowler in his book of the same title, offers a particularly vivid example of these images.) I have refrained from discussing in depth this highly ambiguous aspect of some abduction reports for a simple reason. Of the seven abduction cases which make up the core of this book, and which I have investigated myself, only Virginia Horton's abductions involve this kind of extended "conversation" and display of cryptic imagery. The telepathic communications involved in the five other abductions apparently consisted only of minimal physical orders, words intended to calm the abductee, and warnings not to remember the encounter.

Throughout my own study of the UFO abduction phenomenon, I have tried, in the recently hoary phrase, to separate the signal from the noise. When one examines all seven of these abductions, and then adds the many other cases to which I have alluded, one finds that every experience has its quasi-medical aspect—which often remains visible in the form of scar tissue. The inference is inescapable that these "medical" operations are part of the *signal*, while the occasional extended conversation may well be only part of the *noise*. Simple logic requires us to search for the clearest, most specific patterns we can find within the sometimes misleading mass of UFO reports. The physical operations are, indeed, central.

II

If the UFO phenomenon has been so active for such a long period of time, how, one might ask, has it managed to escape the attention of various world governments and intelligence networks? The answer is simple but not immediately obvious. There is reason to believe that the Air Force and other official agencies possess a great deal of photographic and even physical evidence attesting to the reality of extraterrestrial craft.[13] However, there is also reason to believe that there has been *no communication* between these spacecraft and any governmental authorities. If the UFO occupants are involved in the long-term monitoring of many human specimens, and/or experimenting with various genetic structures, there would be no reason for them to communicate directly with anyone, officially or unofficially. In other words, the government might not know anything more about the UFO phenomenon than you or I—they would simply have better pictures.

Consider what kind of announcement a president could make if this were the case. An apprehensive population is asked to turn on their television sets for an extremely important proclamation by the nation's commander-in-chief. This is what they hear:

"My fellow Americans: It is my duty to inform you of a nearly unbelievable fact. The joint chiefs of staff and the CIA now pos-

sess incontrovertible evidence that extraterrestrial space vehicles
are operating within our atmosphere. We have numerous films,
close-up photographs, and radar tracking reports of these objects.
They can outfly any aircraft in our defensive arsenal. Their means
of propulsion is at this moment completely unknown to modern
science. There has been no communication between these alien
craft and ourselves. We have no idea of their intentions, or whether or not they are peaceful. We will simply have to wait and see."
If that is all an American president could say to the people—and it
is my guess that this is *precisely* all he could say—it is fair to
assume that near-panic might ensue. Surely, most long-range
planning would suffer. Who would save carefully for his children's education? Who would invest in any area requiring long-
term economic stability? How would real estate and life insurance
and other similar economic sectors fare under such an uncertain
future? I can imagine that the policy of any government would be
to withhold information about the UFO phenomenon *until* there is
some official communication between extraterrestrials and ourselves.

III

When we consider the unfolding history of the UFO phenomenon in recent times an interesting sequence presents itself.[14] In
the 1896–97 wave of sightings alluded to in the introduction, the
craft often were described as moving slowly—though more familiar UFO maneuvers and great bursts of speed were also reported—seemingly to observe our towns and cities from a low altitude. It was, of course, an infinitely simpler world in those far-off
days, and there was little anyone could do to interfere with these
overflights. In almost all of the many contemporary newspaper
accounts about these craft, they were assumed to be nothing more
than the remarkable product of an Earthly inventor, whose identity and the location of whose factory excited great curiosity.

The second major UFO wave, as I pointed out, was during
World War II when hundreds of pilots on both sides found their
war planes accompanied by small disks, occasionally only a few
feet in diameter and often only a few inches away from wingtip or
cockpit. Relatively few overflights of cities were reported; the
UFOs' interest was apparently focused on our airborn achieve-
ments. Again, the reports show that most everyone assumed these

so-called "foo-fighters" were terrestrial secret weapons of some sort. (Immediately after World War II, in 1946, a number of rocketlike craft were sighted over the Scandinavian countries. So sure was the Air Force that these UFOs were Russian secret weapons that General James Doolittle was dispatched to Sweden to investigate.[15] So it is a simple matter of historical fact that UFO sightings preceded by years any idea that they may be extraterrestrial spaceships. The widely disseminated theory that UFOs have been "wished" into existence by people in need of quasi-magical space people is untenable. There are cases, however, in which people have, *after the fact*, seized on the UFO phenomenon and adapted it for their own cultist purposes, in the same way certain primitive people have erected effigies of airplanes and made them objects of worship. The overflights of real craft in each case provided both the pretext and the symbol. The theory of an extraterrestrial origin for the UFO phenomenon only began to be formulated around 1947 after observers like General Doolittle and others found absolutely no evidence that UFOs were Russian, American, or some other nation's experimental hardware.)

The sequence of events I am theorizing follows a logical course to the present interest by UFO occupants in genetic experimentation and observation. Originally, at the end of the nineteenth century, our cities and towns were seemingly the objects of extraterrestrial surveillance. Infrequent UFO sightings continued to be made until the Forties, when earthly airborne technology apparently became the target of avid UFO curiosity. By 1947, extensive UFO flights over the United States and Europe were in progress, with particular attention being paid to military and atomic installations.[16] By 1950, as we have seen, the abduction phenomenon has begun. Whether or not this sequence of events will stand up to scrutiny as a systematic escalation of UFO curiosity is uncertain; the iceberg of unreported UFO cases may have a different shape than its documented tip so far indicates.

IV

One of the many perplexing facets of the UFO abduction phenomenon is what seems to be an externally induced amnesia, forced, perhaps by post-hypnotic suggestion, upon the abductees. Several interrelated questions present themselves. How is the process accomplished? Why is it done, especially if the UFO occupants know it can in many cases be broached by our own terrestrial hypnotic techniques? And why have there been cases where it was apparently not used at all?

A speculative answer to the last question also bears on the first. One major exception to the imposition of amnesia occurred in the October 11, 1973, abduction of Charles Hickson and Calvin Parker in Pascagoula, Mississippi.[17] The men were fishing when a bluish UFO landed near them and three robotlike figures emerged, moving towards them. At this moment, Parker fainted. Hickson (and possibly Parker) was floated into the UFO; he remembers being examined. When they were returned to the riverbank, Parker regained consciousness and both men immediately went to the police to report their encounter. Hickson remembered nearly everything and Parker recalled everything that happened before he fainted. Apparently, little or no amnesia had been induced. The reason, it seems to me, has to do with Parker's actually fainting; unconscious, he could not be hypnotized by his captors, and so long as he remained that way, no post-hypnotic suggestions could be implanted. And since Parker could remember the beginning of the abduction, there might have been no reason to block the recall of just one witness; Hickson's memory, therefore, was left relatively unimpaired. The Pascagoula affair is a possible example, it would seem, of a semibotched abduction.

If the amnesia that follows an abduction has been induced when the individual is in a trance very like our own hypnosis, we should expect a wide variation in its effectiveness and longevity. The reader by now should have a strong sense of this range in the ease or difficulty various abductees have had in piercing their own amnesia, but an additional case will help demonstrate the problem.

A woman friend of mine, whom I shall call Mary, is a painter with the kind of deep-seated and uneasy interest in the UFO phenomenon that often indicates a buried UFO experience. Mary is happily married, successful, and the mother of three children. In the summer of 1979, in my Wellfleet studio, I told a group of friends a little about the Virginia Horton and Philip Osborne cases. Mary was there, and her eyes were wide. A week later, she called me and said she wanted to drop in for a chat. She arrived looking nervous and uncertain. She said that as I had outlined the two cases and described the unusual wounds and the lack of memory about their causes, a memory of her own came vividly back to her. She had been a little girl, playing in a neighbor's garden in Chapel Hill, North Carolina.

"I don't know if there's anything to this," she said, using a phrase I have heard many times, "but I had an experience a lot like Virginia Horton's." Mary had also been struck by a further coincidence; like Virginia and Philip she, too, was born in 1943, and the incident, again like theirs, happened in the summer of 1950.

It was one of the strongest memories of her early childhood. As she was playing outside, she glimpsed a hummingbird, "the most beautiful thing I had ever seen. It was absolutely gorgeous. I followed it around the garden as it went from flower to flower. I remember everything as being so vivid, the smells, the sunshine, the tall hollyhocks, and that beautiful hummingbird."

Deciding to try to capture the hummingbird, she went into the house to get a glass jar to catch it with. She remembers later running back into the house holding the jar with her prize inside, and proudly raising it up for her friends to see—but the jar was empty. And, on top of this disappointment, she was scolded for something she cannot remember—perhaps for having been gone too long—and it was pointed out to her that her leg was bleeding.

She felt no pain whatsoever, and assumed the blood had gotten on her leg from someone else. The shock when she found out that she had not, after all, caught the hummingbird was more profound to her than the sight of blood on her leg. She felt as though she had been somehow tricked; the hummingbird *had* to have been in the jar. She was angry and hurt, and the experience remains vivid in both its beauty and its disappointment across the intervening thirty years.

I asked if the cut on her leg had left a scar, and she said that it had not. Mary has striking red hair and the myriad summer freckles that often go with it. And, at this point in August, she also had a handsome suntan.

"Would you mind," I inquired, "if I looked at the backs of your legs?" I turned on the overhead studio lights and knelt down; on the back of her left calf was a thin, straight, horizontal scar close to the location of Virginia's vertical scar. Mary's freckles and suntan made the scar quite faint, so I called my wife, who was once a registered nurse, to examine the mark. "Yes," said April, "it's a straight, hairline scar all right." Mary looked at me, her eyes wider and rounder than I had ever seen them. "I never knew I had that scar," she said, "and you knew just where to look."

This story is in a kind of investigative limbo. Mary has had six hypnotic sessions with Dr. Clamar, and through them all, she vividly remembers everything *except* what happened between her chasing the hummingbird and her arrival in the house with an empty jar and a bloody, painless incision on the back of her calf. She experiences the block as a wall that she can neither see through nor outflank. But there is a positive significance to this absence of recall. Thirty years ago, *something* cut her leg neatly and deeply across a relatively inaccessible place, the back of her calf; the still visible scar and her memory make this virtually certain. If the wound had a prosaic cause, it would most likely have emerged by now.

Mary has had several disturbing dreams which seem to link her experience even more closely to Virginia Horton's. In late September of 1980, she woke up from a frightening near-nightmare which began benignly enough. She was looking at "a decorative thing, the way you'd see a map on a wall . . . and I don't know where it was, but it seemed to go through transitions. First, it was essentially a piece of decoration to me, and when I looked more closely, I realized it was a map that related to the heavens . . . and then it seemed to be almost a window, and that I was actually looking out into space. . . .

"Also, there was someone with me who was explaining this to me, but this person was sort of like a voice over my right shoulder, and not anyone that I *saw* in my dream. The thing was flat at first, like a chart, and then it was as if I was looking past it into the thing that it represented, or it sort of melted away and I could really see what he was talking about.

"And the other image was looking down on a group of figures approaching me. This seemed to follow the thing with the chart, but I think probably it should have come before. The figures approaching me had a weird light on them . . . there was something artificial about them, and the light shining on them was not a light I'd ever seen before. The voice was telling me that they weren't regular people, that there was something very different about them, and that's when I got frightened and woke up. I know there was more to the dream, but I think I blocked it because I was quite frightened when I woke up."

I asked Mary about the chart. "It started like a colored drawing. It had, like, a black background with the stars and planets in reddish tones. There were white tones and green colors, too."

The disembodied voice was so like Virginia's "patient explainer," who spoke to her telepathically, that I asked Mary about the actual sound of the voice in her dream, and she gave the answer I expected: "I don't remember hearing it as an actual sound." I inquired about its effect.

"Explanatory. Like a teacher, or a lecturer. The voice seemed like it was explaining things to me. Sometimes I didn't like what it was explaining, but it didn't seem malign. The voice was not at all threatening."

In the specific details of the star map and the particular way she perceived the neutral, explaining, but soundless voice, Mary's dream parallels both Betty Hill's and Virginia Horton's experiences. Dr. Clamar has hypothesized that the mind generally releases only those traumatic memories it can safely handle, and at a pace which also is manageable. It seems to me that fissures are appearing in the wall of Mary's amnesia, and that soon she—and we—will know more about how she received her scar, and what else occurred on that summer day in 1950. I suspect that Mary's beautiful hummingbird eventually will undergo the same transformation as Virginia's soulful deer.

If, as I have suggested, abductees have their memories blocked through a process not unlike our own method of post-hypnotic suggestion,[18] and their memories demonstrably can be "unblocked" by hypnosis, why do the UFO occupants bother to do it in the first place? And especially why if they know the authorities have strong—perhaps absolute, physical—evidence that extraterrestrials are operating in our atmosphere?

Two related answers to these questions should be considered. First of all, there is the possibility that the abduction experience is blocked from conscious memory for the good of the abductee. Virginia Horton said that she felt the amnesia "was for our protection just in general. I probably would have told my friends in school and they probably would have given me a hard time." A rather immense understatement! One has only to read the account of Hickson's and Parker's turmoil after their Pascagoula abduction to realize the advantages offered by not knowing, immediately afterwards, what has just transpired. In fact, in the years after their abduction, these two men have had unusually difficult experiences in their personal lives dealing with the mind-wrenching thing that happened to them. Knowing too much, too vividly, and too soon may actually strain to the breaking point the fabric of one's previously accepted world view.

Memory blocks may also have to do with the abductee's role as a "human specimen" unwittingly being studied over a period of years. If people are being picked up as children, implanted with monitoring devices, and abducted a second time after puberty, at the very least the first abduction would have to be concealed. If the study is truly long range, the subjects would have to be kept in the dark about their role for many years, and a strongly effective block would have to be imposed.

The theory that amnesia is used as a way simply to conceal the presence of UFOs from government investigators is not persuasive, it seems to me, when one considers the frank and open "showing off" UFOs have indulged in over the decades. But above everything, finally, there lurks the disturbing possibility that these enforced memory blocks may be extremely effective; the few hundred cases in which the amnesia has been pierced may ultimately represent only a tiny percentage of the actual number of abductees. The epidemic, I believe, may be almost entirely invisible.

10

WHAT CAN BE DONE?

I

Our collective human ego is about to suffer the same profound dislocation it experienced centuries ago when Copernicus established that we were no longer the center of the universe. Having got used to the idea that the Earth is merely one of several planets circling the same star, we will soon have to adjust to the idea that we may not even be the most advanced intelligence operating within our own atmosphere. And we must now take certain steps to minimize the inevitable damage to our collective ego that will occur when the evidence of extraterrestrial visitation becomes overwhelming.

First, I believe, we must try to make the invisible epidemic visible; we must try to take the measure of the UFO abduction phenomenon. How many people have actually been "used," and for what purposes?

A recent experience of mine provides a textbook example of how we must be alert for clues in attempting to learn more about the extent of UFO abductions. A casual conversation at a Whitney Museum opening led to my being told—second-hand—about a recent UFO sighting. The witness was a microbiologist at a New York City hospital, and his April 2, 1980, sighting was a rather routine nighttime observation of an oval object with lights. The thing that caught my attention was my informant's feeling that the witness, a close personal friend, had been unusually disturbed by the event. The disparity between a powerful, emotional reaction

231

and its relatively negligible cause—a distant night sighting—is a
sign that the case should be looked into; a buried traumatic episode can easily be the hidden fuel for such a reaction.

At the time I heard of this incident, I was very near the end of
my work on this book, so I was reluctant to investigate further. But
since my thoughts were focused on the issue of just how widespread the abduction phenomenon might be, I decided after all to
pursue the matter. I called the scientist, whom I shall refer to as
Dr. Geis and asked him about his sighting. Apparently, the UFO
had never been closer than perhaps five or six hundred feet, and
circumspect questioning led me to believe that there was no time
lapse involved. He told me that, when he stopped his car to look
up, and saw that the UFO had also stopped, he became extremely
frightened. So frightened, he said, that he was afraid he was going
to die there.

I asked about his subsequent memories and feelings.

"I've dreamed about this thing coming over my house and
trying to get me, or engulfing my house. The first three weeks, I
was even getting up at two or three in the morning and looking out
the window, making sure that everything was all right. And, when
I walked the dog, I had the strangest feeling that I should seek
cover . . . that I don't want to be seen from the air."

So great was the sense of fear he transmitted to me that, a few
days later, I interviewed two of his closest associates to find out if
he was a particularly timorous, nervous man. Separately, they assured me that he was firmly self-reliant and controlled, a man of
greater than normal fortitude. It was the unusually intense fear
that he radiated about this one incident which had been so striking
to both men in the first place. I phoned Dr. Geis's wife, and her
casual attitude toward the UFO sighting confirmed my feeling that
there had been nothing more to the April incident than they consciously remembered. Therefore, I turned to the possibility that
Dr. Geis had had an earlier encounter, and that this long-buried
trauma had been reactivated by his recent sighting.

"Have you ever had any other experience like this?" I asked,
and his answer was immediate. "Yes, when I was a kid. It probably doesn't mean much, though."

He was a teenager then, staying with relatives in a cabin near
Wurtsboro, New York. While walking alone one night, heading
towards Yankee Lake to view the spectacular night sky, he saw "a
glowing thing that seemed to hover in the forest. That's all I

remember. I felt that something would come over the trees . . . and grab me. I remembered that feeling when I saw that thing last April."

It was significant that he had immediately connected the two incidents. I pressed him for more details. "I couldn't make out much more than that it looked large, it looked low, and it was aglow when it went into the bushes. It was like you're expecting something to come out and surprise you. . . . That's the feeling I had when I saw this thing. . . . What it was, I don't know, but it stuck in my mind at that point. It was sort of light green, a soft green with maybe a little yellow in it.

"I had no time to study it. I don't know if it was there a long time or not. It went into the trees beyond my ability to see it, and I was waiting. I had the feeling that something was going to grab me . . . that's why it stayed with me and I had nightmares about that for quite some time." His phrase "and I was waiting" is a curious one, but then every detail he related was suggestive of the abduction scenario. He had no specific recollections of any time problems, but the incident had happened years before, when he had been only about sixteen years old.

I phrased my next question with a sense of foreboding. I asked what year he was born.

"Nineteen-forty-three," he answered. "What has that got to do with it?"

I said something about "various patterns," and then came out with it: "You don't remember any kind of unusual childhood injury or accident involving, say, a laceration or an unexplained time problem or . . ." His answer interrupted the question.

"There is one thing that's always been a mystery. My mother even gave me a beating because I said I didn't know how I did it. It is a cut on my knee and I don't know how I did it. I was playing in the back yard and I don't remember gashing it, but I had a tremendous cut on my knee, and I have the scar to this day. The flesh was open to a fairly deep level. My family doctor said to me, 'My God, you must have been playing hard. What did you tear yourself up on, metal?' 'No, I was just jumping,' I said. That was the only thing I could think of that might have caused it. I realized after I jumped that there was a little bit of blood."

I asked how old he was when this happened.

"Around seven, I'd say, because I was still in Brooklyn."

When I inquired about the surroundings, he said that there

was open land near his house, with a small woods nearby. "The scar," he said, "is peculiar. It's directly in the center of the knee, right *above* the patella, the knee-cap. That's what's so peculiar." He told me that he has "lots of scars, but I remember how I got every one. Except this one, and this is the one that's always puzzled me. You're welcome to see my scar. You're the first person who's ever wanted to see it! But it's in a peculiar spot. It's hard to imagine how I got it."

Dr. Geis's final recollection was particularly interesting:

"There was an old table in the back yard and I was jumping from that, and it was almost as if the wound just burst open. I don't actually remember it bursting open, but that's what crossed my mind at the time.

"I told the doctor that's what happened: 'I didn't cut myself on anything; it just burst open. I never came in contact with metal.' Ordinarily, I would have cried, but there was no pain. None. I never felt anything."

I thought immediately of Virginia Horton's and Philip Osborne's descriptions of their deep, yet painless wounds. Philip recalled that he was cut open "very cleanly, and something taken out, and then just put right back together." He does not remember bleeding as profusely as one might expect, judging by the depth of his wound. Virginia felt that her incision "just closes up and stops bleeding." Geis, however, was *jumping* off a table, flexing his legs perhaps minutes after his incision had "just been closed up." One can surmise that the UFO experimenters in 1950 had a healing technology that was not quite adequate for a hyperactive seven-year-old boy from Brooklyn!

Dr. Geis is the *fourth* person I know who was born in 1943 and who suffered a mysterious wound, most likely in the summer of 1950, when he or she would have been about seven years old. The parents of each have been consulted; they remember the *fact* of their child's accident, but not its cause. Dr. Geis's father vividly remembers carrying his son to the doctor's office since the cut was so deep. Interestingly, Dr. Geis's wound—the one that "burst open"—was the only one of the four requiring stitches.

I met Dr. Geis in late September at his office in a New York hospital. He is a strong, vigorous, no-nonsense kind of man, holding a Ph.D. degree and an important research position. I took the chair he offered and sat amidst the paraphernalia of his scientific projects. He stood up and delivered what was almost a harangue

on the subject of why UFOs *cannot* be extraterrestrial in origin—it
is *impossible* for spacecraft with living beings to cross such vast
reaches of space, they would *never* look like us in any way, and so
on. What he saw in New Jersey *must* have been some kind of
American or Russian experimental craft. I have never seen a witness so obsessively bent on discounting the UFO phenomenon,
nor have I ever seen a man so frightened of what he is sure can't
possibly exist.

I proposed a scientific experiment. It would involve his
agreeing to undergo hypnosis on the origin of his scar and the
sighting he made as a teenager. Prior to this, I would have written
down what I thought would emerge from the process. My accounts
would be sealed and handed to his research associates, to be
opened after his third hypnotic session. If I could effectively describe what these two experiences of his entailed, there would be
definite evidentiary benefits.

He instantly declined my offer. He could never be hypnotized, he told me, because he hates ever to relinquish control. In
fact, I could see that my proposition had deeply unnerved him.

"What if I found out something so upsetting that I might die?
What if it caused a heart attack?"

His fear is a powerful adversary. During lunch, as he and his
friends and I discussed the issue of hypnosis, the conversation
veered to the subject of science fiction. I asked Dr. Geis his reaction to some of the recent sci-fi films.

"I'm probably the only person in New Jersey who still hasn't
seen *Star Wars*," he answered. "In fact, the television commer-
cials for that new one, the sequel, are disturbing to me. I can't
watch them." He *had* seen the movie *Close Encounters of the
Third Kind* and it, too, was upsetting. (This might be the place to
reassure the reader about one detail: Steven, Philip Osborne, Virginia, Mac McMahon, and almost all of the abductees we have
been examining had *not* seen that movie prior to the recall of their
abduction experiences. Actually, the film, in its junk-jewelry vision of the UFOs themselves, its noisy, chaotic *Exorcist*-type epi-
sodes, and smiling, babylike humanoids provides a kind of control
on witness accounts. Almost nothing within these pages resembles
in any way the "Hollywood version" of the UFO phenomenon.
The contrast is actually startling.)

Dr. Geis is steadfast in his refusal to undergo any hypnotic
exploration of his experiences, though I remain hopeful that some-

day he will change his mind. A psychotherapist friend of mine made an interesting remark after I told her of the many cases like Dr. Geis's in which the witness has a deep-seated fear stemming from a UFO encounter, *and* an equally intense fear of undergoing hypnosis to explore this experience:

"Think of all the energy a person in a situation like that wastes, just trying to keep something unknown and disturbing out of his thoughts. It would be so much better to explore the experience and undergo whatever temporary pain there might be, just to not have to waste all that energy keeping the memory buried."

This witness-reluctance to explore a suspected abduction is undoubtedly abetted by the kind of veiled threat against "remembering" that is apparently implanted in the minds of so many abductees. Steven Kilburn, under hypnosis, said that he was not to remember anything, that it was serious, that he might die. He knew, of course, that the threat was not literally true, but it unnerved him nevertheless. I thought of this when Dr. Geis said, "What if I found out something so upsetting that I might die? What if it caused a heart attack?" His remark suggested to me a buried threat, half-remembered and rankling. Hundreds of abductees have been hypnotized and no one yet seems to have been the victim of a reprisal. Ventilation of the experience is, I believe, therapeutically helpful for almost everyone. Fear of the unknown is the greatest fear of all.

II

By now, the reader is familiar with many clues, both obvious and subtle, which indicate the possibility of a buried abduction experience. If someone should strongly suspect such an encounter, the final page of the book provides information on how to go about reporting it. We will try to investigate as fully as we can.

The efforts of the many individuals and organizations throughout the world to investigate and record the UFO phenomenon in all its complexity are, despite the best of intentions, inadequate. What is needed now is an official governmental effort, an agency whose purpose would be fourfold. (I make these recommendations despite the present national economic and political climate, which makes their implementation highly improbable.

Nevertheless, the urgency I feel about these measures requires me to list them here.)

First, the government has an obligation to prepare the public for the day when the extraterrestrial presence is obvious to everyone. The potential for panic and economic disruption must be recognized and effectively reduced by careful advance planning.

Second, an open and official UFO investigative arm should be established, preferably internationally through the United Nations. That way, everyone would know where to file a UFO report, and also would know that the world's governments recognize the UFO phenomenon as a serious reality. Ridicule and the fear of ridicule must be eliminated once and for all.

Third, a major central repository of UFO material must be created for use by the world's scientists, if we are ever to understand the mystery of UFO intentions. The efforts of Dr. Allen Hynek, Dr. David Saunders, David Webb, and Ted Bloecher to establish data banks in various categories of UFO information can serve as the nucleus for an international undertaking.[1]

Fourth, and most difficult to imagine, there must be some kind of effort made to communicate with the UFO occupants. I have no more of an idea of how that can be managed than the next man, yet I believe it should be attempted. Intentions *must* be gauged.

The realities are clear. Very likely a majority of the world's scientists believe that the existence of extraterrestrial life is probable. And if that is true, some of this extraterrestrial life must be more advanced than we, and thus capable of technological feats far beyond ours. We, ourselves, have proved the feasibility of space travel, and so eventual contact of some kind appears inevitable. That inevitable day, however, has been placed by most of us in a vague and distant future. For many, it is literally unthinkable. But the comfort of that distance, I am afraid, is the comfort of the ostrich's sand. Our desert oasis is not as isolated as we wish to think.

For me, the conclusion is inescapable: They are already here. Though I do not *want* to believe this, and feel decidedly unnerved by it, I believe it is true; extraterrestrials have been observing us in our innocence for many years, and we have *no idea* of their intentions.

I began this book, not with the idea of answering questions, but with the simpler goal of raising them. The evidence I have presented establishes the existence of a clear, hard-edged, and disturbing phenomenon, one which is far more pervasive than any of us may imagine. In these last few pages, I have tried to theorize as carefully as possible what it all may mean, but my theories remain only educated guesses. It is the reality of the abduction phenomenon itself which the reader must confront, not one man's speculation about its meaning.

In 1964, when my curiosity was first piqued by the dull aluminum-colored disk I saw in the clouds above Cape Cod, I could never have guessed where it would lead. Since that time, I have become enmeshed in the lives of many witnesses whose encounters were, unlike mine, truly unnerving. I have spent scores of hours watching in helpless silence as these men and women relived through hypnosis the often harrowing abduction experiences of earlier times. Their resistance and calm and fear and fortitude have at times been almost physically palpable, and I have been moved, sometimes, to tears. For each of these people, at a certain moment in their lives, something happened, something almost unimaginable for the rest of us.

I have tried to relate these encounters, these events, as directly, and with as little adornment as possible because I want the reader to experience them as I did. I have no solutions to the open-ended problems they raise, and least of all to the profound issue of their human toll. I do not believe the UFO phenomenon is malign or evilly intentioned. I fear, instead, that it is merely indifferent, though I fervently hope to be proven wrong.

NOTES ON THE HYPNOSIS OF

UFO WITNESSES

A New York Times article on Saturday, November 3, 1979, describes a situation which closely parallels the use of hypnosis in recovering information in traumatic UFO abduction cases. It begins:

SYRACUSE, November 2: A jury in a rape trial here in Onondaga County Court found the defendant guilty last night, in part on the basis of testimony drawn from the witness through hypno-sis. . . .

The victim, married and twenty-three years old, was said to be so traumatized by the assault, in the spring of 1978, that for three months she could recall neither the circumstances of the rape nor the identity of her attacker.

In a hypnotic state, however, she identified the assailant as Kirk Hughes, twenty-one, her neighbor and former babysitter.

Further on in the article, the Times quotes William Fitzpa-trick, the assistant district attorney who prosecuted the case, as saying that hypnosis was gaining acceptance as a forensic tool.

"I can't think of a better example than this case," he said. "She was with him long enough to identify him, but was unable to do so because of the horror of it."

The New York Times' science page of October 14, 1980, car-ried an article by Jane E. Brody in which she discussed hypnosis as a weapon against crime. Though she warned about areas of possi-ble abuse, she cited the successes of hypnosis in helping to solve some well-known criminal cases:

The rescue of twenty-six schoolchildren kidnapped at gun-point from a school bus in Chowchilla, California, in 1976 was facilitated by hypnosis of the bus driver, who then recalled enough of a license plate number to enable police to find the get-away van.

Last summer, a ballerina who had seen a man with a young cellist at the Metropolitan Opera House shortly before the cellist's brutal murder was able, under hypnosis, to describe the man well enough so that a police sketch led to the arrest of a suspect.

In the same article, Brody cited an interesting statistic:

In the Los Angeles Police Department, eleven police officers have used the technique in about six hundred cases, with ninety percent of the hypnotic investigations yielding information that led to the arrest of a suspect. . . .

Hypnosis, then, is accepted as a valid tool by both courts and

police departments. Properly used, the technique can be an avenue to truth, particularly so when traumatic events have buried
specific details beyond immediate recall.

The following is an account by psychotherapist Dr. Aphrodite
Clamar of her experience in using hypnosis in the investigation of
the UFO abduction cases discussed in this book.

AFTERWORD

By Aphrodite Clamar, Ph.D.

It was neither by design nor out of any interest in the subject
of UFOs that I became involved with Budd Hopkins's witnesses
and with the effort to ascertain what might lie behind their incom-
plete recollection. A colleague, Dr. Robert Naiman, knowing that I
use hypnosis with some of my patients, asked me if I would be
willing to hypnotize a woman UFO witness who had requested a
woman practitioner. I agreed.

I had never read anything on UFO abductions, and I never
had had a patient who reported such an experience—nor, indeed,
had I even given the subject anything more than the most fleeting
thought. It was only some time later, after I had become involved
with the UFO world, that I realized that the amount of available
information on the use of hypnosis with UFO witnesses was limited at best. Having little if anything to go on in terms of the experience of others, I was forced to develop my own procedures. Thus
far, Budd Hopkins has brought me more than a dozen men and
women from all parts of the country, five of whom are the subjects
of this book. Some of them told under hypnosis of events they had
never previously reported. For others, the hypnotic state led to the
recounting of additional details of reports made earlier. For all of
them, the experience under hypnosis had positive results, provid-
ing a sense of release and relief for people who—as they told it—
had undergone frightening experiences that both mystified and
disturbed them. As in psychotherapy generally, the act of repeating the story robbed it of some of its fearful aspects. Here, under
hypnosis, experiences—real or imagined—buried in the unconscious were brought to the surface and released. The mystery of
the time lapse—the missing hours when the abduction was alleged

to have taken place—was solved for some. And the subjects were helped to be at peace with themselves, and with the experiences they had reported.

I began by employing techniques that I had used with the patients in my practice as a clinical psychologist and psychotherapist, making whatever changes I found useful as I developed greater experience with UFO witnesses. On the assumption that reliving the UFO abduction (if this was indeed what it was) might prove to be traumatic, I sought to make the experience of hypnosis as easy—even comfortable—as possible, while at the same time giving the subjects a sense of control over what was happening to them.

With these considerations in mind, I started each opening ninety-minute session with an information-gathering interview, asking for a short life history and other relevant background material. Then I offered an opportunity to experience hypnosis for its own sake, unrelated to the UFO encounter. This trial run, I suggested, would acquaint the subject with hypnosis, so that in future sessions the process of being hypnotized—and what it felt like to be under hypnosis—would be familiar rather than strange. In this way, the subjects would be free to concentrate their energies on the experiences which they were reliving.

I also wanted to dispel the notion that hypnosis was a "knocked-out," unconscious experience for those who undergo it. I emphasized that they would still be aware of things going on around them, that they would be able not only to hear my voice, but also to talk with me, to open their eyes if need be, move around and even write—all while still remaining under hypnosis. For our purpose, I explained, hypnosis would be a useful tool—though not necessarily a precise one—that would enable us to explore, relive, and possibly understand the mysterious events they had reported earlier. Finally, I said, there was no way of predicting in advance what, if anything, would emerge.

I then asked the subject to lie down on a deep and comfortable brown leather couch in the darkened, cozy, book-lined room that is my office. I took my place on a high-backed wooden chair at the head of the couch. When the subject was comfortable and at ease, I began what I came to think of as the "build-your-own-cloud" exercise, using standard progressive relaxation and deepening techniques to induce hypnosis. In the hypnotic state, the subjects were asked to visualize a fluffy, inviting cloud of any shape, design, or color they wished, sturdy enough to support their weight and equipped with whatever objects or devices they might need when the cloud became the vehicle to return to the past experiences we would explore together. When this image was in focus, they were asked to imagine themselves stepping into the cloud, exploring it, making sure that it was satisfactory, then letting themselves lie back, relax and go on a short ride.

Thus the cloud becomes a private environment, one that fits the subjects' specific needs, a friendly object they can control and direct, a personal image of unequaled possibilities.

Other than David Oldham, none of the people whose case histories appear in this book were ever hypnotized before. All accepted the cloud image except one—Steven Kilburn, who preferred a sturdy house of his own design, three-quarters of which was underground, the rest hidden from view by thick trees. His fear of reliving his UFO experience was strong enough to require a well-fortified environment for his return trip.

After the first get-acquainted session, the subjects returned to my office for two or sometimes three follow-up sessions, each lasting one-and-one-half to two hours. Like most persons under hypnosis, these subjects had a distorted sense of time. Speech was slow and often labored as they groped to recall the past. There were long silences. At the end of a ninety-minute session, they emerged from hypnosis astounded to find that so much time had gone by. "It felt like twenty minutes" was a standard reaction.

Two of the five subjects whose UFO encounters are described in this book—and at least half of the others I have put under hypnosis—complained of being cold when they were reliving their experiences; a blanket is now kept ready when UFO witnesses come to my office. About half of them also asked me to turn off all the lights in an already dimly lit room. Aside from these two unusual requests, I cannot say that these subjects exhibited any different responses from patients I have put under hypnosis in my regular therapeutic practice. Their emotional needs appeared to be diverse, like those of other client populations I have known.

I did not find any drug users among the subjects whom Budd Hopkins brought, nor any alcoholism, nor any strange habits or exotic perversions. Persons who claim to have had UFO experiences, I now know, come in all sizes, shapes, ages, and sexes. Some are close to their families; others are not. They are handsome or ordinary-looking, neat or sloppy. Most are satisfied with their choice of careers and relatively successful. The five whose experiences are reported in this book are all college graduates, but it is not necessary to have a bachelor's degree in order to report a UFO experience. The people I have seen who claim to have had a strange encounter of whatever kind are run-of-the-mill people, neither psycho nor psychic, people like you and me. I could find no common thread that ties them together—other than their UFO experience—and no common pathology; indeed, no discernible pathology at all.

Their fantasies are different from those of "ordinary" people—but only if you assume that the experiences they report are fantasies. The common variety of fantasy most of us indulge in at one time or another creates a special and pleasurable situation in which we succeed—like the five-foot-six-inch accountant who fantasizes himself leading the Boston Celtics to the National Basketball Association championship. But the UFO experience is not at all pleasurable; it is frightening, mysterious, deeply disturbing.

If there is anything that links these people to one another, it is that all of them are deeply perplexed and troubled by their experience. Most often they are troubled by the time lapse or amnesia they have experienced, and by the question: "Why me?" And because we live in a society which—like most societies—does not hold the "different" person in high esteem, the UFO witnesses I have seen are apt to feel marked or stigmatized in some way—ashamed and embarrassed by what they believe happened to them. They are hesitant about sharing it with others; boasting about it is usually furthest from their mind. Perhaps this accounts for the lack of conscious memory of the details of the experiences they report. They feel something "strange" or "weird" has occurred, but until they go under hypnosis, their memory fails them—in effect, protecting them from painful recollections until they grow strong enough to handle or integrate them.

The sense that the UFO experience is a taboo experience, to be recalled or shared only reluctantly, soon becomes apparent to the hypnotherapist who works with these subjects. One reason for this reluctance may be that the memory of the UFO abduction has been repressed because of its traumatic nature. The mind has a way of protecting itself by repressing painful or frightening experiences. In extreme cases of this kind, we call the repression amnesia. In the case of the five UFO abductees described in this book, the amnesia was temporary. Under hypnosis, facts and events they had not previously told about came to the fore. In my judgment, if they were to undergo additional hypnotic sessions, additional details would rise to the surface.

The question persists: is the UFO experience genuine, or are those who claim to have been abducted the victims of hysteria—or their own delusions? After spending more than fifty hours with a dozen subjects under hypnosis, I still cannot answer the question. "Aliens" from outer space are the stuff of science fiction. The photographs and other physical evidence that would establish these experiences as something more than fantasy remain disturbingly elusive. And yet, and yet . . . the events recounted by a variety of people from scattered places are strikingly similar, suggesting that there might be more to the whole business than mere coincidence. In different years, different people from different parts of the country all report nearly identical experiences. All of these people seem quite ordinary in the psychological sense—although they have not been subjected to the kind of psychological testing that might provide a deeper understanding of their personalities. Yet, they report details of the experience that are startling in their similarity. The content of these accounts is markedly different from most of the fantasies reported in psychological literature. Far from the pleasurable, whimsical, wish-fulfilling fantasies most of us have, these bring fear and terror.

Are these, then, hallucinations? Are they false perceptions which have "a compulsive sense of the reality of objects, although relevant and adequate stimuli for such perceiving are lacking?" English and English, in their *Comprehensive Dictionary of Psychological and Psychoanalytic Terms*, describe hallucinations as "abnormal phenomena, though occasionally experienced by normal persons."

The five subjects whose reported experiences are recounted in this book may be described as "normal." That would not rule out hallucination. It is the curious similarity of their experiences that gives pause. But the answer to the question has not yet been devised, the key to unlock the secret not yet found. Budd Hopkins hoped that by inducing hypnosis among the five UFO abductees, I might be able to find a final answer. But what was revealed under hypnosis only deepened the mystery: new details were added, new experiences described, new questions raised.

In the two years that I worked with the subjects whom Budd

Hopkins brought to me, I used a variety of hypnotic techniques to help them "return" to the incident, relive their reported experience and try to make sense of it. I can not say whether the experience was "real" or not; that is, I do not know—nor could hypnosis claim to establish—whether the UFO experience actually "happened." I am persuaded, however, that all of the subjects do, in fact, believe that something strange and unknown did occur. It happened for them; it happened to them. Who of us is to say that it did not? Since it is difficult to provide a consistent explanation for these similar accounts, a real problem remains—a problem requiring further exploration.

HOW TO REPORT
A SUSPECTED UFO EXPERIENCE

If you believe you have seen a UFO relatively closely and clearly, you can report it to your local police department, asking them to relay your account to the Center for UFO Studies via their twenty-four-hour hotline. All police departments have this private telephone number on file, and are requested to use it to relay such reports.

If you believe you may have had the kind of experience dealt with in this book, you may wish to write your recollections in detail to:

Budd Hopkins c/o Richard Marek Publishers, Inc. 200 Madison Avenue New York, New York 10016.

As time permits, an investigator will be in touch with you. All letters will be kept strictly confidential.

Notes

Introduction

1. The United States Air Force lists twelve thousand sighting reports in its Project Bluebook files, and Dr. David Saunders of the Center for UFO Studies has some sixty thousand reports in his data bank. For a thorough historical account of the many civilian and governmental studies of the phenomenon, see Dr. David Jacobs, *The UFO Controversy in America* (Indiana University Press, 1975; New York: New American Library, 1976).
2. Dr. J. Allen Hynek, *The Hynek UFO Report* (New York: Dell, 1977), pp. 223–229.
3. Robert Emenegger, *UFOs Past, Present and Future* (New York: Ballantine Books, 1974), p. 65.
4. The Bloecher-Webb *Catalogue of Humanoid Reports—HUMCAT*—will be published when completed.
5. Jacobs, p. 40.
6. Jacobs, pp. 30, 31.
7. Ted Bloecher, *Report on the UFO Wave of 1947* (Washington, D.C.: published by the author, 1967. Available from the Center for UFO Studies, 1609 Sherman Avenue, Evanston, Illinois, 60201.) Bloecher quotes one witness, Mr. Kjell Quale, as having been "one of the very few UFO witnesses in the 1947 wave—one of two, to be exact—who openly expressed the opinion that the objects seen could have been 'spaceships.'" (p. II-5).

8. See in particular the Goodland, Kansas, abduction as reported in *International UFO Reporter*, Vol. 2, no. 10, published by the Center for UFO Studies.

9. When lecturing on the subject of UFOs, Dr. Hynek frequently asks members of his audience to raise their hands if they believe they have ever seen a UFO. He then asks how many *reported* their sightings, and invariably about eight out of ten hands go down. My own inquiries suggest that the percentage of reported sightings is even less, since those attending a lecture on UFOs are more highly motivated than the average witness, and thus are more likely to have filed reports.

10. This case is still under investigation by Ted Bloecher and myself. Three of the seven witnesses have undergone hypnosis, but no details can be presented here lest we jeopardize the validity of future hypnotic explorations. See page 53 for further discussion of this case.

11. A "probable" abduction is a sighting in which several clues suggest the likelihood of an abduction. These include the witnesses' awareness of a time lapse, the presence of physical marks or wounds after such a hiatus, dreams or vivid waking recollections of an abduction, again following a time lapse, and so forth.

12. This figure is based on the nearly three hundred individuals listed in the Bloecher-Webb *HUMCAT* as probable abductees, plus a percentage of the largely uncatalogued hundred and five cases uncovered by Dr. James Harder (see page 217). Still uncatalogued abduction cases investigated by Dr. Leo Sprinkel of the Aerial Phenomena Research Organization and others have been estimated to bring the total of individual abductees to "roughly five hundred." The number of investigated *incidents* is far less, since many abductions—perhaps half—involve more than one abductee.

1: CAPE COD GENESIS

1. John Fuller, *The Interrupted Journey*. (New York: Dial Press, 1966.)
2. Paraphrase of remarks on "The Stanley Siegel Show."
3. See page 226.

2: THE LANDING IN NORTH HUDSON PARK

1. For example, on July 17, 1975—seven months after O'Barski's encounter—Emiliano Velasco was in his tractor ploughing a field near Valladolid, Spain. A cylindrical UFO approached him, moving in circles around the tractor and coming as close as ten feet. There was a flash, a high whistle, and one of the panes of glass in the tractor's cab was cracked. See FSR (Flying Saucer Review), Vol. 22, No. 3.
2. FSR, Vol. 22, No. 3, and No. 4.

3: A SHARP RIGHT TURN ON THE NATIONAL ROAD

1. This is not Kilburn's real name. Both the fear of ridicule and the possibility of adverse reactions among employers and acquaintances has led me in many cases to conceal the witness's identity.
2. Charles Fort, 1874–1932, wrote four books in which he collected bits of information about odd, unexplained phenomena. Included in these books, but certainly not central to them, is a variety of unusual aerial phenomena.
3. This case is still under investigation by Ted Bloecher and myself, so no information from one witness's recollections can be presented here without jeopardizing the validity of future hypnotic sessions with the other witnesses.
4. Travis Walton, The Walton Experience (New York: Berkley, 1978), pp. 108, 109.
5. Coral and Jim Lorenzen, Abducted! (New York: Berkley, 1977), p. 77.
6. Wayne Laporte, "The Charleston Close Encounters," UFO Report, December 1979, pp. 20–23.
7. David Haisell, "The Missing Seven Hours Revealed," Journal UFO: Vol. 1, No. 1., pp. 2–10.
8. Lorenzen, p. 47.
9. This case, like several others discussed in these pages, is still under investigation. For many reasons, those involved do not wish to publish any details prior to a hoped-for hypnotic regression with the principal witness.
10. B. Ann Slate, "The Story of the Kendall Abduction," UFO

Report, December 1979, pp. 55–62. Also a telephone interview with the author.

11. This case, very probably an abduction, is still under investigation. The two thoroughly reliable witnesses live in different parts of the country from the Tennessee town where the
incident occurred. I hope someday to be able more fully to
explore the matter
12. Lorenzen, pp. 52–69.
13. *HUMCAT*, from case abstract by Ted Bloecher.
14. Lorenzen, pp. 114–131.
15. Ibid., pp. 38–51.
16. Ibid., pp. 114 131.

4: THE BLUE LIGHT IN THE PINE BARRENS

1. Ted Bloecher and Patrick Huyghe had been handling the
investigation of this case, but neither was available to attend
the October 5 session. David had been hypnotized a few
years earlier by another psychologist, and once before, in
September, by Dr. Clamar; this final session was the most
informative and dramatic of all.
2. Though it is not absolutely certain that David's friends were
not taken, there are clear precedents in the Larson (Lorenz-
en, pp. 52–69) and Andreasson cases (Fowler, *The Andreasson Affair*, New York, Prentice-Hall, 1979) for this kind of
selective abduction. Sandy Larson and her daughter's boy-
friend were taken while Sandy's daughter was held "rigid"
in a field outside the ship. Betty Andreasson was apparently
selected from her ten-member family group, and again the
others were held in a state of suspended animation until Betty's abduction was over.

5: NBC—THE CATALYST

1. His name, and the names of his two friends, have been
altered to protect their anonymity.
2   McMahon and Federico were both surprised to learn that
Sharkey had been with them. Their memory lapse is odd.

Even odder is the fact that when Ted Bloecher finally located Sharkey, he had only a vague recollection of the incident himself. He remembered, hazily, that they had seen a light, and that it had been above their car as they drove to the police station, and nothing of the other details. He vividly recalled a sighting he and his mother made around that time, though it was of a distant object, and not nearly as detailed as this DeForest Lake incident. I suspect that only Federico and McMahon were actually abducted, and that all three had their perceptions of the event somehow manipulated after the fact. See page 109 and note.

3. McMahon's sudden, spontaneous recall of his abduction experience is not without precedent; it occurred, for instance, in the Sergeant Charles Moody case. (*See Lorenzen, Abducted!, pp. 42, 43.*) The immediate recall of Hickson and Parker in the Pascagoula kidnapping is discussed, along with other vagaries of abduction-case amnesia in my Chapter 9. It is, however, very significant that McMahon's account is extraordinarily similar to those retrieved through hypnosis. Since the same essential details come to light through normal, immediate memory (Hickson, Parker), through delayed but spontaneous recall (McMahon, Moody), and through regressive hypnosis, there is no way that the abduction experience can be tied to a particular *method* of recollection. It is not a function of the hypnotic process.

4. Fuller, *The Interrupted Journey* (New York: Berkley, 1974), p. 116.

6: THE VIRGINIA HORTON CASE

1. Lorenzen, *Abducted!* (New York: Berkley, 1977), p. 129.
2. Fuller, *The Interrupted Journey*, (New York: Berkley, 1974), p. 305.
3. Lorenzen, p. 78.
4. Ibid., p. 29.
5. Ibid., p. 117.
6. Fuller, p. 194.
7. David Haisell, *The Missing Seven Hours Revealed*, (Markham, Ontario: by the author), p. 2.
8. Lorenzen, p. 76.

9. Fuller, p. 193.
10. Lorenzen, p. 127
11. Ibid., pp. 9-24.
12. Betty Hill gives a particularly vivid account of her captors taking skin scrapings, strands of hair, even fingernail cuttings. *(See Fuller, pp. 193–194.).*
13. The John Fuller book on the Hill case, *The Interrupted Journey*, is also a classic account of a UFO investigation, and is highly recommended.
14. She requested, and was given, a booklike object, but it was taken from her when she left the craft, to her intense dismay. *(See Fuller, pp. 207–212.)*

7: PITTSBURGH AND THE MOUNTAINTOP

1. The Travis Walton case, detailed in Lorenzen, *Abducted!*, pp. 80-103, and *The Walton Experience* by Travis Walton (New York: Berkley, 1978).
2. Ralph Blum, with Judy Blum, *Beyond Earth: Man's Contact with UFOs* (New York: Bantam, 1974), p. 32.
3. Lorenzen, *Abducted!* (New York: Berkley, 1977), pp. 80-103.
4. Ibid., pp. 38-51.
5. Ann Druffel and D. Scott Rogo. *The Tujunga Canyon Contacts* (Englewood Cliffs, N.J.: Prentice-Hall, 1980), p. 190.

8: THE ALSATIAN DEER

1. Lorenzen, *Abducted!* (New York: Berkley, 1977). p. 47.
2. See, for example, the Higdon case in Lorenzen, and the Betty Andreasson affair in the book by the same title by Raymond Fowler. Many other cases exist in the UFO literature.
3. Some of the earlier books on the subject of UFOs detail this kind of activity at length. See, especially, Dr. J. Allen Hynek's two books, *The UFO Experience: A Scientific Enquiry* (New York: Ballantine, 1974), and *The Hynek UFO Report* (New York, Dell, 1977).
4. Raymond E. Fowler, *The Andreasson Affair* (Englewood Cliffs, New Jersey: Prentice-Hall, 1979), pp. 51 and 57-58.

5. Lorenzen, p. 58.
6. Fuller, The Interrupted Journey, (New York: Berkley, 1974), pp. 210–211.
7. Gray, "The Heavenly Deception," New York Review of Books, Vol. XXVI, No. 16, October 25, 1979, pp. 8, 10.
8. Fuller, p. 195.
9. Lorenzen, p. 43.
10. Fuller, p. 240.
11. Lorenzen, p. 63, 64.
12. Fuller, p. 157.

9: Speculations Both Grim and Hopeful

1. See the Introduction, Note 12, page 247.
2. Raymond E. Fowler, The Andreasson Affair (Englewood Cliffs, New Jersey: Prentice-Hall, 1979) pp. 51 and 57–58.
3. Curtis G. Fuller, ed., Proceedings of the First International UFO Congress (New York: Warner Books, 1980), pp. 362, 363.
4. In this context, Jastrow was posing, and answering, hypothetical questions. His position in regard to the UFO problem is not one of deep interest; he is cautiously curious.
5. This investigation is awaiting the decision of one or both of the witnesses to undertake hypnosis. Unfortunately, many of our potentially most interesting cases exist in this particular limbo.
6. Each of the witnesses has had mental "flashbacks" of a suggestive nature. One has recurrent dreams of lying helpless on a hospital-type table and looking out into the dark night through a rounded window. The other has had images of himself being carried, a rare experience, as he points out, since he weighs two hundred and forty-five pounds.
7. Fuller, The Interrupted Journey (New York: Berkley, 1974), pp. 195, 196.
8. Ibid., p. 157.
9. B. Ann Slate, "Against Her Will—The Kendall Abduction," UFO Report, December 1979, New York, p. 58.
10. Raymond E. Fowler, p. 53.
11. Lorenzen, Abducted!, (New York: Berkley, 1977), pp. 25-37.
12. Ibid., p. 27.

13. As an example of suppressed evidence in government hands there exists a film of four UFOs taken over Australia by that nation's Air Force, and a good friend of mine, a former U.S. Air Force sergeant with top secret clearance, was shown the film in the late 1960s. Together with other personnel with equally high security ratings, he viewed this short movie shot from an Australian B-29 converted to a photo-mapping function. It showed a huge, hovering, windowed craft with three small UFOs attached to it as a kind of tail. A door on the "mother ship" opened—two vertical panels and two horizontally aligned ones sliding apart—and the three small ships zipped inside. The panels closed, the large craft canted at an angle, and in seconds it was gone. The filmed image of the UFO was extraordinarily large and clear, filling the entire movie screen.

14. The general history of the phenomenon reported here is drawn from Dr. David Jacobs's excellent overview, *The UFO Controversy in America* (New York: Signet, 1976).

15. Ibid., p. 31.

16. Dr. David Saunders's county-by-county statistical study of UFO sighting reports seems to have established this fact beyond doubt. Unfortunately, his material is largely unpublished, but is available to investigators through the Center for UFO Studies.

17. Blum, *Beyond Earth: Man's Contact with UFOs*, (New York: Bantam, 1974), pp. 9–36.

18. See my discussion on pages 61–62.

10: WHAT CAN BE DONE?

1. The Center for UFO Studies as it now exists is a kind of prototype of this undertaking.

SELECTED BIBLIOGRAPHY

BOOKS

Bloecher, Ted. *Report on the UFO Wave of 1947.* Washington, D.C.: By the Author, 1967. (Available from the Center for UFO Studies, 1609 Sherman Ave., Evanston, Ill. 60201.)

Blum, Ralph, with Blum, Judy. *Beyond Earth: Man's Contact with UFOs.* New York: Bantam Books, 1974.

Bowen, Charles, ed. *Encounter Cases from Flying Saucer Review.* New York: Signet, 1977.

Condon, Edward U., project director. *Scientific Study of Unidentified Flying Objects.* New York: Bantam Books, 1969.

Davis, Isabel, and Bloecher, Ted. *Close Encounters at Kelly and Others of 1955.* Evanston, Ill.: Center for UFO Studies, 1978.

Druffel, Ann, and Rogo,D. Scott. *The Tujunga Canyon Contacts.* Englewood Cliffs, New Jersey: Prentice-Hall, 1980.

Emenegger, Robert. *UFOs Past, Present and Future.* New York: Ballantine Books, 1974.

Fowler, Raymond E. *The Andreasson Affair.* Englewood Cliffs, New Jersey: Prentice-Hall, 1979. Bantam, 1980.

Fuller, Curtis G., ed. *Proceedings of the First International UFO Congress.* New York: Warner Books, 1980.

Fuller, John. *The Interrupted Journey.* New York: Dial Press, 1966. Berkley, 1974.

Haisell, David. *The Missing Seven Hours.* Markham, Ontario, Canada: Paperjacks, 1978.

_____ . *The Missing Seven Hours Revealed.* Markham, Ontario: by the author. (Available from Paperjacks, Ltd., 330 Steelcase Rd., Markham, Ontario, Canada, L3R 2M1.)

Hynek, J. Allen. *The Hynek UFO Report.* New York: Dell, 1977.

_____ . *The UFO Experience: A Scientific Inquiry.* Chicago: Henry Regnery, 1972. Ballantine, 1974.

Jacobs, David Michael. *The UFO Controversy in America.* Indiana University Press, 1975. New York: New American Library, 1976.

Jung, Carl G. *Flying Saucers: A Modern Myth of Things Seen in the Sky.* New York: Harcourt Brace, 1959; Signet, 1969.

Lorenzen, Coral with Lorenzen, Jim. *Abducted!*. New York; Berkley, 1977.

_____ *Encounters with UFO Occupants*. New York: Berkley, 1976.

Ruppelt, Edward J. *The Report on Unidentified Flying Objects*. Garden City, New York: Doubleday, 1956. Ace Books, 1956.

Sachs, Margaret. *The UFO Encyclopedia*. New York: G.P. Putnam's Sons, 1980.

Sagan, Carl, and Page, Thornton, eds. *UFOs: A Scientific Debate*. Ithaca, New York: Cornell University Press, 1973. New York: Norton, 1974.

Saunders, David R., and Harkins, R. Roger. *UFOs? Yes!: Where the Condon Committee Went Wrong*. New York: World, 1969. Signet, 1968.

Story, Ronald D., ed. *The Encyclopedia of UFOs*. Garden City, New York: Doubleday, 1980.

Vallee, Jacques. *Anatomy of a Phenomenon*. Chicago: Henry Regnery, 1965.

Walton, Travis. *The Walton Experience*. New York: Berkley, 1978.

Webb, David. *1973—Year of the Humanoids*. Evanston, Illinois: Center for UFO Studies, 1974.

ARTICLES AND PERIODICALS

The *A.P.R.O. Bulletin*. Edited by Coral Lorenzen. Tuscon, Ariz.: Aerial Phenomena Research Organization.

Bloecher, Ted. "The Stonehenge Incidents of January, 1975." *FSR (Flying Saucer Review)*. Edited by Charles Bowen. Maidstone, Kent, England. Part I-Vol 22. No. 3, Part II-Vol 22. No.4.

Gray, Francine du Plessix. "The Heavenly Deception." *New York Review of Books*. Vol. XXVI, No. 16. Oct. 25, 1979.

"The Goodland, Kansas, Abduction. *International UFO Reporter*, Vol. 2, No. 10., pp. 4-7. Edited by Dr. J. Allen Hynek. Evanston, Ill.

Laporte, Wayne. "The Charleston Close Encounters." *UFO Report*, December, 1979. New York.

The *MUFON UFO Journal*. Edited by Richard Hall. Seguin, Texas: The Mutual UFO Network.

Slate, B. Ann. "Against Her Will—The Kendall Abduction." *UFO Report*, December 1979. New York.

INDEX